The Undersea Discoveries
of Jacques-Yves Cousteau

OCTOPUS AND SQUID
The Soft Intelligence

In the same series

Jacques-Yves Cousteau and Philippe Cousteau
THE SHARK: Splendid Savage of the Sea

Jacques-Yves Cousteau with Philippe Diolé
LIFE AND DEATH IN A CORAL SEA

Jacques-Yves Cousteau and Philippe Diolé
DIVING FOR SUNKEN TREASURE

Jacques-Yves Cousteau and Philippe Diolé
THE WHALE: Mighty Monarch of the Sea

Jacques-Yves Cousteau and Philippe Diolé
THREE ADVENTURES: Galápagos – Titicaca
The Blue Holes

The Undersea Discoveries
of Jacques-Yves Cousteau

OCTOPUS AND SQUID

The Soft Intelligence

Jacques-Yves Cousteau

and Philippe Diolé

Translated from the French by J. F. Bernard

DOUBLEDAY & COMPANY, INC., GARDEN CITY, NEW YORK

Translated from the French by J. F. Bernard
ISBN: 0-385-06896-4
Library of Congress Catalog Card Number 72-76141
Printed in the Federal Republic of Germany
9   8   7   6   5   4   3   2

Contents

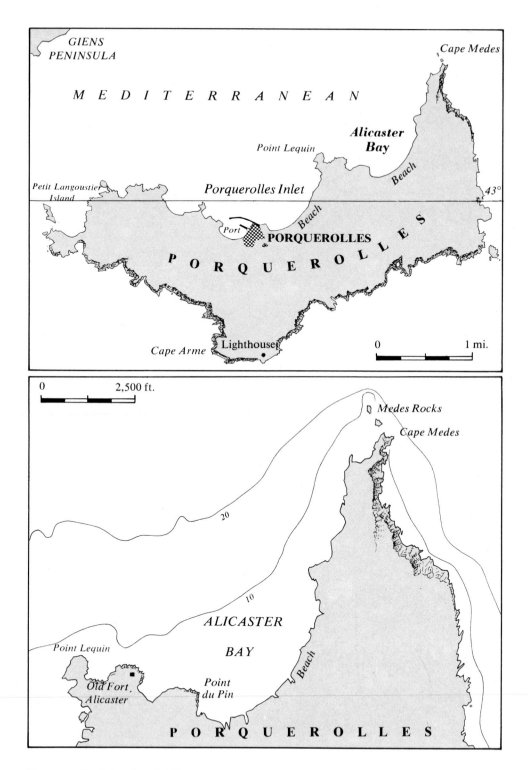

Porquerolles Island and Alicaster bay.

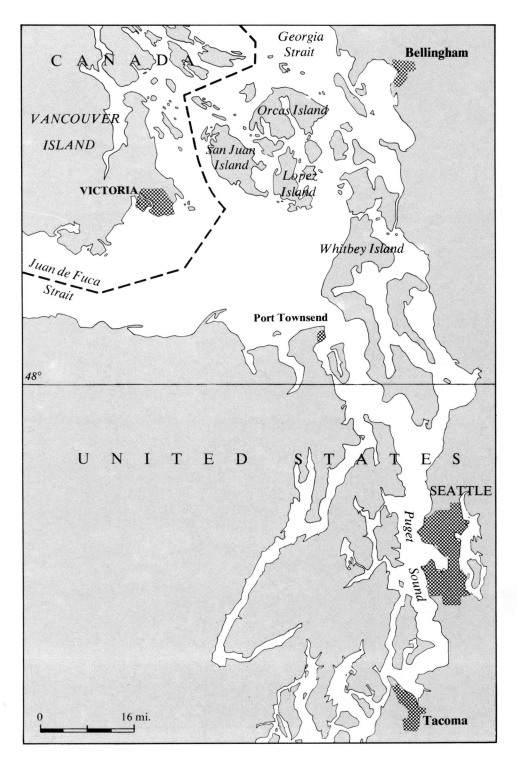

The Pacific coast in the Seattle area.

Captain Cousteau, aboard *Calypso,* observing the mating of octopuses in an aquarium. *Calypso* is anchored in front of the Oceanographic Museum of Monaco.

ONE

Champions of Freedom

I know this flat, sandy, grayish bottom very well. I can see, here and there, pebbles scattered; and, farther on, there is a hole. To my right there is a scattering of greenish seaweed. The surface of the water is a bit choppy, and the sun's reflections dance on the sand. Looking up, I can see the sky as a silver-blue light in the sea.

This stretch of bottom is not one that divers ordinarily find attractive. It is a plain, twenty-five or thirty feet beneath the surface, stretching as far as the eye can see. There are few fish, but there is a great deal of debris. For years, pleasure boats have used this place as a dumping ground for their empty bottles. It is a sorry sight.

And yet I cannot help smiling behind my mask. My being here somehow has the spirit of a homecoming.

Falco is swimming ahead of me. I can see that he is pleased at being able to introduce his friends to me and to show me how talented they are.

His friends are the octopuses* that live here.
But they were my friends before they became his.

The Builders of the Sea

It is very easy to come here and not see a single octopus. The octopus, far
from being the aggressive monster so dear to fiction writers and filmmakers, is
a shy, retiring creature. Octopuses do not lie in wait for divers, or rush out to
attack them on sight. They are out of sight, in their holes under the large rocks
that we call their "houses." And, in order to find the octopuses, one must be
able to recognize such houses. Their architecture has a great variety of forms,
and there is a large assortment of models which reflects the nature of the
building materials available locally. Here, the houses are large rocks, or form-
less piles of different materials patiently gathered and heaped together:
stones and bits of metal, often with abalone shells lying, glistening on the
bottom around them, like the uncertain ornaments of a suburban garden.

I have known this spot for twenty years. The inhabitants of course are no
longer the same as the ones who were here then. Those that I first knew are
now dead. Octopuses do not live for very long; but their houses still stand,
occupied by other inhabitants. It seems very long ago that our team, which
was then just beginning its study of marine life, first came here. There were
Frédéric Dumas, Philippe Tailliez, and Falco—who was very young then, and
had just joined us.

This dreary stretch of sand, which we happened upon by accident, had
taken on great interest for us when we discovered that it was inhabited by
strange animals who were little understood by land-dwellers, but who, we
hoped, would little by little reveal their secrets to us.

We had named this place Octopus City—in French, *Poulpeville*. Our
work in the sea has since taken us to many other places, to the Red Sea and
the Indian Ocean and to the Pacific Ocean as far as Alaska. But I never forgot
the thrill of our first discoveries here, off the little Mediterranean island of
Porquerolles, in the Bay of Alicaster. On our first visit in 1950, we had immediately noticed the series of small hills spread over this plain. In each one
of these hills, there was an octopus, living proudly in his own little cottage. At
that time we were inexperienced enough in the ways of the sea to be astonished whenever we happened upon something new. We felt like intruders in

---

*There are a number of acceptable—or at least accepted—plural forms for the noun "octopus." The most
frequently encountered of these are octopi, octopus, octopussies, and octopuses. We have adopted the latter
form, not necessarily because it is the most correct, but because it is the most usual.

the presence of the life forms that we encountered. We cautiously put our heads into the doors of the little houses that we saw, and we could make out the globular black-pupiled eyes of the octopuses. They looked back at us, just as curiously. It had been an unexpected discovery, and, for years afterward, I had been haunted by the memory of Octopus City.

It is true that the common octopus, *Octopus vulgaris*, is found just about everywhere in the Mediterranean. But Alicaster is an especially suitable place for them, because it has not too much swell and not too much wind. This plain is therefore ideal for octopuses, for it is both sheltered and, at the same time, on the edge of a current—a location that they find particularly desirable. On the other hand, Alicaster has none of the rocky caves that octopuses usually favor and so they are forced to make other arrangements. (Fortunately, octopuses are clever about getting around problems—even though people who do not know them may think otherwise.) Here, they live at a depth of less than 35 feet, though they can make themselves comfortable at depths of up to 300 feet so long as they are sheltered and well housed.

Today, after twenty-two years, we have returned to Porquerolles. We have more men, better equipment, and, especially, the experience of over two decades of observing marine life. This time we hope to be able to do more than exchange puzzled stares with *Octopus vulgaris*. We have decided to live with them a while, to observe them, touch them, film them, and study their behavior and their makeup. Up to now we have only suspicions concerning their degree of development.

Falco and Friend

Falco points out a large plate of rusted iron, the relic of a sunken ship. We head for it. When we are about fifteen feet away, I see the elusive form of an octopus come out from under it. Its arms are extended, cautiously feeling the bottom as it comes toward us. Its great alien, dark-barred eyes are fixed on us. Or rather, they are fixed on Falco; for it is Falco who is its friend and who has brought a few tokens of affection; small crabs, bits of fish and of lobster carried in a basket. A feast for an octopus.

Falco stretches out his hands toward the octopus and tries gently to take hold of it. It extends its arms and begins a sort of dance, in the course of which it strokes Falco's mask, his shoulders, his hands. Finally, it settles on his chest and, with its long arms, tries to reach into the basket in which Falco carries his offerings.

It is truly a large octopus; the largest, it seems, in this whole area. Even though it weighs only a few pounds, its arms, when extended, must have a

Left. Two divers go down *Espadon*'s ladder in search of octopuses at Porquerolles in Alicaster bay.

Right. Octopuses live in amphorae from a sunken Roman ship (third century B.C.) at Grand Congloué.

Below. An octopus in a "herbarium" at Alicaster.

spread of over six feet. Not only has this fine specimen befriended our team, but he has also turned out to be a fine actor. We have already filmed several sequences; but there are many more left to do, both here and elsewhere, in order to capture on film the fascinating world of the cephalopods.

First Contact

The over-all aspect of this place has not changed since 1950. Most of the octopuses' houses are still located under large, flat rocks, but the inhabitants we saw then are all gone. Octopuses do not live for more than three years. I remember that one of them had taken up residence under a tree trunk that he had raised and buttressed with bricks. Dumas and I had been astonished to discover the ingenuity of this octopus in making use of available construction material. Was it a form of intelligence? I still believe it was. We had not

Frédéric Dumas playing with an octopus in 1946. (From the film, *Silent World of Jacques Cousteau*.)

Right. Dumas' playmate lets him have it with a jet of ink.

Following page. An octopus hides among sea-fan branches and takes on their color.

disturbed the animal. It would have been wrong, somehow, to trespass on the house that it had built so painstakingly.

In 1953, we made a short film on Octopus City and its houses. We had been surprised to find octopuses there to begin with, for topographically, the flat, sandy bottom is not suitable for them. What made the difference, apparently, was the presence of large slabs of stone, probably very old—perhaps going back into antiquity—which had come from a shipwreck. These stones are now buried in the sand, with only sections of them showing above the bottom. They are also scattered about—which, no doubt, appeals to the octopuses, for they are creatures who value privacy. Under these slabs of stone they have dug holes; thus, they have houses with solid roofs. Outside the entrances to the houses one sees accumulations of strange objects, carried one by one in the octopuses' arms and deposited there: bottles, line, sandals, cans, old tires, and so forth. It is hard to decide whether they are natural-born collectors, or ragpickers.

The octopuses' holes are often dug vertically under the rock. This makes it very difficult to enter—except for its proprietor, who is a miracle of suppleness. An octopus is capable of passing through openings that to the observer seem absolutely impassable. One must be able to see them slip, slide, and actually "flow" like water to understand that the absence of a skeleton in a marine life form constitutes a form of perfection.

A Marine Marvel

I sometimes wonder whether today's divers are able to imagine what our first encounters with octopuses in the water meant to us. What it meant to be able to touch them and even to be able to play with them.

When we first began using the Aqua-lung, we knew hardly anything about the behavior of marine animals. Every new dive brought a new experience. At the very beginning, we sometimes felt a sense of revulsion when we touched the sticky surface of a rock covered with an unfamiliar form of animal life. Then we noticed that in the water our fingers did not "feel" certain unpleasant sensations that we knew from life on land. Even so, we were still apprehensive about being stung or burned simply by brushing our hands over creatures that, as yet, we knew nothing about.

It did not take us long to get interested in octopuses. We saw them often during our first dives, living in caves and hiding behind ramparts made out of debris, pebbles, and shells; and sometimes we saw, like a flower in a garden, a sea anemone nearby. When we approached one of these caves, the octopus would first swell up, as though by increasing its volume it could better take advantage of its fortifications. It would send a protective arm around its rampart and, without taking its eyes away from us, would begin to pile up its defensive bric-a-brac as though to bar our way to its lair. It also demonstrated that its psychic makeup was far more advanced than we had thought. It changed color—but we did not know whether this was a sign of fear or of anger. Then a moment would come when the octopus would decide to flee; it would begin slowly, sinuously, its arms and body almost flat against the rock. And then, suddenly, it would shoot away, its arms stretched forward. When we were able to catch one of the animals, it would stick to our hands and fight desperately to get away. But its suction cups left only faint marks on our hands; and these disappeared quickly.

The Olive Branch and the Octopus

At this time, Frédéric Dumas had had more experience with octopuses than the rest of us. When he was only ten years old, he had found some octopuses off Port Issol and had brought them back to the beach to show the young daughter of friends of his parents. The girl had been delighted and had let the octopuses crawl up and down her arms. This display became an instant center of attention on the beach, especially to the girl's horrified parents and other adults. Fathers shouted, and mothers clutched their children.

In those days, of course, the scuba had not been invented and even underwater goggles did not exist. What young Dumas had done was simply to find a medium-sized octopus, grab it, and bring the soft mass, with its arms writhing, back to the beach to show its white suction cups. Dumas admits that, at first, he had to overcome a certain physical disgust. But he quickly learned to lure octopuses into the open water by waving an olive branch before their holes. It was an old trick inherited from the Greeks. Octopuses quickly seize anything that moves in the water, and, once entirely out of their holes, they are easily brought to the surface.

An Underwater Ballet

During our first scuba dives, Dumas had finally found himself face to face with a species of animal which until then had been interesting only as a victim and which he had never considered to be more than a simple piece of flesh, flaccid and sticky. Upon first observing the octopus in its environment, he was particularly struck by its yellow, expressive eyes with their black pupils. He discovered that there existed in this mass of flesh a spark—a spark directed toward him, one which contained an expression of intense interest.

It was at Port Cros that Dumas captured his first sizable octopus. After having held it for a moment in his hand, he let it go, and the animal moved away jerkily, its arms trailing behind, in what seemed to us to be no great hurry. The octopus swims by inflating its mantle and suddenly expelling the liquid forward through a sort of tube: the funnel. Thus, the octopus swims backward. But, in this rapid motion to the rear, the real means of locomotion is the animal's muscular apparatus, by virtue of which it is able to expel the water with sufficient force to enable it to move.

Didi patiently followed the octopus, despite its elaborate maneuvers and ruses designed to throw a pursuer off the track and despite its marvelous camouflage. For the octopus had sensed Didi in pursuit, and, several times, had spurted a jet of ink toward his mask. However, this ink does not form, as has been said often, a "smoke screen" behind which the octopus hides. Instead, it is used to cover a change of direction in the octopus' course. The ink forms a rather thick cloud in the water, which ends in a tail; and its pigment, since it does not dilute in sea water, prevents the cloud from dissipating quickly. One

The Mediterranean octopus makes its home amid magnificent colors.

hypothesis is that this cloud, since it has the same general form as the octopus, is supposed to serve as a decoy while the octopus makes its getaway.

All the while that Didi was following the octopus and the octopus was trying its bag of tricks, I was filming away with our only underwater camera. It was a scene that had never before been captured. Finally, when the octopus was tired of fleeing, it lay on the bottom and took on immediately the color of the sand. But we were quite close to it and did not allow ourselves to be fooled. Whereupon, the octopus began swimming again, climbing upward toward the light, but with its arms spread out in the shape of a fan as though to acknowledge defeat; and then it allowed Dumas to take it in his hand. There followed a long and enchanting scene, with Dumas stroking the oc-

Genest attempts to make friends with an octopus on a rocky bottom off the island of Riou.

topus gently, then letting it go for a moment, so as to calm it. This was the first of our series of underwater ballets, and its rhythm became more and more peaceful. Finally, Dumas was playing with the octopus as with a cat. For once a man had attempted to convince an octopus that no harm was intended.

An Experiment

Our friend Dumas has always had a bit of the pyromaniac about him. He loves fireworks and rockets and he was the first man to introduce fire into the sea. At the beginning of our exploration of the sea, he invented an underwater light—which worked perfectly well, but to the accompaniment of a dreadful roaring and cascades of bubbles. This gadget of Didi's was extremely useful. It was also the occasion of a great many surprises, and it provided us with the first sequence of *The Silent World*.

Dumas and I were obsessed with the idea of learning what the reaction of marine animals would be to the sight of fire, in the form of light, in the water. One day at Octopus City, in the Bay of Alicaster, Dumas dived with an underwater rocket and began waving it in front of an octopus' house. Nothing happened. The animal reacted not at all. He did not try to hide, or to escape. Dumas then turned the beam directly onto the octopus, which did not even draw its arms. The game was called off, however, when Dumas saw that it was becoming cruel. The octopus showed signs of having been burned. But even then it had not tried to escape. Obviously, an octopus does not know what fire is, or how to escape from it. It was obvious that he did not learn from this one contact, but it is possible that a second experience would be sufficient for him to learn the proper reaction.

This surprising insensitivity to fire has been confirmed by Guy Gilpatric, one of the pioneers of diving, who told us that he has seen an octopus, which had been brought onto shore, cross through a fire to get back into the water.

The Calumnies of Victor Hugo

There have been many occasions for me in the past two decades to become more and more interested in the octopus. In the course of many encounters they have given ample demonstration of either humor or of a surprising understanding. With an octopus, one must always be ready for anything. For years, Frédéric Dumas, Philippe Tailliez, and I have been observing octopuses; and especially the Mediterranean octopus, the *Octopus vulgaris*, which is intelligent, easy to tame, and apparently willing to play games with us.

In the patches of vegetation of the Mediterranean, which are composed of posidoniae, which are not seaweeds but flowering aquatic plants (phanerogams)—which resemble leeks, we have often found cephalopods other than octopuses, especially cuttlefish. Cuttlefish seem to have three separate speeds. There is a rapid backward movement effected by the contraction of the muscular membrane; a slow swim, in which its ribbonlike fins are used; and, finally, a "neutral" pace, in which the cuttlefish remains almost immobile, its

"Gilliatt and the Octopus," by Gustave Doré. This is an illustration for Hugo's *Toilers of the Sea*. (Maison de Victor Hugo, Paris.)

An octopus gathers its arms around itself for protection. The sucker disks are protruding.

body suspended in the water. Cuttlefish, like octopuses, shoot out clouds of ink when frightened.

As we have progressed in our observation of octopuses, we have been struck by the differences between the reality of these animals and their reputation. Much of the latter is founded upon Victor Hugo's novel, *Toilers of the Sea,* published in English in 1866. We have never run into octopuses as large as the monster described by Hugo. And they certainly do not exist in such sizes in the English Channel, around the Channel Islands. I think that the ferocious giants of Hugo's work must have existed only in the author's imagination.

But what an imagination! "The octopus, O horror! inhales a man," he writes. "It draws him to itself, and into itself; and, bound, immobile, he feels himself slowly ingested by that incredible being which is the monster. The terrible tentacles are supple as leather, solid as steel, cold as night."

In the Mediterranean, the octopus neither looks nor behaves like a monster. It is small and shy. It flees like a frightened bird, and it comes to rest gently on the ocean floor.

A diver flushes out an octopus hidden among vegetation.

But calumny dies hard. Artists and writers have depicted the octopus as a giant being, thirsty for blood and powerful enough to sink ships. Octopuses, devilfish, *Kraken*—they were all hideous, ferocious, and famished. And, for some reason known only to the weavers of such tales, they all shared an insatiable appetite for human flesh. Man, of all the animals, is probably the only one to regard himself as a great delicacy.

Traps for Archaeologists

To us, octopuses are timid animals and—involuntarily—amusing ones. From the standpoint of marine archaeology, however, they represent a booby trap—as we know from our own experience.

Near the island of Grand Congloué, off of Marseilles, there is the wreck of a Roman ship, lying about 150 feet below the surface. The ship dates from the end of the third century B.C., and its cargo consisted of thousands of amphorae and pieces of ceramic. We undertook a systematic dig at this site— a very difficult job, which continued for more than five years. For many centuries before we came, octopuses had taken up residence in some of the amphorae. "It was not very pleasant," Falco recalls. "We would be there working, digging with our hands, when we'd feel ourselves being pulled backward—by an octopus. So, we'd grab the octopus and stick it into the air lift. It became a standard joke. As soon as an octopus would come out of an amphora, we'd send it up the air lift, and it would be regurgitated onto *Calypso*'s deck—to the surprise and horror of our archaeologist on duty, who would then throw it back into the water." The octopus, no doubt as horrified at the sight of the archaeologist as the latter was at him, would swim happily away, greatly relieved to have escaped the clutches of the incredible monster lurking above the surface.

The archaeologist, Professor Fernand Benoit, supervised the dig from the surface, where he kept inventory of the contents of the amphorae and tried to determine their age and origins, for Greek and Roman relics were both there in abundance. Finally, by means of some pottery shards, pebbles, and resin remnants in some of the amphorae, Benoit was able to piece together a chronology. But, for two thousand years, the octopuses of the Mediterranean had lived in the wreckage and the litter; and, in order to build their houses, had moved all the bits and pieces of pottery and the shards from one amphora to another. To make matters more confusing, with these fragments of Greek and Roman artifacts, they had mixed in more recent objects that they had found in the vicinity. Therefore, every amphora had become a trap for the unwary archaeologist. It took Professor Benoit a while to realize that in the sea the octopus was archaeology's resident enemy.

It is true, however, that the octopuses were not alone in playing practical jokes on Professor Benoit. The divers once sent modern coins up the air lift— to hear the whoops of joy from the archaeologists, who at first glance thought that they had discovered coins from antiquity. The last word in this joke, however, came from an octopus two weeks later, who was discovered in an amphora with one of the coins. Apparently, the animal had found it and taken it home with him.

Frédéric Dumas reported: "The movement of water caused by the air lift did not seem to disturb the octopuses curled up snugly in their amphorae. I cannot help thinking of their joy two thousand years ago when they saw this prefabricated palace sinking down toward the bottom; a place of many apartments, spacious yet with entrances so narrow that its occupant would be protected from marauding groupers look for a meal."

The penchant of the octopus for the unexpected had already been noted

Portrait of an octopus, by Frédéric Dumas.

by our friend Gilpatric, who wrote the first book on underwater exploration, *The Compleat Goggler*. He recorded that he brought an octopus home and put it in an aquarium, which he then covered with a heavy lid. A short time later, the aquarium was empty, and Gilpatric found the octopus going through his library, book by book, turning the pages with its arms.

Champions of Liberty

Octopuses are champions of liberty, and I like them all the more for it. It is extremely difficult to keep them in captivity. Their ability to elongate their bodies in such a way as to pass through the narrowest openings has long been

Following page. In a herbarium at Alicaster, Genest tries to approach an octopus without frightening it.

the nightmare of aquarium curators; and it has given us a great deal of trouble aboard *Calypso*. We have often tried to keep specimens in jars on the rear deck, but it is almost impossible to do so because they lift the heavy covers and slide out of the tiniest crack. On the other hand, we are so delighted at their ingenuity in escaping that we have never had the heart to try to prevent them from doing so. What we usually do, in fact, is to film the escape.

In spite of ourselves, we have been unable to withhold our admiration of such cleverness and perseverance in this body without a skeleton; in a being so far-removed from ourselves, who yet will go to any length to recover its liberty. We learned, too, that there are many qualities that are not restricted to animals in possession of vertebrae.

During the fifteen or so years in which I have traveled the seas aboard *Calypso*, we have come across octopuses, cuttlefish, and squid. Falco has even seen, from the minisub, in the Indian Ocean, one of those gigantic cephalopods from the deep about which we know practically nothing. We know only that, at depths of between 2,000 and 5,000 feet, there are giant squid. Prince Albert of Monaco, during his expeditions, found fragments of their corpses; and, since that time, other corpses, partially decomposed, have been found. But nothing is known about their shapes, their habits; and it will be a long time before more information is available, because it seems impossible, so far, to catch specimens by trawling or similar methods. Even observers in diving bells have never sighted one. The giant squid is one of the great secrets of the sea, and one of the last ones. But it is one whose solution is worth waiting for.

Providential Animals

One thing is certain. Cephalopods, whatever their size, are a very important link in the alimentary chain of the oceans. Cachalots dive down to almost 4,000 feet to find the giant squids on which they feed. White tuna, dolphins, pilot whales, and sharks all swallow, by the mouthful, the small squids of the genus *Loligo*, which meet in large groups during the mating season. Cuttlefish, squids, and octopuses are the primary food of several species of marine mammal and of certain fish.

Man also has long since learned to make use of the cephalopods in many ways. The most striking example I have seen of this is at Madeira, an island small in size but with 350,000 inhabitants. The island itself rises almost vertically from the ocean bottom, and its population would not have been able to subsist without a providential fish, the espada (*Aphanopus carbo,*) which is found only there. It is black, with bronze specks and red eyes, and weighs

THE KRAKEN SUPPOSED A SEPIA OR CUTTLE FISH.

Victor Hugo, photographed among the rocks of Guernsey. (Musée Victor Hugo, Paris.)

The Kraken, attacking a junk. (Copyright, Frank W. Lane.)

between ten and fifteen pounds. Its teeth are similar to those of the barracuda, and, indeed, its over-all appearance is rather like the barracuda's. The espada, however, is caught only in very deep water, where it lives. At night, it rises closer to the surface. When it is totally dark, therefore, it can be caught at between 3,800 and 5,400 feet; and, when there is moonlight, at between 4,700 and 6,500 feet.

The people of the island fish for the espada by methods hallowed by tradition. Once they are over water of the proper depth, they let down lines from the front and rear of their boats. These lines are weighted with stones and then lowered. On the last 1,500 feet of line, other lines are attached, about six feet apart. These lines have hooks attached—a total of 280 of them. The most extraordinary thing is that all this equipment of line and hooks, which remains in the water all night, never gets tangled.

While waiting for the first light of dawn, the fishermen build a fire on the rear of their boat to attract squid, which they harpoon with spears. These are used the next day to bait the espada lines. It is because of squid, therefore, that the inhabitants of Madeira have been able to exist for centuries on their sterile little island.

The Eggs

In 1954, *Calypso* was on her way out of the Persian Gulf, having completed a mission of oil exploration that was to enrich the emirate of Abu Dabi. She was heading toward Aldabrat, by way of the Seychelles Islands. In

The floor of the Mediterranean is covered with sedentary multicolored life forms. This is one of the favorite hiding places of the octopus.

the middle of the Indian Ocean, two days from Ormuz and with the ocean at a dead calm, I saw a bright red object in the water. We moved toward it and brought it aboard. It was a rectangular substance about 36 by 54 inches—a thick piece of membrane the purpose of which was to carry cephalopod eggs. It was obviously supposed to float beneath the surface. We could see that it was covered with millions of eggs, in which we could make out the silhouette of embryos.

This was not the first time that eggs of this kind had been found, though they are found rarely enough. It is not known what kind of giant cephalopod is capable of secreting a nursery of this kind.

A Physiological Success

The octopus is a fascinating creature. We have always found it so, and we do still. But it is not because it is a "devilfish," as the English say; and even less because it is a "monster." It is because it is exceptional, unique among animals marine or otherwise. A "cousin" of the oyster and the clam, the octopus has attained independence, obtained mobility without using the means

An octopus rises toward the surface.

of locomotion of other animals in the sea or on land.

To man, the soft and unprotected flesh of the octopus seems very vulnerable. Yet, the octopus as a species is not in danger. It is adept at escaping the perils of the sea. Skillful at hiding, quick to flee, the octopus is protected by the high degree of development of its organs of sense and its nervous system. It has excellent eyesight—eyes that are almost the equal of those of the vertebrates, almost the equal of man's eyes. It can change its shape, its form, and its color.

The octopus' sense of touch is much more developed than that of man; and it is a sense that man does not possess at all, or only in a rudimentary form, which is very important in the kind of life that an octopus leads. It is a sense that is both chemical and gustatory; one that alerts an octopus to the presence of other animals within range—and especially of the prey that it prefers, such as crustaceans and certain small mollusks.

A cephalopod is a very sensitive receiver and analyst, capable of registering information that escapes man and, indeed, is alien to him.

The most important and the most individual characteristic of the cephalopod is its ability to change its appearance. It can transform itself, cover itself with excrescences and granulations, or change its color. Sometimes this is done to provide camouflage by taking on the color of the environment—of the seaweed where it hides, of the rock on which it rests. Sometimes an octopus will turn red, either with anger or with fear. But who can interpret these signs? As yet, we can only note the fact that they exist.

If we want to understand the octopus and to understand what is said in this book, we must first of all admit that the octopus has a world of its own; that it belongs to a world apart, in which sensations and reactions are different from those of most other forms of marine life. In order to preserve its existence, the octopus has found effective and unusual means: its arms, its suction cups—which are almost as dexterous as our hands—and a supply of poison. Everything about it is mysterious.

An End to Prejudice

It is our intention to put an end to the calumnies of which the unfortunate octopus has been the target; to demythologize the fabulous monsters of Victor Hugo and Jules Verne, which were capable of destroying divers and dragging ships to the bottom of the sea. In order to accomplish that purpose, we must be able to do only one thing: to live with octopuses, to enter into their world. The prejudices against these marvelous animals, whose dexterity and grace is so admirable, are based on ignorance. The trouble has been that, for thousands of years, man has seen octopuses only out of the water. Perhaps only the Aegean artists, some three thousand years ago, had an idea of what beauty lay in the octopus.

We have never met, in the Mediterranean, the Red Sea, the Indian Ocean, or the Atlantic, an octopus of sufficient size to be dangerous to *Calypso*'s divers. All those that we have seen were small enough for us to be able to play with them, to tame them, to observe their intelligence, their memory, their love life, and the skill with which they build and fortify their houses.

Even so, Victor Hugo was not altogether wrong. There are actually giant monsters; octopuses thirty feet across and weighing 125 pounds. But these are not found in the English Channel, on the coasts of Guernsey, but in the Pacific, on the North American coast, near Seattle. And it is of these giant octopuses that we will speak first.

TWO

Formidable—but Lazy

The water is calm, flat, and slightly cloudy around a ring of islands. There is a complex network of canals and small lakes. Despite its quiet appearance, the water is in motion and at each tide it is crossed by rapid currents; for the irregular lagoon opens onto the sea. At one end of this fjord stands one of North America's largest cities: Seattle. It is at once a great natural port, an industrial center for naval and aeronautical construction, and an outlet for the agricultural and lumber products of northwestern United States.

A series of lakes, rivers, and sounds, running among wooded hills, gives this region an air of natural grandeur, and makes it a paradise for pleasure-boating.

The very irregular coastline of the region played a role in the Age of Discovery. In the seventeenth century, a Greek explorer, Juan de Fuca, sailed for three weeks through a strait which he thought was the passageway between the Atlantic and the Pacific; a corridor between East and West that

Left. A diver contends with a giant octopus of the Pacific (*Octopus dofleini*).

for over a century had been the dream of seamen everywhere. He was convinced that he had found the famous "Northwest Passage." He was wrong, but he left his mark on the area; and the strait which separates the state of Washington from Vancouver Island is called today the Strait of Juan de Fuca. The gulf which penetrates deeply into the American continent is called Puget Sound.

In the muddy, grassy maze formed by a sprinkling of rocky islands along both sides of the Sound, we find the largest octopuses in the world, the *Octopuses dofleini*, which in North America are also known as *Octopus apollyon*. They live in waters bordered by currents, which is what they prefer. And they find here, on the alternately rocky and muddy bottom, rich in vegetation and restocked by the currents, the kind of food they most enjoy: crabs, shrimp, and shellfish.

When *Calypso*'s divers first arrived at Seattle, they were somewhat surprised at the abundance of the waterways. They had never before seen anything like it. Simply to explore the innumerable canals would require a great deal of time. Moreover, visibility was often poor—sometimes only a few yards.

The waters of the area were rich in alluvial deposits. A diver had only to strike the bottom with his palm to raise a cloud of mud that made it impossible to film, or even to see, the octopuses. Simply working in one spot for a few minutes disturbed the bottom sufficiently for us to be forced to start looking for another location. Occasionally, however, it was possible to find an area with relatively clear water on the edge of the currents' path. Many of the underwater surfaces were covered with algae, and others were carpeted by sea anemones resembling large white bubbles—all of which added to the strangeness of the landscape. The water was never very deep; usually between 25 and 35 feet, and never more than 65 feet. But the currents were very strong, especially toward the center of the lagoon, and the divers had to be very careful in that respect.

The divers' most dangerous enemy, however, was the cold. The water's temperature stayed around 48°F. Bernard Delemotte, Raymond Coll, and Louis Prezelin, who were our advance party on this expedition, equipped themselves accordingly. Under their wet suits, they wore special vests, which were a constant hindrance in the water; and they could never work without their gloves. Even so, they often returned aboard shivering from the cold.

Something to Kill a Man

Prezelin and Coll were soon joined by our cameraman, Michel Deloire, and Henri Alliet, his assistant, to begin exploration of the zones of relative calm at the edge of the currents. The water here was somber, the bottom greenish; but animal life seemed abundant, especially with sea urchins, abalone, mussels, crabs and sea squirts. It seemed to have been created as a hunting ground for the giant octopus.

As it turned out, this was exactly what it was. An octopus was already there, swollen, its arms moving slowly to and fro, its head covered with bristling flesh, staring fixedly at the divers with its great yellow eyes and black pupils visible in the dim light.

The divers' first impression was one of size. The "giant" of Victor Hugo's imagination was, in fact, a reality.

It was both exciting and disturbing. Exciting, because the octopus seemed to be at least as large as the "monster" of maritime legend; and here, at last, was an opportunity to discover what would actually happen when it came face to face with man. And it was disturbing too, because the local newspapers had to be full of warnings and advice to our divers. A short time before, it was said, some divers had had a long and bloody battle with an octopus weighing over two hundred pounds. In addition—and this was perhaps more serious—specialists from the Seattle aquarium had warned our divers about the bite of the giant octopus, which, they said, was sufficiently poisonous to kill a man. Now, the beak of the giant octopus is very small—less than an inch; and there was no official record of either a bite or a death. Yet, according to all reports, the relationship between local divers and the giant octopuses was one of continuous violence.

Our divers were therefore more inclined to caution than otherwise. But they soon discovered that their biggest problem was not to get away from the octopuses, but to get near them. They were timid animals, quick to disappear in the first available crevice. They were wary of man and apparently had often been disturbed and even hunted.

The first giant octopus that the divers encountered slid immediately toward an opening in a rock and flowed into it. It succeeded, despite the fact that it was obviously impossible, in getting its whole enormous body through a crack so small that it was hardly visible. The whole operation seems contrary to the laws of nature; and we have concluded, only half-jokingly, that the larger an octopus is, the smaller the opening through which it can pass. It has a fantastic ability to stretch itself thin, like rubber; or lengthen its arms, one after the other; to flatten its body. Even its head changes shape, and the eyes can be moved obliquely.

The giant octopus changes color more slowly than does our Mediterranean octopus; but, when it is disturbed, mishandled, or brought up to the surface, it takes on a vivid reddish, almost violet tincture—the color of great emotion. Usually, the octopuses of Seattle do not have the same degree of mimetic ability as their smaller cousins, or the varying shades of color. Their flesh sometimes bristles, especially on the head; but we do not know if this is the effect of fear or of anger.

One must remember that an octopus measuring from ten to thirteen feet in diameter, and sometimes as much as twenty feet, is at least as impressive as a gorilla encountered on a jungle trail. The diver finds it easy to resist the temptation to experiment with the emotions of such an animal. Curiosity, even scientific curiosity, must be limited by prudence—particularly when the object of one's curiosity is an animal whose size and strength is such as to make it capable of adequate retaliation if it is even inadvertently offended.

"At the beginning," says Henri Alliet, "we tried to stay out of its line of vision, and we were very wary of its arms. It was not very reassuring to think that it has eight of them, and that, at any moment, one of them might grab you."

Here was a chance to see whether the octopuses lived up to the reputation that Hugo had created for them. "What can be more horrible," Hugo wrote, "than to be clasped by those viscous thongs which adhere closely to the body by virtue of their many sharp points? Each of these points is an eternity of terrible, indescribable pain. It is as though one were being eaten alive by a hundred mouths, each of them too small. But the wound of these points is as nothing compared to that of the sucker disks. The points are the beast entering into your flesh. The disks are you, entering into the flesh of the monster."

The Timid Monsters

We very soon managed to locate five or six places in which the water was usually clear. We dived at the foot of the Orcas Islands, almost at the entrance to the Sound; and also farther inland, near Tacoma, where we are almost always sure to find octopuses. Local diving clubs also flocked to this area to engage in their favorite sport: teasing the octopuses. This, in fact, seems to be Seattle's favorite outdoor sport; especially since one can, in some places, drive right up to the side of the canals.

It is not surprising, therefore, that the octopuses usually stay out of sight, and that they rarely hunt in the open water. Most often, they stay near their own caves, on a rock, and they disappear at the first sign of an intruder. Every octopus has its own permanent lair. The Seattle octopus is much more sedentary than its Mediterranean relative.

The giant octopuses, far from seeming ferocious, bloodthirsty, and hungry for human flesh, appear to be very retiring. They do not like to be seen.

Calypso's team going down into the water among the rocks of Elliott Bay.

We could sometimes catch sight of them in their holes, watching us go past, but it was impossible to lure them out.

The giant octopus is further distinguished from the Mediterranean octopus by its relatively limited talent as an architect. Like the *Octopus vulgaris,* the giant octopus builds a barricade in front of its house, but it is hardly a wall. It is hardly even a row of pebbles. We do not find the clever dwellings that we became accustomed to among the octopuses of Alicaster and Riou.

These comparative limitations are more than compensated for the first time that one watches a giant octopus swim for even a short distance—say, fifteen or twenty feet. It is a marvelous spectacle. Its great hydrodynamic form seems to fill the water. Giant octopuses do not curl up their tentacles when they flee, as smaller octopuses do. Instead, they open up like incredible flowers and show their white sucker disks.

Despite their shyness, the octopuses of Seattle, are very mobile creatures. This made our task rather difficult. We had to follow them in cloudy water, bringing with us our batteries and lamps to light the divers and the octopus, and pulling our electric cables behind us. At the same time, we had to continue filming the sequence from an acceptable angle. But, in these circumstances, the weight and size of the octopus was in our favor. Its body was rather easily visible, and its mass seemed disproportionate to its means of locomotion. Between the giant octopus and the *Octopus vulgaris,* there is as much difference as between a Boeing 747 and a Caravelle.

The Perils of Octopus-Hunting

We very quickly made some interesting friends in Seattle. One was a young woman named Joanne Duffy, a diving monitor, who holds a master's degree in marine biology. Another was Gary Keffler, who operates a nautical sporting-goods store in Seattle. The common bond among all divers quickly became evident between these two Americans and *Calypso*'s team. We had a great deal of fun, and we were very impressed by the way our new friends handled themselves in the water.

One of the great favors they did for us was to place at our disposal their own wealth of knowledge on the habits of cephalopods. They told us that, since 1957, a yearly octopus-hunting competition has taken place in Elliott Bay of Seattle, with the prize in this cruel sport going to the diver who brings in the heaviest octopus. The participants in this hunt have discovered how to lure the octopuses out of their holes. They spread a small amount of copper sulphate, or a chlorate solution, outside the octopus' den. The animal, which is very sensitive to chemical variations in the water, comes out immediately. At that point, a diver needs all his courage. A cephalopod in the open water is virtually helpless. But heaven help the diver who lets his prey get two or three arms around a rock. Even a small octopus is capable of dragging twenty times its own weight; and an octopus weighing a hundred pounds can exert traction of about a ton. (Man, with the greatest effort, can move double his own weight.)

One of our Seattle friends, Jerry Brown, was very disappointed that he was not able to find, and show us, the largest octopus that he has ever seen. It measures, he says, over thirty feet in diameter, and probably weighs over 200 pounds. No doubt, octopuses of such size do exist, but they are rare. It is possible that Jerry's giant had decided to move to deeper waters.

Danger

How serious is the danger to a diver from the giant octopuses of Seattle? I think that there is real danger for a diver without scuba equipment, let us say, who swims past an octopus' hole carrying a shiny object. He might be grabbed by one or more arms. In such a case, it would take much time and effort for him to get free; and, if he were without breathing apparatus, he would drown before he could do so. The clasp of the octopus' arm is a strange thing, rather like that of a noose. The more one pulls on the arm, the tighter its grip becomes. And there is little hope of being able to neutralize the octopus by turning over its mantle as one can sometimes do with smaller specimens. It is one of the parts of its body that the animal defends most diligently, for it is a weak point that plays a large role in combat between octopuses. It is therefore the object of a defensive instinct.

Even in the open water, it requires much courage to tackle such a mass of writhing flesh, with its serpentlike arms constantly trying to recircle the diver, to tear off his mask or to rip out his mouthpiece. On the other hand, it is certain that an octopus, if given the opportunity, would willingly let go of the moving support, which is the diver, in favor of a stable rock.

Because these octopuses are of incredible size, it is difficult to believe that they are really inoffensive creatures; and one therefore experiences a certain apprehension in confronting them on their own territory. Their sucker disks alone are sometimes one or two inches in diameter. When a diver sees a giant octopus in the dim water, its great eyes fixed on him, he feels a strange sensation of respect, as though he were in the presence of a very wise and very old animal, whose tranquility it would be best not to disturb. Then, too, there is always the nagging thought in the back of one's mind of Hugo's monster and its sucker disks: "The disks are you, entering into the flesh of the monster." The myths on which we are raised die hard, even in those of us who pride ourselves most on having conquered fear through knowledge.

Bernard Delemotte, Louis Prezelin, and Raymond Coll, guided by Joanne and Gary, roam through the Seattle waters, going from crevice to crevice and poking under rocks in search of octopuses. Our friends from Seattle know every cave in the area, and they know almost every octopus by name. They each choose the largest one they know, and coax it out of its house by creating a small cloud of copper sulfate. Since the octopus is so sensitive to chemical emanations, a very small amount is enough to make it come out of its hole. These holes, or caves, are comparatively very narrow, and are natural crevices.

It is not the chemical solutions of the divers that are a danger to the octopus, but the necessity for the animal, when pursued, to swim in open

Left. An octopus attempts to "cover" a diver as it would an intended victim.

Above. The diver foils the octopus by holding it at arm's length.

Below. He turns the octopus around and pulls it toward him.

water. The effort exchausts him. Pursued by a diver, without the chance to stop and breathe, the octopus becomes very vulnerable.

"They also show an undeniable curiosity about the diver," Michel Deloire says. "They try to hide; but they also try to see everything that is happening around them. It is rather flattering. We can see that the octopus' eyes are following every move we make, and that it knows perfectly well what we are doing. They are very intuitive animals. They seem to know when we are going to approach them, and they change color even before we make any move toward them. If there is really something "diabolical' about the octopus, as was believed for so long, it is that divinatory sense, that apparent combination of apprehension and attraction with respect to man."

What makes the Seattle octopuses so timid, no doubt, is the annual octopus hunt, as cruel as it is unsportsmanlike, mentioned above. Even so, the octopuses show no sign of hostility. They do not attack divers. They try only to get away and lead their own solitary lives. The octopuses of Seattle live even farther away from one another than those of Alicaster, and they are even more timid. They are hermits by preference, and the presence of the diver seems an intrusion.

Three Battles

Gary has no luck. His octopus is unwilling to come entirely out of its hole. It does take hold of him, but only while remaining solidly anchored to its rock with its rear arms. The diver and the octopus wrestle in a confusion of arms. Gary's mask is ripped off, and he cannot see. It is necessary to get the water out of the mask, clean it, and replace it—all while Gary is held prisoner in the octopus' arms, almost unable to move. He is virtually covered by the octopus' arms and mantle, as though he were the customary prey of the cephalopods— a giant crab or lobster.

Deloire films the entire scene with great enthusiasm, while a circle of divers watches the struggle. The ghost of Victor Hugo walks in the waters of Washington State. Is Hugo perhaps right? Is the animal "ferocious?" No. Gary, latter-day hero of *Toilers of the Sea,* is experienced in this sort of thing. He does not lose his head, and he succeeds in getting his opponent out into the open water. He handles it very well and is even able to calm it. It is a fine

Right above. After a dive, divers from *Calypso* and Seattle exchange information on octopuses.
Right below. One of the Seattle divers holds up an octopus' arm to show its length.

example of the technique of mastering an animal, reminiscent of the prehistoric age when man tamed animals with his bare hands.

Joanne, meanwhile, has had an easier time of it than Gary, and has succeeded immediately in imposing her will on the octopus. She leads the animal away from the rocky wall so that it cannot grasp it, and holds it in front of her. The octopus turns red, but then calms down and its color becomes paler. Joanne strokes it on the mantle, on the head, and then turns it loose. It leaves, propelled by the powerful jet of its funnel. Then it slows and continues at a more leisurely pace. Compared to it, the most graceful diver is clumsy, heavy. The cameras and lights follow. The octopus reaches its rock and attaches itself. Joanne goes behind it: an unusual pose. Beyond a doubt, the giant octopuses of Seattle are born actors.

Prezelin now comes near the octopus and tries to hold it, but the animal does not show the same docility that it did toward Joanne. Its arms whip out and encircle Prezelin's arms and body. He simply waits. When the last arm has left the rock, the octopus is now resting entirely on the diver. Prezelin still does not move. One hand holds his mask and his mouthpiece—toward which an arm is advancing. The diver has been observing the technique of his American friends. He now raises the animal's body in his arms—it must weigh about 65 or 70 pounds—and carries it over to the rock. Hugo would be very disappointed, for the octopus shows no aggressiveness. It is merely looking for support. When the octopus is at the rock, the pressure of its arms relaxes around Prezelin's body, and the sucker disks are lifted one by one and transferred to the new support.

What makes the Seattle octopus comparatively easy to handle is its weak musculature, which is not proportionate to its size or its weight. Comparatively, it is more poorly armed for combat than the small Mediterranean octopus whose weight is ten times less.

It must also be said that the giant octopus is much less inclined to battle than the *Octopus vulgaris*. It is not that it is cowardly, but that it is lazy. Even its sucker disks do not stick as quickly, or hold as long, as those of its Mediterranean cousin. If the giant octopus had the same reactions as the latter, it would be a truly formidable adversary.

Bernard Delemotte showed himself to be especially adept in handling the giant octopuses. He could drive them before him, make them turn, keep them at a certain distance—all of which seemed quickly to exhaust the animals. The Seattle octopuses, in fact, have little stamina once they are out of their homes. If they are pursued even for a short time, they become listless and without defense unless they are allowed to rest. *Calypso*'s divers, in noting the lack of energy among these so-called monsters, called them "paper octopuses." It is possible that these large animals are so quickly exhausted as to be easily on the verge of asphyxiation. Octopuses need a large supply of oxygen—so much so that the pelagic species exist continually at the outer limits of their respiratory potential.

An American specialist, accustomed to the relatively slow reactions of the Seattle octopuses, was astonished at the vigor and speed of the small octopuses at the Biological Station of Banyuls-sur-Mer. It was very difficult even to catch a specimen in one's hand.

Truth and Poetry

Thus, the divers of *Calypso* had their first confrontation with those mythical beings who, for centuries, have been "monsters" to land creatures and have held an honored spot in the folklore and legends of the West.

Face to face with the largest octopuses in the world, our team was able to measure the strength and estimate the danger which they represented. And it has been demonstrated that, for an experienced diver, it is possible to handle a cephalopod weighing 125 pounds and measuring 20 feet in diameter. Once our prejudices have been demolished, man and octopus will be able to live together in harmony in the same sea.

Never did the Seattle octopuses seem so beautiful and so worthy of consideration as when we watched them "walking" on the bottom. It was then that we were able to observe and appreciate the complexity of a movement which is neither a crawl nor a slide, but an extremely supple motion whose component parts are difficult to determine. The animal goes forward, its arms stretched in the shape of a fan, as though he were exploring what lay ahead. The first two dorsal arms are extended; the next two follow and take the weight of the octopus' body and move it forward, while the body is carried at a slant. It is almost an indecipherable motion in which the entire body participates, while the arms are moving slowly and surely.

This is the usual mode of locomotion for giant octopuses, who do not move by jet propulsion except in case of panic. Otherwise, they would not be in a position to hunt, since, when they move by expelling water through the funnel, they are moving backward and cannot see where they are going.

We kept aboard *Calypso*, for some time, an aquarium containing a giant octopus from Seattle. It looked even larger in the aquarium than it had in the ocean. We wanted to examine a specimen at our leisure, and so Bernard Delemotte had brought us one—wrapped around his arm. The octopus was red with emotion. Once in its aquarium, however, it calmed down and took on its normal coloration, especially after we gave it its first meal.

I already knew from experience the strength and ingenuity that an octo-

On *Calypso*'s rear deck, several octopuses are kept for observation in a tarpaulin filled with water.

Left. An octopus, red with anger, is brought aboard *Calypso*.

pus can bring to the task of escaping from confinement. The aquarium at Monaco has taught me something about this, where I saw octopuses, living in constantly renewed and oxygenated water, struggling to escape so as to end up on the floor, without hope of survival.

I knew too that, at the end of a certain amount of time, octopuses become accustomed to captivity and to man's presence—especially if small stones are put into their tanks for them to hide among and to build houses out of.

I was hoping that, aboard *Calypso*, our giant octopus, being well treated, well fed, and living in water, temperature of which was kept constant, would accept his situation and become accustomed to us. As it happened, however, the tank was too small and the octopus too large. It succeeded in raising and removing the cover that we had placed on the aquarium, and which we had weighted with several 20-pound weights. We saw its arms emerge one by one, then its eyes, then its body slide down onto *Calypso*'s rear deck. We did not try to stop it. The sea was only a few feet away, and we were already feeling guilty about having deprived an animal of its liberty—a splendid animal made for freedom. Sitting in one's office or home, or working in a laboratory, it is very easy to reconcile oneself to the belief that animals must be captured and observed for the advancement of knowledge and for the sake of human progress. But when we are brought face to face with a creature like an octopus, with its appearance of *knowing*, then it becomes difficult to maintain one's detachment. I think that each of us, in our hearts, was happy to see the octopus slide over *Calypso*'s side and drop into the sea.

The last news received from Seattle was encouraging. Jerry Brown, a good friend and an excellent diver who spent several days aboard *Calypso*, has found a giant octopus in a sunken ship, and he has succeeded in taming it. Which shows that communication between cephalopods and man is not impossible, and that reconciliation between man and his legendary enemy in the sea is around the corner.

THREE

The Lady and the Octopus

A Heroine for James Bond

The most surprising thing that we found in the waters of Seattle was not the giant octopus, but Joanne Duffy, the diver and marine biologist whose exploits I have just touched on briefly. Joanne is very feminine, well rounded, quite striking in a bathing suit. At the same time, she is a superb athlete, surprisingly strong, and very levelheaded. Apart from her professional qualifications, she is an intriguing woman, with just enough reserve about herself and her private life to create a faint air of mystery. Altogether, a James Bond heroine. We have seen her pass her air bottle over her head with one hand, and yet, under her delicate skin, there is scarcely a sign of muscle.

Joanne does not talk about herself much, and this makes her of more than ordinary interest to us. How and why had she become an expert diver? And, above all, why does she take such a special interest in octopuses? We have all had ample opportunity to see and judge the way that divers, both men and women, behave in the water, especially when they come face to face

Right. Joanne Duffy at the Seattle laboratory.

Left. Joanne Duffy with her favorite octopus.

Below. Joanne pets an octopus which she has tamed.

with an animal of the size and weight of a giant octopus. As a result of our experiences, we have perhaps become overly critical. But Joanne, in every one of the dives she has made with us, consistently handles herself in a way that elicits our respect and unreserved admiration.

In the water, she is perfectly at ease. She swims around, searching among the algae and the anemones and sticking her hand into crevices in the rocks to flush out "monsters" the very sight of which has horrified men for three thousand years. And, when she succeeds, she handles 125-pound octopuses as though they were trained dogs in a circus. It is a memorable sight to witness: Joanne working at close quarters with an eight-armed animal at least as big as herself.

Joanne was a great help to us, and from her we have learned many things. Without her, we would have spent much more time than we have exploring the strange underwater world of Seattle, learning how to lure octopuses out of their houses, taming them, photographing and filming them. Joanne, among her other accomplishments, is a fine actress, and she has shown a perfect willingness to co-operate in any way that she can while we are filming. Upon request, she can hold an octopus in her arms, lead it out into open water, or even bring it up to the surface.

"Joanne," I asked, "how do you manage to stay so calm all the time? I've never seen you make a wasted motion in the water."

"It's because I'm studying karate," she answered. And, when she saw us exchange glances, she added, "Oh, it's not to defend myself against men. I use it for self-confidence, as a kind of training. It's also a sort of mental and spiritual discipline for me. When I get home after a session, exhausted, covered with sweat, I have the feeling that I've accomplished something. I have three sessions a week. But I'm just a beginner."

We are determined to learn more about this young lady, this octopus trainer who is happiest when she is exhausted and covered with sweat.

A Vocation

Joanne, although reserved, seems willing to tell us about her background. She was born in Montana. As a young girl, she loved to swim and often entered contests. She came to Seattle with her parents when she was

Right. "It was a squid of colossal size." Neuville's illustration for *Twenty Thousand Leagues under the Sea,* by Jules Verne.

Following page. Gary and Joanne struggling with a giant octopus.

sixteen, and it was then that she first saw the ocean. All of her swimming until then had been in the lakes of Montana, and she had never done any diving. Neither of her parents had any taste for swimming. Her mother, in fact, was horrified at the very idea of going into the water.

Joanne found few friends, either boys or girls, in Seattle. Her great interest was watching underwater films on television—especially Lloyd Bridges' "Sea Hunt" series. In order to meet other young people interested in diving, she joined a diving club; and, finally, without asking her parents, she signed up for an underwater-hunting contest. Her reason was that "it sounded like fun."

The contest required that a participant stay in the water for five or six hours in free dive, catching fish. The one who caught the most fish was the winner. Joanne's largest single catch weighed about twenty pounds. The contests were held at the local, state, and national levels. Women were eligible to participate in all of these. The international competition, however, was closed to them. Only men were eligible for that.

Even now, when telling the story, Joanne's nose wrinkles in resentment. She does not hide the fact that she has a few accounts to settle with the male chauvinists.

In 1967, she stopped participating in these contests.

"Why?" I asked.

"Oh, nothing was happening, and it wasn't fun any more."

"Did you think that these hunts were harmful to marine life? That ecology was affected?"

"It wasn't so much ecology as the fact that people weren't very pleasant when, at the end of a contest, they would see all those fish stacked up on the beach. It didn't seem to matter that everyone eats fish, or that we always gave the fish away to hospitals or charitable institutions."

"Joanne, when did you begin to dive?"

"I received my first certificate in March 1963. It's just nine years ago, but it seems forever. In 1967, I received my certificate as an instructor, and I became chief instructor here in Seattle."

Octopuses Grow on Trees

The thing that interests us most is why Joanne has taken up octopuses as her specialty. "Every year," she explains, "Seattle had an octopus-fishing contest. Whoever won it was the world's champion octopus fisherman, if for no other reason than that it was the only octopus-fishing competition in the world.* It was held in Tacoma, where most of the octopuses are. We would

---

* The authors condemn this type of hunt, and Joanne herself has given it up.

catch them, weigh them, and then put them back into the water. The contest took place in April or May, and the first one was held in 1967. I took part only in a few of them, because people couldn't accept the fact that a woman really could be interested in octopuses. There aren't many people who are able to catch them, you know.

"The first time I was in a contest it was held in the area of Port Townsend. We had to dive among enormous logs that had been thrown into the water by lumber companies. And of course we were told a lot of stories about those logs. Some of it was true, and some of it was pure fantasy. People said that huge, ferocious octopuses would latch onto the underside of the logs and then drop, like spiders, onto a diver's head. So far as octopuses hanging onto the logs was concerned, it was true. They did. But I don't think that one ever actually attacked a diver. Even so, it wasn't very pleasant, swimming along and thinking that, at any moment, a giant octopus might drop on you. I've heard that it has happened; but it certainly doesn't happen often. In any case, I spent my whole dive looking upward at the underside of the logs, trying to see if there was an octopus lying in wait for me. Nothing happened, of course, which is just as well. If I had had an unfortunate experience so early, I would probably never have gotten over it, and I wouldn't want to have anything to do with octopuses today.

"The problem in dealing with octopuses is that there is something about them which causes a diver to panic. Then you don't know what you are doing any more, and the situation becomes dangerous. An octopus can rip off your mask, or your mouthpiece; then, you can't see and you can't breathe. Unless you're a very experienced diver and you know exactly what to do, you are really in trouble."

"How do you go about getting out of trouble?"

"Oh, it's really quite simple. You hold the octopus at arm's length and, at the moment that its arms start coming toward you, you rock it from side to side. Its arms then turn soft and drop."

"Our small Mediterranean octopuses never react like that."

"That is probably because they are fighting so hard that you can't get a really good grip on them. The octopuses here are large and heavy, but their movements are relatively slow, and if you hold them firmly they soon relax. They try to climb onto you, of course; but they don't mean any harm by it, and they soon give up. The whole trick is to hold them at a distance, and not to let their arms rip off your equipment—your mask and your mouthpiece. It's really a matter of getting used to it. What I do, as I said, is to make them lie down in the water; that is, I put their bodies in a horizontal position. In that position, it seems that they calm down and are easily handled. The thing to avoid is being rough with them, or frightening them. If they sense that you

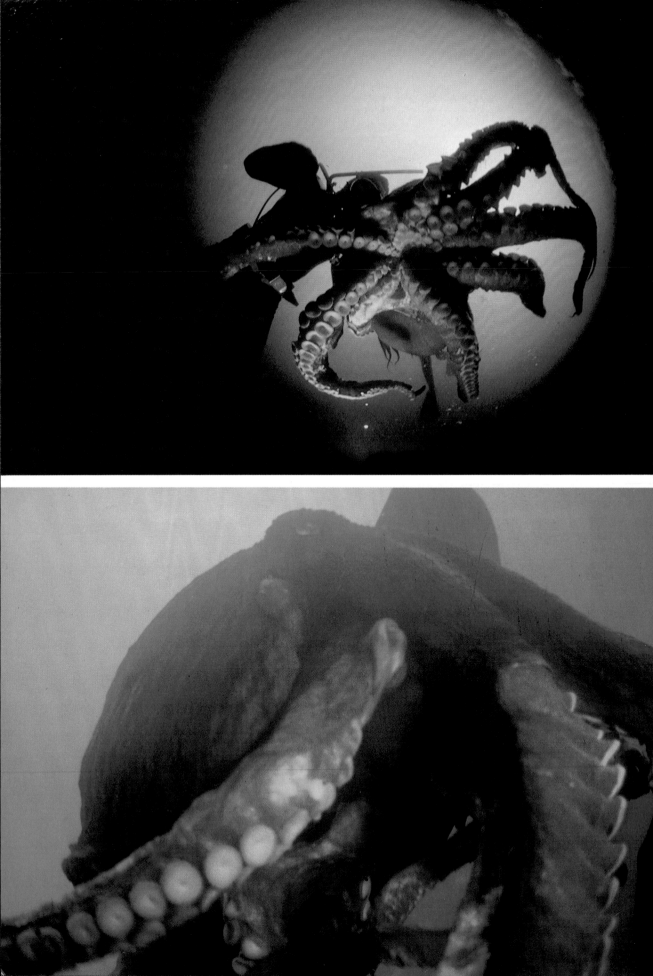

are nervous, they tend to panic, and then anything can happen."

In listening to Joanne's matter-of-fact approach to the giant octopus, we cannot help thinking of Victor Hugo, Gilliatt, and the monsters of Guernsey. There is some discussion of Jules Verne, too; and, aboard *Calypso*, a worn copy of *Twenty Thousand Leagues Under the Sea* is passed from hand to hand. Of particular interest are the illustrations, which everyone inspects with mixed nostalgia and irony. One caption reads: "It was a gigantic squid." The illustration shows Captain Nemo, booted and bearded, standing in the observation chamber of the *Nautilus*, his arms folded, calmly contemplating the monster lurking outside. The trouble is that the "gigantic squid" is an octopus, as is easily seen from its eight arms. Another illustration showed the monster seizing an unfortunate sailor from the *Nautilus* in one of its arms.

Left above. The Seattle octopus can reach an impressive size: over thirty feet in spread and a weight of seventy-five pounds.

Left below. *Octopus apollyon,* the North American octopus, is as large as the "monsters" which excited such terror during the nineteenth century.

Below. Joanne, carrying one octopus, goes to help Gary, who is struggling with another.

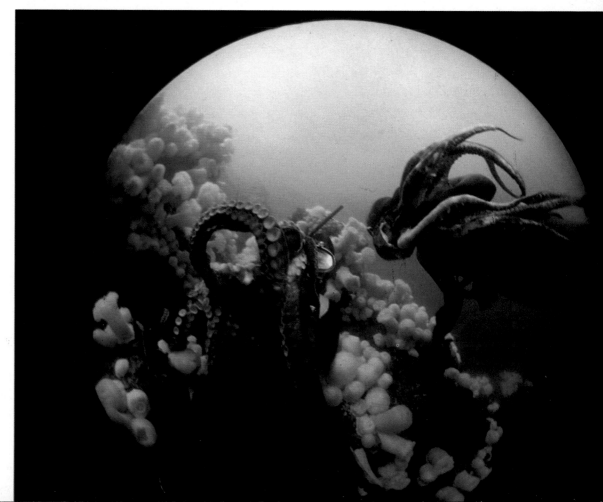

The giant octopuses are not much smaller than those created by the imagination of Verne's illustrator, though they are surely less aggressive.

To the Kelp

"Before you can wrestle with an octopus," Joanne cautions us, "you have to find one. And that's not easy. Octopuses are so good at camouflage that finding them is an art in itself. You can swim right past a dozen of them without ever knowing that they're there. They hide under kelp, and they change their appearance and their color so well that they are easily confused with the algae. They also change color with the tide, and you can look in the kelp all day without finding one."

We ask Joanne more detailed questions about her relationship with octopuses. Has she encountered the same octopus more than once? Has she ever found an octopus house and gone back to visit it several times? Is it possible to establish friendly relations with a particular octopus? We are particularly interested in these things, we explain, because they are precisely what we ourselves have done in the Mediterranean.

"In this respect, at least," Joanne says, "the giant octopus is no different from the small octopus. The giant octopus finds a house and stays in it. If the house is one it likes, it will come back to it every year. I know of one place in the bay, at Alchive, where one octopus has returned to the same hole several years in a row. I know that this is true, hard as it may be to believe. We have been able to do some marking of octopuses, and from this we have learned that, when octopuses go out to deeper water, they return eventually to the place they started out from; and some of them even go back to the very same holes they had before. Their homing instinct is very well developed. At Keystone Jetty, for example, there is one particular hole that has always been occupied, so far as I can tell, by the same octopus."

A Movie Star

"Even before I began to dive," Joanne tells us, "Jerry Brown had filmed an episode for "Sea Hunt' that involved a killer octopus. It was one of the giant octopuses found in cold water, especially in the northern Pacific. The star of this episode was a specimen that weighed 115 pounds. They kept the animal four days, while filming the sequence; and, at the end of that time, it had become so docile that they could get it to follow them around by using one of its arms as a leash. They kept the octopus in a large rubber dinghy, in which it seemed perfectly content; at least it did not try to escape. They fed it well, of course—crabs for dinner every night. The octopus worked very well, and, for all practical purposes, was fully domesticated.

"There was one sequence in the film in which the octopus was supposed to be lured out of its hole by offering it a scallop as bait. The opening of the scallop shell under water was part of the sequence. It worked better than anybody had thought. As soon as the octopus saw the shell, it tried to grab it away from the divers. There was a big fight which, naturally, the octopus won. It had not lost all of its natural instincts."

A Co-operative Octopus

"There used to be a marine garden of sorts at Keystone Jetty, at which divers served as guides for visitors. I worked there for two years. The main attraction consisted in carrying a large octopus to the window of the observation chamber for the customers to see. Which meant that, first of all, I had to find an octopus of the right size, and then find a proper house for it where it would be easily available. I found an animal, but, since it was new, it was not very co-operative at first. After two or three tries, however, it seemed to understand that I was not going to hurt it; and, from then on, it was willing to do whatever I wanted it to do. This made my job a lot easier.

"It was at that time that I learned to appreciate the intelligence and judgment of the octopus. They seem able to think, and even to reason.* In the two years I spent working there, I had ample opportunity to see to what extent they were able even to measure the passing of time. The visitors' tours usually lasted twenty minutes, and, when we were very busy, the schedule was followed strictly. My octopus behaved as though it knew all about the schedule. By the time I would get to its hole, it was ready to come out. And it seemed able to adapt itself to the routine.

"Each diver had a particular way of taking it to the visitors' observation window. The first two times that I was on duty, I carried it in my arms. After that, all I had to do was tickle its arms a little and it would swim right up to the window. Afterward, I would swim back to its hole with it. We didn't reward it in any way after each performance. We fed it regularly, of course—crabs and clams—but its food didn't depend in any way on the quality of its

---

*There is Joanne Duffy's opinion, based upon her own observations. Scientists, although they concede that the octopus has a memory and that it learns quickly, do not use the word "intelligence" in describing it.

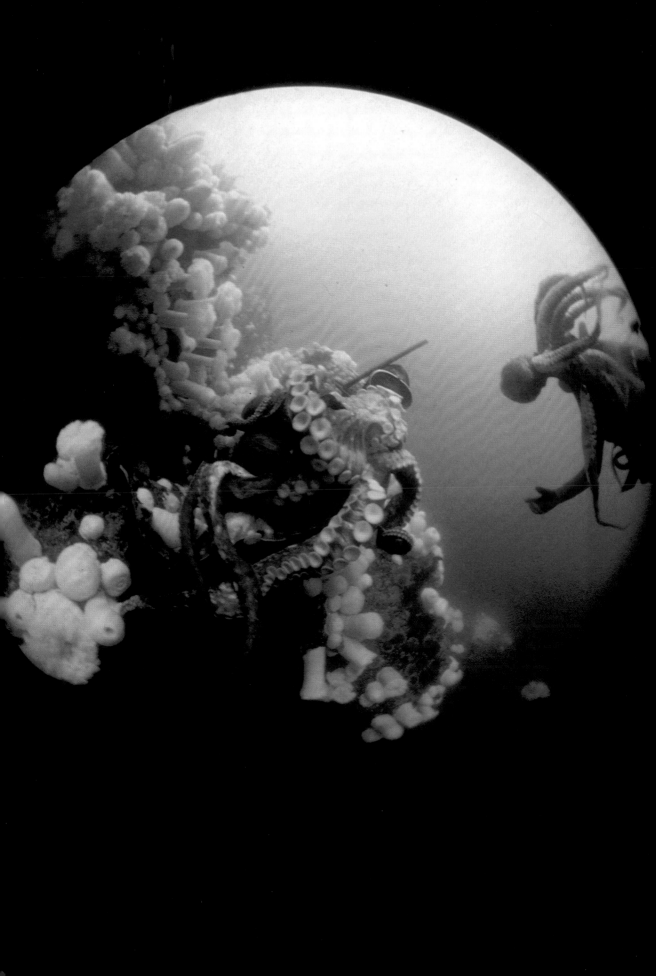

Left. Gary, carrying an octopus, swims toward Joanne.

Above. Joanne brings an octopus ashore.

Below. Captured octopuses are weighed and then put back into the water.

performance. I got the impression that it did what it did simply because it wanted to."

"Did it obey, do you think, because it liked you? Or was it because it liked to be around humans and liked being petted?"

"Octopuses like to be petted, certainly. But it has to be done very gently, and one has to be careful. There were several divers at our marine garden, and the octopuses showed a decided preference for some of them, and an aversion for others. If a diver handled an octopus too roughly, it was difficult to get that octopus to do its number for the visitors. It could also happen that an octopus which had been treated roughly became quite docile, simply because it was in bad shape. I am not talking about hitting an octopus, or pinching it, but about not being sufficiently gentle with it. If it is handled roughly, it seems to lapse into a state of complete exhaustion.

"It is hard to keep in mind that octopuses of the size and weight of these are really very fragile animals, highly developed and with a very sensitive nervous system. They seem to succumb easily to nervous disorders. If a diver is too rough with an octopus, even without actually hurting it physically, it happens that the animal goes into a state of emotional shock and sometimes dies.

"When an octopus is angry, it often changes color. If, for example, you surprise an octopus on the bottom and touch it near the head, it turns white, and then brick-red—which is the color of discontent. It takes about two seconds for the entire body to change its color. Then the animal holds its arms over its head, like a protective helmet, and runs away in that position."

The Most Beautiful Creature in the Sea

To me, it would seem normal for a young lady to feel an almost instinctive disgust at a creature as sticky and slimy as an octopus. I asked Joanne whether she had ever experienced this reaction.

"No, never," she answered. "I don't know why. The only thing I can say is that, so far as I am concerned, the octopus is the most beautiful creature in the sea. Even when it is not moving, it is something marvelous to look at. I've never felt the repugnance that people say they experience around octopuses. Maybe such people have never seen or touched an octopus in the water. After all, we have to judge animals in their own environment, and not in ours."

"How about the octopus' ink cloud," I asked. "Does it bother you?"

"No, not at all. I can't really say whether an octopus uses its ink often or rarely. It depends upon the individual octopus and upon the circumstances. If it's an octopus that doesn't know you, then you can expect a healthy squirt of

Left. To approach an octopus without frightening it requires much patience and a "feel" for octopuses.

ink right at the beginning, especially if it is an aggressive octopus. It will try to get away, change its color, and shoot out some ink. But if you hold it firmly, it will stop trying to escape—regardless of how angry it seems or how much ink it shoots. It will calm down very quickly, and the ink will stop."

Poisonous Bites

"There is a lot of talk about octopus bites and about their deadly poison. I once saw a fight between an eel and an octopus. I think that these fights are frequent, because they often want the same hole as their lair. In this case, the match was a draw, and both animals swam away. It looked to me as though the eel had not been bitten. In any case, it was not paralyzed. There is only one species of octopus whose poison is fatal to man, and it lives in the waters around Australia. Cuttlefish and squid are well equipped to bite; but the same thing is not true about the octopus, since its beak is located at the base of its arms and is surrounded by them. So, in order to be able to bite, the octopus must either be right up against its victim, or it must somehow bring it up to its beak. And this is not easy for an octopus to do with a diver.

"If you are holding an octopus and it begins to wrap its arms around you and to press up against your body, then you can be sure that it regards you as its prey. In that case, all you have to do is put your hand under its body and

Joanne Duffy after a dive in Seattle Bay.

Right. Long before Joanne's time, Hercules was battling monsters. One of these was the famous Hydra. This *lékuthos,* or oil jar, dating from the sixth century before Christ, is attributed to the painter Diosphos. (Louvre Museum, Department of Greek and Roman Antiquities. Photo: Chuzeville.)

make it straighten its arms to put it in a horizontal position. At that point, it will make use of its funnel to shoot away from you. It's much easier for them to defend themselves with their arms than to use their beaks; and that is what they do. But even that does not happen when an octopus is accustomed to humans."

I must say that, at least so far as octopus bites are concerned, I am not of the same opinion as Joanne. As willing as we may be to believe that octopuses do not bite, no one in our team thinks for a minute that it is because they *cannot* bite. It has happened more than once that Delemotte or Michel Deloire has had a hand, an arm, or even their faces, within biting distance of an octopus' beak—which is, after all, a rather terrible sight. An octopus can rear up over a diver, and then its beak can easily reach the diver's flesh. Or the animal can assume what we call the "flower position," which we have often photographed, with its arms extended, and its mantle opened wide, and its beak fully exposed. The beak, in appearance, is a formidable weapon. And yet, it does not seem that the octopus uses it. Joanne is quite certain on that score. None of us has ever been bitten, and I have never heard reports of anyone in the Seattle area having been bitten. I do not know why the beak is not used. It may be because the octopus has a better weapon: a poison which paralyzes, and which is produced by the salivary glands. But this poison is not injected by means of the beak. Instead, the octopus brings its prey close to its mouth and "spits" the poison onto it. Victor Hugo seems not to have known about this, for, in all the imaginary horrors he dredges up to describe the octopus, he never once mentions its real weapon.

Other species of cephalopods, however, use their beaks to attack their

prey. It is well established that cuttlefish bite. Albert Falco has seen a diver seriously wounded by the bite of a cuttlefish. "But," he says, "I have never seen an octopus bite anyone, and I have never heard of an incident of this kind."

How to Tell Your Friends from Your Enemies

We ask Joanne to tell us how she recognizes the octopuses with which she was on friendly terms—how she distinguishes them from the others.

"Oh," she says, "it's easy. I never get them mixed up, because octopuses don't really all look alike. They don't live in the same holes, of course. But, more than that, there are differences in size. Some have long arms, and some have short arms. Some have battle scars, and so forth. The real problem is not how we tell octopuses apart, but how they tell *us* apart. And they are able to distinguish among us, you know, even though every diver wears more or less the same sort of suit. It may be that the octopus can tell by the way in which a particular diver swims or holds himself in the water. Not all divers have the same manner in the water, and not all are equally skilled. That, I think, is very important. There are also differences in the way that different divers approach an octopus and touch it on the head or on the mantle. When I approach a strange octopus it takes a certain amount of time before I can handle it, and I am not always successful on the first try.

"I have a favorite octopus. I can tell it from the others by a scar on its mantle which does not change color when the rest of the body does. It looks as though the skin had been worn off at that spot."

"Is it a male or a female?"

"A male. You can tell by the suction disks. A male octopus, once he grows beyond a certain size, has one or more suction disks which are noticeably larger than the others, and which look unusually white. It may be that this is the sign of sexual maturity among males.

"Mating among the octopuses does not take place here, in Elliott Bay. The octopuses leave in April or May and head for deeper water, and they mate there. They return in October or November. I have never seen them mate, but I don't think that the female dies after reproducing. Certainly, they must mate several times during their lives. It takes a while for a cephalopod to reach the size of those here—up to 250 pounds. But, even though we have tagged some of them, we have never been able to discover just what their life span is.

"Sometimes," Joanne says, "I wonder why I feel as I do about octopuses. It's very complicated. What I like about them is that they seem to be very intelligent and sensitive, and yet very different from us. It is not sympathy that I feel for them, but an emotion. It is not a mutual friendship, but an attraction—something physical. I want to protect them, to prevent their being hurt. I want them to be able to continue to live here, in their natural environment, without people coming to bother them too much.

"To tell you the truth, I am very partial to everything that lives in the sea. I'm studying biology at the College of Fisheries at the University of Washington, and I will take my last exams at Christmas. After that, I hope to be able to work for the National Wildlife Service, especially at its research laboratory in Seattle. It's very hard, however, for a woman to break into that field. There is a systematic opposition to women that is difficult to distinguish from outright discrimination. There is too much prejudice about what women should or should not do. Too many people still feel that a woman's place is in the home, or in the kitchen."

In these circumstances, it is understandable that Joanne has much sympathy for the fem lib movement. She regards herself as being realistic and reasonable, and she denies being an extremist; but when she handles her octopuses, or takes her exams, she impresses me as being determined to prove that women are every bit as capable as men.

Joanne's profession by no means excludes domestic happiness, love, and marriage. When we asked her what kind of man she hopes to be able to find, she answers: "Someone I can admire. Someone who is a better athlete than I, who dives better than I, and who is a black belt in karate. And that, of course, eliminates about 91 per cent of men—for most men are vegetables."

This, no doubt, is an expression common in Montana.

I hope that Joanne will forgive me if I say that her case is by no means unique. It is even possible that we may have discovered the reasons for her friendship with the octopus. In Greek mythology, one of the twelve labors of Hercules was to overcome the nine-headed Hydra, which was an obvious symbol of the male principle. For a woman determined to liberate herself, an eight-armed octopus is, no doubt, the equal of a nine-headed Hydra.

An underwater cliff covered with sea fans—an excellent hiding place for octopuses.

FOUR

The Battle of the Amphora

The giant octopuses of Seattle, so far as size was concerned, were everything that we could have wanted, and our film sequences of them are quite spectacular. Nonetheless, it must be admitted that we were rather disappointed at their lack of strong reaction when they are held in the open water.

Following our experiences with these giants, the Mediterranean octopus, when we returned to it, suddenly seemed very small indeed; but it compensated for this by being extremely active. At this time, *Calypso* was still on an expedition in the Pacific, and I placed Albert Falco at the head of a group of divers whose assignment it was to study these cephalopods. For this purpose, they made use of our Marseilles boat, the *Espadon*, a converted trawler.

Falco, who has been one of our team for twenty years, grew up in the environs of Marseilles, and he is completely familiar with the bottom along that coast. He had already explored the grouper holes in that area, and he knew where to look for octopuses. At his instructions, the first dives of the mission took place near a small island at the entry to the port of Marseilles: the island of Riou.

Riou is a historic place. Since the time of the Greeks of Phocaea, 2,500 years before Christ, it has been a ship's graveyard, and wrecks have followed one another with depressing regularity at the entrance to the "old port." Divers who know the place see the whole spectrum of man's history in the Mediterranean on the bottom, from the vestiges of Roman galleys to the shells and depth charges of World War II.

Falco knew all this. And he knew especially how to find the numerous octopuses who are able to make themselves invisible to a less experienced eye by melting into the smallest opening, and, through their extraordinary mimetic talent, by taking on the color of the bottom.

The Water-jug Trap

The unusual abilities of the Mediterranean octopus, however, have not always been sufficient to save them, for the Mediterranean fishermen have a few tricks of their own. In order to catch octopuses, they make use of a method which goes back to the Greeks and the Romans—who, in turn, borrowed it from the Egyptians. They let down into the water a group of jugs, about ten of them fixed to a frame. The frame sinks to the bottom. The octopuses, with the affection that they have for jars and containers of any description, quickly take up residence in the jugs. It sometimes happens that, when the fishermen pull the frame up to the surface, they find an octopus in every one of the jugs.

The *Espadon*, having left the port of Marseilles, sailed past the Chateau d'If—celebrated as the setting chosen by Alexandre Dumas for his novel, *The Count of Monte Cristo*. Not far from there, a fisherman, in the sort of small boat that we call a *pointu*, had already lowered his octopus-catching apparatus into the water. The *Espadon* stopped, and our men could see that it was a good catch. Almost every one of the jugs was occupied. The fisherman removed the octopuses one by one and quickly killed them by biting them at the base of the eyes. This is the classic method of dispatching an octopus. It appears cruel, but it is effective and quick. The animal has no time to suffer. It assumes a fair knowledge of the octopus' anatomy, and its effect is to destroy the brain. There is another method, not so humane, which consists in turning back the octopus' mantle so as to expose its gills to the air. The animal then suffocates. But an octopus out of water can survive for as long as one hour—which represents a long period of agony for an animal with a nervous system as highly developed as that of the octopus.

The Wall

The *Espadon* dropped anchor off the island of Riou. Falco, Deloire, and Genest suited up immediately and dived, with lights and an underwater camera.

The first experiment was to observe the reactions of an octopus when the wall of its house was destroyed. For this, Falco and his team chose the largest octopus they could find. First, they removed the stones blocking the entry to its den and installed a camera, operated by remote control, on a tripod. Then they withdrew. They had to wait almost an hour before the octopus put one arm out of its hole. Little by little, without leaving the hole, the octopus extended its arms toward the material still lying around outside of its house. It touched a pebble with the end of an arm, and felt it to determine its size and weight. Then, with its arm extended, it passed the pebble from sucker disk to sucker disk until it reached the hole where, with the help of another arm, it was used in the construction of the wall. The process continued until the wall was entirely rebuilt; and it was identical in every respect with that which the divers had demolished.

The problem of housing is of primary importance for the octopus. Its life depends upon its ability to find shelter. It is without other defense against its mortal enemies, eels and groupers. For this, it needs not only a shelter, but one which the octopus alone can enter and which will keep out large predators.

The octopus' den is also its center of operations. From there, it explores the surrounding area, hunts, and, in the case of males, goes out in search of a female.

Pottery fragments are, from the standpoint of the octopus, an ideal home, and octopuses will fight to the death over them. For the first time, it was possible to film one of these encounters in open water. And this is how it came about. Michel Deloire placed the lower part of an amphora—which makes an excellent octopus house—on the bottom in an area where there were an unusually large number of octopuses. This was at Riou, in exceptionally good weather, in water between 35 and 45 feet deep. There was a ferocious battle between two large octopuses for possession of the amphora, and Deloire and his companions stayed in the water for five hours, filming the battle from beginning to end. When their air gave out, as it did several times, the bottles were replaced by others sent down from the *Espadon*.

For a long time, it was difficult to make out exactly which way the battle was going. It seemed a free-for-all, with sixteen arms thrashing about. There were feints, thrusts, sneak attacks, shows of force, with each of the octopuses managing to avoid the other's grasp. The combatants were of about the same

size, weight, and strength. The objective seemed to be for one octopus to succeed in getting an arm under the mantle of the other octopus. But both of them defended themselves very well and were able to parry any thrusts. Finally, one of the two animals succeeded in wrapping its arms around the other in such a way as to immobilize its mantle. The defeated octopus began to smother. It lost its color, while the other was a bright red. In the sequence filmed by Deloire, the victor was able to penetrate so deeply as to have the tip of its arm emerge from the funnel of its enemy. Now, the defeated octopus was grayish, and, on the point of death by asphyxiation, it became almost completely white.

Before the octopus could die, however, the divers—who, after all, had started the fight—separated the combatants. The winner occupied the amphora which he had just won, while the defeated octopus took refuge in a rusted pail.

We do not know whether such a battle between octopuses may be interpreted as the kind of territorial defense which is so common in the animal world. Fish defend their territorial waters, it is true, but the octopus seems to defend only its house. It fights to defend its shelter, its den, the vital spot in which it feels protected, rather than the area in which it hunts or mates. Its drive seems to be to build walls and to find stones to shelter its sensitive flesh; to acquire, as it were, a surrogate shell.

It seems that there are frequent housing crises in the world of the octopus. For they are often seen wandering around, looking for a cave, a hole, or any kind of opening into which they will fit and which they can protect by building a wall.

Even though octopuses are concerned first with fortifying their houses, they also take pains to keep them clean and even to make them comfortable. Inside, they smooth the sand with jets of water from their funnel, and they are careful, above all, to remove the debris of their meals. As soon as they have finished eating, any shells or other leavings are pushed outside. And this debris, of course, is one sign that a particular hole or artifact is the home of an octopus.

The Octopus as a Loner

It is clear that octopuses are not social animals. Although a group of octopuses may live together in the same general area, they live separately, except during the mating season. They seem to prefer living alone. As soon as

Left. At Riou, Jean-Pierre Genest plays with a Mediterranean octopus (*Octopus vulgaris*).

Left. Aboard the *Espadon*, Falco and Bonnici suit up for a dive.

Right. Limestone algae, sea fans, and red coral on a wall of the Sormiou *calanque,* or cove.

Below. A diver evicts an octopus living in a fragment of amphora.

one octopus approaches the den of another, either there is a fight, or the resident merely extends an arm and the intruder takes the hint and leaves. Falco has, on occasion, brought octopuses near a house that was obviously occupied. As soon as they saw that there was already an octopus in the neighborhood, they left. "In an underwater area of about 600 square feet," Falco says, "there are between ten and fifteen octopuses. But they live from 60 to 90 feet apart." This, apparently, is the acceptable social distance.

Falco believes that octopuses hunt virtually without leaving their houses, except at night—and especially at dawn and dusk. But, in fact, the habits of the octopus are not very predictable, for even during the day one sees them on the bottom, or on rocks and algae; and, at the same time, one also sees some of them in their holes. It may be that if an octopus is hungry and nothing edible comes within reach, it goes out to hunt for prey. The preferred diet of the octopus is crab, for shrimp are a bit too fast for octopuses.

The Octopus as Actor

The unpredictable habits of octopuses made life difficult for Falco and Deloire when they were diving to shoot various sequences, for they seldom were able to use the same specimens from one sequence to the next.

"It's not as bad as one might think," Falco says. "To begin with, some animals are more talented than others. Our first job was to pick out the best ones and to confine our efforts to those. We learned how to avoid frightening them and how to calm them. The important thing for an octopus is to have a shelter. Unless one is available, the octopus is afraid and is constantly looking for a place to hide. It is impossible to do anything with it. But, as soon as it has found a hole, it feels secure. It takes only a few minutes for it to learn that we don't intend to harm it, and it quickly gains confidence in us. It then comes halfway out of its hole—though it is rare for an octopus to come completely out of it. If an octopus is a 'good subject,' it becomes curious about the divers and seems to be watching what they do.

"If we put a crab in front of its house—and, of course, we do so quite often—it concentrates completely on getting it. It changes color, and we can see its eyes on the crab. One might almost say that the octopus is thinking about the crab. It is the marine animal which most gives the impression of being able to 'meditate.' It watches the crab, then suddenly, it seems to arrive at a decision. It puts out an arm, seizes the crab, and pulls it into the hole if it senses the presence of a diver. But it also happens that the octopus will eat the crab outside its hole if it is not afraid.

"Sometimes the octopus glides smoothly over the bottom until it is six or eight inches away from the crab, and then suddenly covers it with its interbrachial membrane and takes it back to its hole. During this procedure, it changes color, gets darker, and shows granulations and spots. It appears that there is some conflict between the hunger which makes it approach the crab, and the wariness which makes it retreat to its hole; a conflict which is manifested by a variation in color and also by a muscular tension in the whole body."

It is easy enough to work with octopuses. They are much less "alien" than is commonly believed.

"I had often encountered octopuses while diving around Marseilles," Falco relates, "but I had never tried to approach them. I had no idea, I must confess, that one could do so much with them. I thought that, as soon as an octopus saw you, it would scurry into its hole and stay there, and that would be the end of it. But that's not the case at all. We've been able to film scenes that I would have thought were impossible. For instance, an octopus in its hole uses all sorts of gestures to attract its prey. It curls up in front of its house, and it twists its arms in every conceivable way. It is likely that these movements attract crustaceans. But if this does not work, it has other tricks. It is a very clever animal.

"The octopus itself is attracted by a waving object, or by one that shines. But it always approaches with great caution, and always feels the object first with the tip of an arm. But it very quickly becomes accustomed to taking whatever we bring it to eat.

"The sight of an octopus eating a crab is really extraordinary. But it is difficult to observe this spectacle, because the first thing the octopus does is to hide the crab under its interbrachial membrane. And, once that has been done, we cannot see what is happening. But we have been able to get hold of some octopuses and turn them over when they are eating, and so we know how they go about it.

"An octopus, depending on its size, may have as many as 240 sucker disks per arm, for a total of 1,920. These disks are very effective weapons. Experiments made at the Zoological Station at Naples have demonstrated that an *Octopus vulgaris* weighing three pounds can exert a traction of forty pounds. Its victim, therefore, has almost no chance of escaping. Once the crustacean is under the interbrachial membrane, it is given a close-range spurt of venom from the octopus' salivary glands. This poison, cephalotoxin, is capable of killing an animal the size of a rabbit. The crustacean is paralyzed almost instantly. An octopus can seize a lobster larger than itself and immobilize it by its poison, without using its beak. The octopus will then wait as long as twenty minutes before beginning to eat. It may be that it is not immune to its own poison. It then uses its beak to open the crustacean at the joining of the cephalothorax and the abdomen (just as humans do), and it

An octopus on a bed of Roman amphorae off the island of Riou.

first eats the soft parts. The tips of the octopus' arms penetrate into the small-est joints of the lobster's legs and claws, and all the meat is carried from sucker disk to sucker disk to the octopus' mouth. In this way, the crustacean is wholly drained of meat, and is then pushed outside the octopus' hole. By then, it is empty—but absolutely intact.

"It has not been possible, so far, to establish the presence of enzymes in the octopus' salivary glands* which would facilitate ingestion of its prey. But

*There are arguments for both sides of the question.

An octopus house, with pebblestone fortifications.

it is likely that the octopus makes use of a liquid which is capable of softening flesh. It is even possible that a part of the digestive process takes place outside the octopus' body.

"A crab of medium size is eaten, and the shell entirely emptied, in a half hour. A lobster requires more time—as much as an entire afternoon. But the octopus' digestive process is slow, lasting from eight to twenty-four hours."

The tips of the octopus' arms are very delicate and sensitive. They are able to penetrate almost any opening, and they also serve to provide the animal with essential tactile information.

The octopus' buccal system, which is located at the center of the brachial crown, is very complex and also plays a part in the ingestion of food. It comprises two beaked jaws, of which the lower covers the upper. This parrot's beak is concealed under two lips, a radula composed of successive rows of five teeth, and the tongue, which is reinforced by a cartilage to which the muscles are attached.

Some marine animals, the echinoderms—sea stars, sea urchins, sea cucumbers—do not seem to fear the poison of the octopus. We brought a sea star to one of our octopuses, and it appeared to wish to avoid contact with the star.

Eyes Almost Human

What struck our divers most about the octopus were its eyes. Cephalopods are invertebrates, and, among the invertebrates, they are the ones whose eyes have attained the highest degree of perfection. The eyes of cephalopods are almost the equal of those of men. Their eyes, like those of vertebrates, have lids, irises, crystalline lenses, and retinas. But a diver does not have to be aware of this to sense something strange in the look of the octopus. One has the sensation of lucidity, of a look much more expressive than that of any fish, or even any marine mammal.

The eye of the octopus is altogether exceptional among invertebrates. And although it has things in common with the eyes of vertebrates, it has also a peculiarity which no doubt contributes to the unique character of its look: the pupil is a black rectangular bar across the center of the eye. Even so, it is likely that the image registered is rather imprecise, because the cells receiving the image are fewer and larger than those of the human eye. The result would then be that the image on the retina is a relatively loose and poorly defined mosaic.

When an octopus is calm or resting, its eyes are immobile, rather fixed, with the black bar of the pupils giving it the appearance of a creature from a sensory world other than our own. But as soon as a prey comes within sight, or if a diver appears and startles it, the eyes of the octopus rise up like periscopes. They are mobile, and can be turned to look in different directions. They not only convey that the octopus is alert and curious, but they also manifest, being large and colorful, a certain beauty.

The Octopus as Wanderer

The octopus' sharpness of vision, the result of its highly developed retina and optical lobes, is a practical weapon of great value, for it enables the animal to observe the outside world from the safety of its hole. This does not mean, however, that the octopus never ventures into the open, or that it does not, from time to time, change its house.

Falco is convinced that the octopus is not a truly sedentary animal. That is, it does not take up residence in a particular hole and remain there forever. It may stay only a day or two, and then go out looking for food without ever returning to the same hole. If it finds another vacant house, it may use it for a while. What is essential, in other words, is a shelter of some kind, wherever the octopus may be. It is rare that an octopus will remain in the same house for as much as a week. Falco and Michel Deloire have found excellent "houses," empty and abandoned, which had been occupied the day before and which would remain empty for several days.

One finds octopuses both in three feet of water and in sixty feet, in algae or on rocky bottoms, living in a tin can or an amphora. They prefer calm water, however, and, since they usually live in shallow water, they are sensitive to the swell which disturbs the stones of their houses and raises up mud and sand which works its way under their mantles and irritates them. During the winter, or even when bad weather approaches, they go down into deeper water to avoid being disturbed.

On one occasion, when it was very windy, the *Espadon* was taken to the nearby coves of Sormiou, at Morgiou. When the divers went down there, they found that the octopuses had also taken shelter in the coves.

When the weather was good, one of the best places for octopuses was off Riou, at a place called La Sablière, where there is an embankment dating, it is thought, from the early nineteenth century. There, one finds a great number of very small octopuses in shallow water. But, in water from 30 to 50 feet deep, many octopus houses could be seen. Falco's guess was that these houses are occupied only when the weather is bad. (In front of one of them, he reported, there was a rampart made of machine-gun rounds, carefully stacked.)

Relics from Antiquity

The octopus film, and the extended exploration which is required, gave us the opportunity to reconnoiter extensively the underwater region around Marseilles. We had thought that we knew this area quite well, but, in pursuit of the octopus, we came across several unexpected discoveries. We had no

Following page. A *pas de deux* with diver and octopus, at the entrance to a cave at Riou.

idea, for example, that the bottom there was so rich in historic relics; and yet, we had spent five years digging out an ancient sunken ship at Grand Congloué, which is close to the island of Riou.

Hidden among the seaweed, or half-buried in the sand, lie anchors from every age. There is sufficient material for one to be able to trace history of anchors for the past three or four thousand years. It is a history which begins with flat, triangular stones, drilled with holes in order to accommodate pieces of wood, which go back to the Phoenicians and the ancient Greeks; it continues through the lead stocks of the Roman era; and it comes up to the grapnels of modern fishing boats.

The amphorae and pots, whether or not inhabited by octopuses and, occasionally, by eels, would be enough to supply a museum specializing in antique ceramics. It is one of the principles of our team to regard the sea as a vast historic site and every work area as a potential Pompei. Yet, we do not have the time both to embark on a course of archaeological research and to study cephalopods. And since we did not want to disturb an area that may well produce valuable information in the future, we tried to leave everything just as we found it—not without a glance of regret occasionally at a particularly intriguing tumulus that we may never be able to find again.

It is certain that the cove of Morgiou, and that of Sormiou, where the *Espadon* took shelter from the wind, had already served as a refuge for the ships of the Phoenicians, Etruscans, Greeks, and Romans when they were not able to reach the port of Marseilles. But, in the Mediterranean, the weather changes very quickly, and one is never sure of what is coming next. In the vicinity of Plane Island, Falco found a bottom of sand and seaweed which had obviously, at one time, seemed ideal for anchorage, but which had become impossible with the coming of the mistral. For us, however, it was an excellent underwater studio, because the bottom was littered with broken amphorae. This must have been the site of many shipwrecks in ancient times. The history of man, however, even going back as far as it does, is very short when compared to the history of life; and it is likely that, long before the foundation of Phocaea, the ancestors of the octopuses found today at Sormiou and Morgiou were already living in holes in the calcium walls of those coves. The habitations of animals change more slowly than those of men and are somewhat more durable.

The Migrants

We must not forget that our Mediterranean octopuses move from time to time, and that the opportunities of encountering them vary from season to season.

These moves, however, are vertical rather than horizontal. They have been studied closely by Mme. Katharina Mangold, an eminent specialist, of the Laboratoire Arago of Banyuls-sur-Mer; and this expert was kind enough to give us the benefit of her guidance while we were making our film on the octopus.

In this area it is in February and March, in shallow water, that one has the best chance of finding the large octopuses which have just come up from deeper water. The males arrive before the females. Other octopuses, the younger ones, come in March and April, and leave in September and October for deeper water (from 250 to 350 feet).

Storms—especially storms from the east, which are particularly violent on France's southern coast—seem to be the reason why the octopuses seek the tranquility of deeper water. They are not happy in rough water. If it happens that a winter is particularly clement, the larger octopuses sometimes do not undertake their usual vertical migration. One can find them then in coastal waters. Only the younger octopuses, or the weaker ones, go to deeper waters at such times.

It is impossible to tell the age of a cephalopod from any of their organs. Among some fish, an examination of the lithocysts or of the scales gives an indication of age; but, so far as the octopus is concerned, only its size conveys some impression of how long it has lived. And even this method is a long way from being perfect. Experiments have shown that the growth rate of the *Octopus vulgaris* is accelerated if its food is abundant. A. Naef, a specialist, has determined that the weight of an octopus can double in a single week if its food is sufficient. It would be a mistake, therefore, to think that the largest octopuses are the oldest. Their size may simply be a function of their nourishment.

"Even though there is a tendency to exaggerate the connection between size and age," says Mme. Mangold, "it is nonetheless probable that the large octopus found by J. B. Verany, for example, which weighed fifty-five pounds, was older than most of other, smaller octopuses of the same species. If the average age of the octopus population is from eighteen months to two years, then large individual specimens are probably four or five years old. According to P. Pelseneer, the maximum age of *Octopus vulgaris* is ten years."*

It should be possible, by close observation during dives, to establish an accurate census of octopuses in order to obtain precise information on their age and longevity. Likewise, studies made during breeding should give valuable information.

*Katharina Mangold-Wirz, *Biologie des céphalopodes et nectoniques de la mer Catalane*. Paris, 1963.

Our divers explore a marine maze inhabited by octopuses in the Sormiou cove.

Right. An octopus, at the foot of Riou island, allows itself to be handled without trying to escape.

The Eledone moschata

Another species of octopus, the *Eledone*, which has only one row of sucker disks, builds its house in much deeper water than the *Octopus vulgaris*, at about 150 feet. Mme. Mangold has caught some in the Mediterranean, off the Algerian coast, at an even greater depth: 750 feet. But, in the fishing area around Port Vendres, none were found beyond 325 feet. The largest specimens were between five and six inches long.

Falco, from the diving saucer, has seen specimens of *Eledone* at 250 feet,

300 feet, and 325 feet. They were dug halfway into the mud at the bottom, and he could see only their arms—and their eyes, shining. When disturbed, they raised themselves and assumed a bell-like position.

The *Eledone* is somewhat more gregarious and less sedentary than the *Octopus*. It seems that it is also somewhat smaller, and, according to Falco, it is rarely seen changing color. The reason may be that it lives on bottoms of sand and mud, and it is not obliged to conform to the color of rocks, seaweed, and algae.

The Chameleon of the Seas

During our dives off Marseilles, Genest was our specialist in cuttlefish. It is difficult to say why the cuttlefish *(Sepia officinalis)* seemed to the rest of us to be less likable than the octopus. The fact is, we did not allow the cuttlefish a single sequence in our film, and we took only a few photographs of it.

The chief failing of the cuttlefish is perhaps that it has no house. It lurks in the seaweed or on the bottom in search of victims. It was when Genest saw one hunting that he became interested in cuttlefish. He described the scene beautifully, but, unfortunately, we were unable to film it.

The cuttlefish feeds mostly on shrimp, and shrimp are usually found half-buried in the sand of the bottom. The cuttlefish has an infallible method of flushing them out. It swims at the level of the bottom and shoots out a jet of water, which uncovers the shrimp. The victim tries to flee, but the cuttlefish's two long tentacles shoot out with the speed of lightning and seize it. It is a fascinating spectacle and a cruel one. Crabs are hunted in the same way. The cuttlefish grasps it with the sucker disks of its prehensile tentacles and, like the octopus, carries it to its mouth, where the crab is paralyzed by the cuttlefish's poison.

Genest has the ability to approach cuttlefish—which are relatively few—in the open water without provoking a cloud of ink. His secret, perhaps, is that he approached them from the front, so that they could observe him at their leisure and without panic—even though their field of vision covers almost a full 360 degrees.

We sometimes encountered cuttlefish in groups of two or three, immobile in the water, three or four inches from one another, their fins waving, their large eyes staring in different directions. The clearness of their gaze, and their slightly comical air, enchanted Genest, and he became their apologist.

But as I have said, Genest notwithstanding, the cuttlefish did not enjoy the same popularity with our team as the octopuses. For one thing, the arms of the cuttlefish are not nearly so active as those of the octopus, and they are much shorter. Only the two long tentacles are always ready to shoot out and seize a victim. Its oval, slightly flat body is bordered by a supple fin, which seems to serve more to keep the cuttlefish stationary than to enable it to move forward. Like other cephalopods, however, it can move by jet propulsion—by shooting jets of water through its funnel. So far as longevity is concerned, little is known about the cuttlefish. It is believed that it lives to a greater age than the octopus—perhaps four or five years.

Another point of inferiority of the cuttlefish, at least in the divers' opinion, is that it is neither an escape artist nor a contortionist. It cannot, like the octopus, crawl through a tiny crack. The upper part of its body is made up of a rigid "bone," which contains gas and liquid in separate chambers, and which serves as its organ of buoyancy.

The single area in which the cuttlefish is markedly superior to the octopus is its remarkable ability to change color or to reproduce on its skin the most complicated designs. Its chromatophores are even more mobile than those of the octopus or the squid, and its mimetic gifts are highly perfected. Its skin, which is either grainy or smooth, and spotted with white, green, and brown, is such a perfect camouflage that a cuttlefish among seaweed is practically invisible.

We were able to judge the extent of that talent for ourselves on one occasion, when Genest captured and brought aboard a specimen. We placed it in an aquarium for several hours and stood around to admire the repertory of color disguises—stripes, brown, black, and wavy zigzags speckled with gold. We then returned it to the sea.

It is widely believed, and it is taught, that cuttlefish live in littoral waters, in the shallows, on sandy bottoms where they dig in until only their eyes and the tops of their backs are visible.

A personal experience, however, leads me to believe that cuttlefish are also found in the open sea. In 1948, off the Cape Verde Islands, the *Élie Monnier* (a ship belonging to the Marine Study and Research Group of Toulon) detected, with its sounder, a very dense layer of some kind at about 700 feet. At the same time, the ship was surrounded by a large number of pilot whales. The whales, for some reason, seemed very tired. I have never seen pilot whales so devoid of reaction. As it turned out, it was because they were overstuffed. When one of the whales was harpooned and dissected, it was found that its stomach contained two hundred and sixty cuttlefish not yet digested, as well as a large number of beaks from cuttlefish already digested. The mysterious layer at 700 feet, obviously, was an enormous school of cuttlefish.

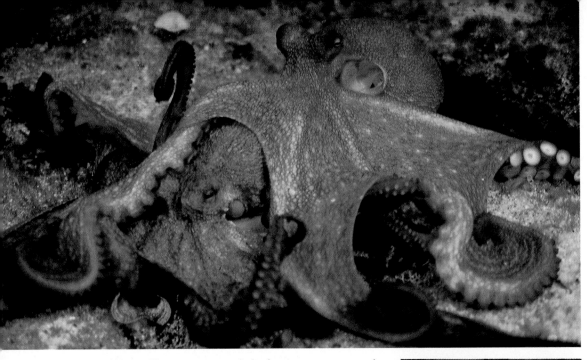

Above. Two octopuses fight it out over possession of a particularly desirable location visible in the background.

Right. One of the fighters begins to get the upper hand, and the other octopus turns pale.

Below. A diver separates the belligerents in order to save the loser.

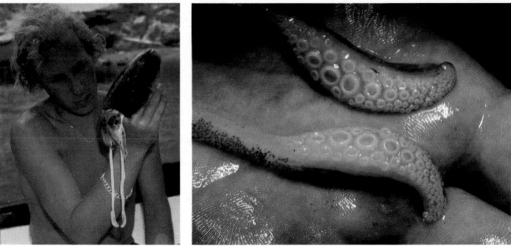

The cuttlefish does not have the sedentary habits of the *Octopus vulgaris*. This one is right over the bottom.

Jean-Pierre Genest holds a cuttlefish. Its two prehensile tentacles are hanging.

The cuttlefish's tentacles end in the shape of a spatula.

The Future of the Deep

In the course of *Calypso*'s expeditions, we have often had the opportunity to reflect, as we did while observing octopuses and cuttlefish, that we live in almost total ignorance of life in the sea. We know practically nothing about the animals that live at 600 feet and beyond. We do not know even how many creatures inhabit those depths. It will only be at some future time, thanks to advances in marine technology, that we will be able finally to know the sea as it really is—as a volume, and not merely as a surface in which animals appear from time to time. For almost all marine animals, life is lived below the surface. Our role, the role of our team, is to hasten the moment when man will be able to exist in the great deep with sufficient facility, and for sufficient lengths of time, to learn what is happening there.

It is our wish to prepare for the future. It is a future, certainly, that we ourselves will never live to see. But we rejoice that others will live in the golden age of oceanography to which our own efforts are but a beginning.

FIVE

Octopus City

The Bay of Alicaster is situated along the coast of the Island of Porquerolles. The marine terrain here is completely different from that of the island of Riou. The beach continues down into the water in a gently descending plain which would be quite bleak were it not for a few tufts of seaweed scattered about.

It is here that twenty-five years ago we discovered our first colony of octopuses, which I baptized Octopus City. The houses are not at all the same as those we saw in the Marseilles area. At Riou, Sormiou, and Frioul, the topography is relatively favorable to octopuses. There are rocks, faults and caves, and also stones with which to build octopus houses, as well as construction material from antiquity: necks of amphorae, and pottery shards. At Alicaster, however, the bottom, which is quite flat, is made of sand and mud. One wonders why octopuses chose this spot to settle, and how they could survive in such unfavorable conditions. The answer, obviously, is that they have been able to make do with what is on hand here.

At Alicaster, apparently, there is a vertical migration of individual oc-

Above. A diver watches an octopus which has crept into a fisherman's trap.

Above right. The octopus succeeds in stealing a lobster from the trap.

Below right. The octopus devours its ill-gotten meal.

topuses or a local displacement made necessary by the condition of the sea and by the wind. I have noticed that, when the mistral is blowing, the wind whistles across the bay and carries debris and algae, which invade the octopuses' houses. This does not please them, for octopuses are fastidious housekeepers. For those who live on the very bottom, I expect that the sand in the water is a source of irritation to their gills.

During the mistral, therefore, the octopus leaves its house and goes into deeper water. And when the east wind is blowing and the weather is good, the animal returns to its house and cleans it. So true is this that at Alicaster it was possible to know when there was going to be a change in the weather and a rough sea. The octopuses would all leave Octopus City beforehand and find other houses in water 80 to 100 feet deep.

Luckily for the octopuses, there are, here and there, large flat stones, obviously quarried and shaped by human hands. Under each of these stones, there is an octopus. Even the disposition of the individual stones suits the

temperament of the octopus: they are a fair distance apart.

Some modifications were required to make the stones actually habitable. Under the slabs, the octopuses dug tunnels sixteen to twenty inches long, and these were their means of access. So far as upkeep is concerned, the octopus-occupant removes sand and pushes outside any shells or other debris. It is therefore easy to tell whether or not a particular hole is occupied. If sand has been allowed to accumulate, and if there is debris, it is a vacant hole.

We have been able to observe octopuses doing their housework. They use their arms in order to remove large objects; but, to rid their houses of sand or mud, they shoot out a jet of water, which does the job very efficiently.

The life of the octopus is made considerably easier at Alicaster by the fact that every year many tourist boats and yachts come to the bay. The bay bottom becomes a garbage dump for these boats—and a windfall for the octopuses. There are rusted cans, bottles, sandals, and even old tires, all of which are suitable for use as an octopus house.

It was at Alicaster that we shot those sequences of our film on octopuses which, for us, were most interesting and exciting.

Worse than Hollywood

For the *Espadon,* it is about a six-hour journey from Marseilles to Porquerolles. Alicaster bay is poorly sheltered and shallow, and the *Espadon,* though more maneuverable than *Calypso,* has about the same draught. We therefore chose a neighboring port, Hyères, as our anchorage. Our cameraman, Michel Deloire, and his team would leave Hyères every morning at dawn; and Frédéric Dumas, an octopus enthusiast for thirty years, joined them.

Dumas' interest in these animals was increased by his new experiences. "Shooting conditions," he says, "were worse than in Hollywood, and had the same drawbacks; which is to say that most of the stars of the film were 'temperamental.' Of course, we must remember that the octopus we chose suddenly found itself facing six divers, two batteries of lights, three cameras of which two were turning. And just as in Hollywood, we had to shoot every scene four or five times. Just as we thought that we must have, for once, a perfect sequence, Michel Deloire would motion 'Cut!' by raising his hand. The lighting had been wrong, or inadequate; or there was another shooting angle that would have been better. And so, we had to begin all over again.

"Three times, we had to take away the crab that we had given to the octopus and start the scene again. Fortunately, the octopus was even-tempered. It had understood that, sooner or later, it would get the crab; and that, after all, we meant no harm. Then, too, the octopus was a natural for the role; all he had to do was what he wanted to do. Only, he would have to wait a bit. It was all a matter of being patient."

The divers and cameramen spent three and a half or four hours motionless in the water. This was in September, when the water is not too cold so long as one swims. But, in shooting, everyone had to stay absolutely still so as not to frighten the octopus. It was essential that the animal decide, freely and spontaneously, to do something. What we wanted were shots of the octopus which would show its natural behavior.

How to Make Friends with an Octopus

At Riou, we had never been sure from one day to the next that we would find the same octopus in the same hole. But at Alicaster, it seemed that every octopus remained in place for two days out of three. It was therefore possible to recognize different octopuses, and to establish individual relationships with them. We could see that reactions varied from animal to animal, and that there were differences in character among the individual animals. Some were very timid, while others were quite curious and even trusting.

The most unusual subject we had was a very large octopus, who seemed more mischievous than the others. It was the first octopus that Falco had showed me, and I had christened it Octopissimus—which doesn't make much sense in English but which, in its French equivalent, means simply "the most possible octopus." It was, in fact, a sizable animal, weighing between ten and twelve pounds and measuring over six feet in spread. It was much smaller than the octopuses we had known in Seattle, of course, but it was much cleverer and more lively than those giants.

Octopissimus' interest in the divers was quite obvious. It is true that this interest first manifested itself in a two-armed attempt to snatch away Genest's mouthpiece, and in a steadfast refusal to let go of it. But, by the divers' second and third visits, it had calmed down sufficiently to come out of its hole into the open water to see if they had brought it any food. After that, it was already outside, waiting, when Dumas arrived. Normally, no octopus would do that. One wonders how it knew precisely when its new friends would come.

What is certain is that Octopissimus enjoyed these visits. We cannot say for sure that it recognized Dumas and each of the divers, but it was obvious

Following page. The marine décor between 100 and 125 feet off the coast of Marseilles: red coral and golden sea fans.

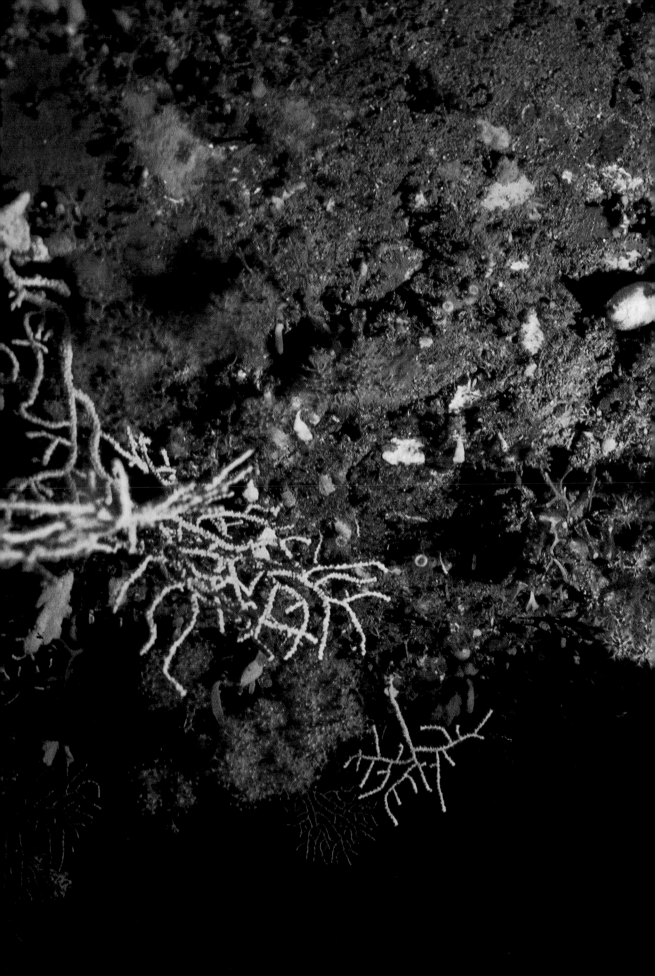

that it had favorites, and that it felt more at ease with some divers than with others.

The game the divers played was to swim away very slowly so as to lure the octopus into the middle of the group. It watched them closely, and it follwed them. In fact, it followed them almost to the *Espadon*. Octopissimus was truly an exceptional octopus.

It happened occasionally that, for no apparent reason, Octopissimus would take fright and swim rapidly away. Then, it would disappear into its hole, or even into the first available hiding place, and no offer of crab or fish could then lure it back.

Octopissimus' home was no ordinary stone slab like those of the other inhabitants of Octopus City. It was a handsome house, large and well dug out, under an inclined sheet of steel, part of which was buried in the sand. Like any well-appointed dwelling, it had several exits, and, occasionally, the octopus made use of them to play hide-and-seek with the camera by coming out of one door when we were expecting him through another.

As understanding as Octopissimus was, his trust of human beings had its limits. I am afraid that the curiosity which we had inspired in him with respect to man, eventually was the cause of his downfall. The same thing had happened to another distant friend, Jojo, the grouper.

It is not that the octopuses of Alicaster were greatly attached to their slabs of rock, but rather that, in this sandy bottom, there was no other shelter.

The Mirror

Frédéric Dumas had devised many octopus experiments which had never been tried before in the sea.

To begin with, we had to find the proper subjects for these experiments, all individuals with different temperaments. For that purpose, each of the houses of Octopus City was marked by a small colored buoy, called a "diver's buoy," the color denoting the character of the occupant.

The first experiment was to present the octopus considered to be the most aggressive of the lot with a mirror. We had already tried this, on several occasions, with groupers in the Indian Ocean. Their reaction was interesting. They mistook their own reflection in the mirror for a rival grouper invading their territory and, furious, charged the mirror and smashed it.

The octopus' reaction to the mirror was more mysterious. It did not make use of any "offensive" means, but, after a moment of immobility during which it stared fixedly at the mirror, it sent out an exploratory arm. The arm was extended and lay flat over the width of the mirror; and then it began a slow, wiping motion across the mirror's surface, like a windshield wiper, as though to wipe off the reflection. The octopus paused, looked again, and began wiping again. Then, it seemed to reflect, and, distressed, returned to its hole and refused to come out.

In the course of these experiments, crabs, which are the favorite food of the octopus, were eaten in great abundance. In order to attract the octopuses and lure them out of their holes, Dumas used not live crabs—since this would have required a large quantity of them—but pieces of crabmeat, which he simply placed in the water. The octopuses were made attentive by the proximity of their preferred dish, and this created a favorable atmosphere. Crushed crabmeat placed before an octopus' hole attracts the animal, and it is soon very excited; which indicates that the octopus' olefactory sense is well developed.

Our team spent hours cracking crabs, but in return, they got much enjoyment from observing the dexterity with which the octopuses would seize the smallest bit of meat and pass it from arm to arm. The tip of each arm is, in effect, an extremely sensitive antenna. It is a tool at least as useful and developed as the hand—but without fingers or opposing thumb. It both grasps, or envelopes, and adheres to an object with terrible efficacy.

The Problem of the Lobster

The best scene devised by Frédéric Dumas had as its purpose to show what the octopus is capable of doing. What we had to do was to present the animal with a difficult problem, but one which its lust for food would motivate it to solve.

One morning, the *Espadon* left the port of Hyères with our entire team. Also aboard was a live lobster and a large clear-glass jar with a stopper. Once in Alicaster bay, the divers went down, carrying with them the jar, filled with water, into which Dumas had placed the lobster.

For this experiment, Michel Deloire had decided not to use Octopissimus, who was still a bit capricious and unpredictable. His choice had fallen instead on an animal known as Number Two, who was not as large as Octopissimus but more calm and deliberate, as well as trusting and friendly.

Dumas deposited the jar and lobster in front of Number Two's house, which was the usual stone slab with its entry protected by means of an old suntan-lotion bottle which, in its turn, had become the home of a few small mussels.

Number Two, already accustomed to divers bearing gifts, was waiting in its doorway. It saw the jar, which had been placed far enough away so that it

Left. A diver takes down a jar, within which a lobster has been placed.

Above. An octopus investigates the glass sides of the jar.

Below. The octopus discovers the jar's stopper.

would have to leave its hole, and it undoubtedly saw the lobster inside the jar.

There was a moment of hesitation. It was surrounded by cameramen and divers, and the floodlights were all lighted. To an octopus, this may be very impressive, and a bit disconcerting. But temptation was strong. Number Two walked forward, stretched out, and with obvious regret came out of its shelter, although two arms lingered until the last minute. Then, it was entirely outside of its hole. The divers held their breath.

Suddenly, an arm shot out like a whip and grasped the jar. Number Two was paralyzed by surprise for an instant. The invisible wall between itself and its prey was something new in its experience. Yet, success must have seemed certain. The lobster, after all, was still there—but it could not be reached. Number Two changed color, turned red, as puzzlement, surprise, and anger affected its pigmentation. There is no way for an octopus to hide its emotions.

Dumas, watching Number Two's predicament, kept repeating: "He is thinking, looking. What is he going to do? Will he be able to figure it out?" And, of course, the cameras were whirling.

The octopus decided first to try the method that had always worked with crustaceans of the lobster's size. It wrapped its arms around the jar, climbed on it, and covered it with its mantle. Under normal circumstances, it would now have been possible for Number Two to paralyze its prey with poison from its salivary glands. Inside the jar, the lobster began moving around; but this only increased the octopus' impatience. It then tried to take the jar back into its house.

"Cut!" Deloire motioned. It was not a good take, and we had to begin all over again. Genest took the bottle away from the octopus.

On the next take, Number Two was on guard. Rather than throw itself onto the jar as before, it explored it slowly with one arm after another, feeling it from top to bottom. When the arm reached the cork stopper (which was protruding from the top of the jar), it stopped there and proceeded even more cautiously—until it found the small hole which had been drilled through the stopper. The tip of an arm was inverted through the hole and touched the lobster. The contact seemed to electrify both the predator and its prey, and the lobster gave a violent jerk with its tail. The octopus was now aware that the lobster was alive. But what next? Should it touch again? Explore the jar once more? Pull? Number Two was no longer an actor, but an intelligence at work. It had forgotten the divers and the cameras and the lights. Its respiration accelerated, and it was now changing color constantly. In the grip of such emotions, would it be able to solve its problem?

Suddenly, the cork stopper was out and shooting toward the surface. The octopus' arm remained glued to it for just an instant. Two other arms were already inside the jar, removing the lobster. The crustacean was raised to

Number Two's mouth, where it was immediately immobilized, and then carried into the octopus' hole.

Number Two deserved the luxury of being able to eat its meal in peace, and we did not disturb it any more that afternoon.

Intelligence?

The event that I have just described as though it happened in unbroken sequence actually had to be begun several times, and it lasted over three hours.

"It was on the third take," Dumas recalls, "that Number Two whipped out the stopper as though it were something that it had been doing all its life. When one thinks of how long it takes to teach a dog something as simple as sitting up or shaking hands, one must admit that an octopus learns very quickly; and that, above all, it teaches itself. We did not show it what to do. Number Two figured it out alone and found the solution to the problem. With a dog, it takes months of patient work before the animal will do what one wants it to do."

The difference between a dog learning and an octopus learning is the difference between training an animal and allowing an animal to exercise its intelligence in determining the means to be used to overcome an obstacle in certain circumstances.

The experiment with the jar is particularly significant because, in the filmed sequence, one can see the octopus adopt, first, its customary course of action when presented with a crustacean; that is, to attack. But, when it saw that the usual approach was useless, it abandoned that tactic and began exploring the object that had come between it and the lobster. It realized that the object was not uniform; and it discovered the presence of the stopper, and the existence of the hole in the stopper. It may have sensed that this was the weak point in the obstacle, since it was through the hole that the lobster was able to be touched. At that stage, the battle was half-won. Then Number Two realized that the stopper could be moved—and it moved it.

Specialists in the field, such as Packard and Sanders, with whom we have worked, are unwilling to speak of "intelligence" in the context of this experiment. But I do not think that the word itself is very important; what *is* important—and astonishing—is the result obtained.

It seems logical to assume that the development of a sense, such as that of touch, must be the source of many intuitions when it becomes necessary for the octopus to extemporize a course of conduct in new and exceptional circumstances. For octopuses, in their way, are very sensitive creatures. Their flesh is sensitive, and even delicate. It happened on several occasions that,

Above. It manages to get the tip of its arm in the hole in the stopper.

Above right. The octopus has removed the stopper.

Below right. The octopus begins to eat the lobster.

when we picked up an octopus to move it to a location more suitable for a particular shot, we discovered, to our consternation, that our fingers left white marks on them, where their flesh had lost its pigmentation because of our touch.

The Fish Rustler

Fishermen often complain that octopuses rob their nets and steal the best of their catch. We wanted to see if that accusation was founded on fact; and so we let down a net near one of the houses of Octopus City, after having baited it ourselves with fish.

Our divers installed lights and cameras near the spot, and then settled back to see what would happen. The octopus came out of its hole, walked

along the bottom, and, by raising itself and extending its arms, removed the fish which were caught by their gills in the openings of the net and took them back to its den to eat.

Its way of going about this was curious. It seemed unwilling to leave the bottom, and it used only one arm—thrown out rather violently, like a whip—to remove the fish. And all the while, it was holding fast to the bottom. We also had the frequent impression that the octopus prefers crawling to swimming. For it to swim, and especially for it to make use of jet propulsion, it must be motivated by fear or some other intense emotion. Moreover, the octopus, when it makes use of its funnel and membrane for this kind of locomotion, moves backward. It cannot see where it is going, and it happens that it collides with rocks.

Respect for the Dead

There occurred an incident at Alicaster which is very difficult to explain. I will therefore confine myself to reporting it just as it happened.

Michel Deloire and Henri Alliet, Michel's assistant, found a dead octopus one day on the bottom. It had turned white and was partially crushed. There was no way of knowing what had happened to it.

Alliet, on impulse, placed the corpse near the hole of another octopus. The two cameramen were astonished to see the octopus immediately come out of its hole, take the corpse, and carry it to a spot twenty-five or thirty feet away. Then, it returned to its house. Why did it do this? We do not know. We would have thought that it might eat the remains of the dead octopus—which is what generally happens when an octopus is killed in a fight.

In the behavior of octopuses, there are subtleties which escape our understanding.

It seems a bit farfetched to speak of "respect for the dead" among octopuses. It is more likely that, given the octopus' highly developed senses of taste and smell, and its sensitivity to chemical emanations, it finds a corpse somehow "disagreeable." Even in this context, however, the octopus' behavior is surprising. The almost human act of picking up the offending corpse to carry it away from the octopus' house presupposes a series of thoughts and judgments of which few animals are capable.

The Trap

Fishermen accuse octopuses not only of raiding their nets, but also of eating the lobsters caught in the fishermen's lobster traps. We therefore decided to conduct an experiment based on this claim. We wanted to see what actually happened in the water.

We let down a lobster trap in which we had placed a live lobster. The trap was placed near an octopus hole, in such a way that, from its hole, the octopus could see the lobster. Then we set up our cameras around the site. We did not have to wait long. Within ten minutes, the octopus was on top of the lobster trap, trying to insert its arms into it in order to reach the lobster. In order to do this, it first examined the trap's exterior until it had found its entry. Then, it paused. It was as though it suspected a trap; and there was a moment of real hesitation. But greed carried the day. The octopus crawled into the trap.

A curious scene followed. The octopus sensed that it was now a prisoner in the lobster trap. It could not find the way out; the lobster—a very large one—was blocking the way, and the octopus, it seems, did not dare attack it. Things were therefore at a standstill. Falco waited, camera in hand, for more than two hours for the stalemate to be broken. Finally, he caught sight of a small octopus a short distance away. He caught it, and put it into the trap with the first octopus and the lobster.

The first octopus, which was relatively large, immediately grasped the smaller one and thrust it under its mantle. But, three minutes later, the small octopus reappeared. It had either been able to escape, or, for some reason, had been freed by the other octopus. In any event, it quickly made its way out of the lobster trap.

This incident seemed to restore the large octopus' self-confidence. It immediately attacked the lobster and, seizing it with its arms, slid it under the interbrachial membrane. The lobster fought back vigorously, but it was suddenly still. The octopus' poison had done its work.

As soon as the lobster had been immobilized, the octopus wished to drag it through the opening of the trap. But it still could not find the opening. The octopus is an animal with a great love of freedom. We saw it panic, change color out of fear, swell up, and then elongate itself in an attempt to find a way into the open water. But it did not succeed. It then returned to the lobster and ate a bit of it. But then fear overcame its hunger, and it began once more to look for an exit. It was as though the octopus could not believe that it was a prisoner. It wandered continually around the trap.

By then, the divers' air was running low, the cameras had to be reloaded, and it was getting late. They therefore returned to the *Espadon*, leaving the octopus to find a solution to its problem. They were certain, at least, that it would not starve.

Early the next morning when the divers returned to the site of the previous day's shooting, they found the lobster trap in place. It contained only the

Left. Jean-Pierre Genest with an octopus in the open water. The animal, as can be seen from its pink color, is not happy.

Above left. Genest offers the octopus a hiding place in a pot.

Above right. The octopus accepts the offer with alacrity.

Below. The animal rolls itself up and refuses to come out of its new house.

empty shell of the lobster. The octopus was back in its hole, from the safety of which it stared out at the divers with an expression that it would have been easy to interpret as one of supreme self-satisfaction.

The "Look"

Everyone—Falco, Dumas, Deloire—talks about these "looks" of the octopuses; and especially of octopuses who are active, those to which we give problems and which we test. No doubt, the animal can examine objects, and the world around it, with its arms; but it also looks, and it is especially by looking that it arrives at its decisions. It is also by looking that the octopus understands, if one may use that term.

"I have seen many fish," Falco says, "and I have seen the kind of look that they give. They are always the same; the eyes are round, fixed, without that special light which evokes a response. We do not even know whether they actually see. They are more sensitive to things in their lateral line of vision than elsewhere. But, with octopuses, the contrary is true. I have often had the impression that they are 'reflecting.' One can feel that they see an object that we hold out; that it has registered; that something is going on in the octopus' brain. This feeling is confirmed when one sees the octopus' reactions expressed by variations in color; and many of these changes express a strong desire to seize the object."

If a diver approaches an octopus very slowly, and if he waves his hand or a piece of white cloth—anything that moves, whether white or colored, attracts its attention—the octopus, rather than withdrawing completely into its hole, will show its eyes. They begin to protrude, to move gently in a circle. Each eye can observe a different area. (Our friend Anig Toulmont has succeeded in hypnotizing octopuses by staring at their eyes. An octopus is then immobilized, and its eyes remain fixed only on her.)

It should be noted that, in all developed beings, it is not the eye which sees, but the brain. The impression of the image on the retina is only the first stage of vision. The image is then transmitted to the brain where it is "processed." It may be assumed that, in an octopus, the interpretation of this image is highly satisfactory, since the animal shows, by its reactions, that it understands quite well what one shows it.

If the object that an octopus sees excites its interest, its look becomes more intense. It puts out one arm, and then another. It tries to touch the object. But, if divers are present, it remains anchored to its den, as long as possible, by two or three arms.

The Sucker Disk and the Hand

Our divers all agree that, contrary to common opinion, it does not appear that the arms of the octopus are identical, or that each one can do whatever any of the others can. The two arms known as the dorsal arms, in the axis of the eyes, are exploratory and prehensile. With these, the octopus feels and grasps. All of the arms, however, can be elongated considerably. Alliet estimates that this elongation is on the order of four to five inches for an octopus of medium size, weighing five to seven pounds. At the same time as the arms are elongated, their diameter is reduced and the arms become very thin, especially at their tips.

The octopus also works with the next two arms, picking up pebbles and seizing crabs. It is able to achieve a marvelous co-ordination in its "offensive" movements; and this is due to a center of co-ordination in the brain which allows the octopus to decide on a particular course of conduct when faced with conflicting circumstances—when, for example, one arm seizes a crab, while another wards off an object that the octopus considers dangerous.

The octopus' ventral arms seem to be used more for anchorage than for any other purpose. One of the main preoccupations of the octopus is to maintain a point of contact with its rock or its hole. From this contact, it derives strength and confidence. The octopus knows that, in open water, it is vulnerable, and that it is in a much stronger position so long as it maintains a grip on a fixed point.

Genest, on several occasions, slowly extended his bare arm toward a friendly octopus. By remaining immobile for a while, he succeeded in getting the animal to send out one arm, and then a second. Its sucker disks felt the diver's arm, moved along it, and pulled on Genest's arm as though the octopus wished to have it in its hole. Genest, however, did not move. With his free hand, he offered the octopus a piece of crab or fish—but held the bait well away from the octopus' hole. The animal finally decided to come out—but it had required much patience on Genest's part, and a willingness to move in slow motion.

Genest was able eventually to induce the octopus to climb onto his body. The animal would sometimes slide between his back and his air bottles; or it would station itself on his helmet, or on his mask. Genest brought one octopus back to the *Espadon* in this way, without having to lay hold of it. An octopus is capable of doing many things—if only one knows how to ask.

In open water, a diver may be able to play with an octopus, but it requires much time and gentleness. Frédéric Dumas has always been particularly adept at this. Yet, if the game is not to be ruined, the diver must be willing to allow the octopus to leave when it has had enough. Once the octopus is back in its hole, it feels protected and secure after an experience which was no doubt an extraordinary one for him. Contact with these monsters, the divers, must be both frightening and satisfying to an octopus, but it is marvelous to see how quickly it becomes accustomed to the experience.

SIX

Death at an Early Age

Falco has seen an octopus employ an extraordinary trick to catch crabs. From the threshold of its house, the octopus extended an arm and moved it slowly back and forth. Falco could see the sucker disks on the arm, standing out like white spots in the water. This was not the first time that he had seen an octopus doing this, and he had a notion of what its purpose was.

To prove his suspicions, he caught a small crab and placed it on the bottom, a short distance from the octopus' house. Then he withdrew to see what would happen. The crab and the octopus, both no doubt disturbed by Falco's interference, did not move. Then, very gently and slowly, the octopus' arm began to sway again, moving the white spots of its disks back and forth in the water. Suddenly, the crab ran across the bottom directly toward the arm. Before it reached it, of course, it had been lassoed and thrust under the octopus' mantle. The octopus obviously fishes for crab in exactly the same way that we fish for octopus: by waving a white object in the water. Many marine animals are attracted by any light spot that moves. How, one wonders, does the octopus know this?

One of our team witnessed an even more surprising scene. He threw into the water a large green and white melon which, after one slice had been cut from it, proved inedible. The melon floated; and, suddenly, it began to move in the water. There were arms around it, trying unsuccessfully to drag it beneath the surface. The melon had been attacked by an octopus; but the octopus was smaller than the melon. It wanted to take the melon to the bottom, but, since it was in the open water and had no fixed point to which to anchor itself, it was simply bobbing up and down with the melon without being able to do anything with it. Eventually, it decided to take the melon to the nearby shore, and it began to tow its prey by contractions of its membrane. As soon as it had reached the shore and attached an arm to a rock, it was able to drag the melon beneath the surface—which escaped and bobbed up to the surface again like a cork. Eventually, with much patience, the octopus succeeded in keeping the melon submerged by wedging it under an overhang—which may have been its house.

Did the octopus go through so much trouble because it likes melon? I doubt it.* I think that the whole struggle was motivated rather by the animal's compulsion to "collect"; that is, by its overriding curiosity which moves it to take whatever it sees that seems strange to it.

There is another factor here which shows up clearly in the foregoing instances. Octopuses, we might say, are animals capable of conceiving and following a set course of action. Their actions, and their stratagems, are spontaneous, effective, and appropriate to the matter at hand. We might even say that octopuses are able to judge, that they are "ingenious."

We shall see in this chapter that numerous experiments show the octopus to be capable of learning. And many of us who have observed octopuses in their natural habitat—that is, in the sea—believe that they are, above all, capable of understanding.

One must have lived in the water with octopuses for months, swum in the same waters, brushed past the same rocks and the same algae, in order to be able truly to appreciate the beauty of the octopus. In the water, the octopus looks like a silken scarf floating, swirling, and settling gently as a leaf on a rock, the color of which it immediately assumes. Then it disappears into a crack which appears to be hardly large enough to accommodate one of its arms, let alone its entire body. The whole process is reminiscent of a ballet. It is somehow ethereal and, at the same time, elaborate, elegant, and slightly mischievous.

Octopuses are much better than divers at dodging and escaping. How, then, are our divers able to approach an octopus, touch it, and become

*One can never be really certain about such things. We know one octopus who likes hard-boiled eggs.

friendly with it? The principal factor in our favor is the octopus' desire for food. It apparently cannot resist the sight of a crab or a lobster; it can hardly resist even the smell of them. The octopus' psychological characteristics, however, also play an important part in our success in establishing relations with it. It is a good observer, a good judge, and it does not run away once it has become clear that we are not enemies.

Prudent—but Curious

We have said in the foregoing chapters that the octopus is a timid animal; that, far from attacking a diver, its first reaction is to flee, to hide, to withdraw into the farthest corner of its house. That is quite true. But we must add that the octopus' timidity is a reasoned reaction, one that is based primarily on prudence and caution. It is not an instinctive and groundless fear that persists regardless of circumstances. If a diver is able to demonstrate that he means no harm, the octopus quickly loses its timidity—more quickly than any "wild" animal. This peculiarity of the octopus made our approach much easier. After a few days—often, after no more than two or three dives—an octopus was accustomed to our presence. He had observed us and made a judgment. This is a much smaller amount of time than is usually required to achieve the same result with land animals.

It must have been obvious to the octopus that we were not his usual, everyday enemies. Certainly, with our cylinders and bubbles, we must have appeared strange, gigantic, and even dangerous. But, within the octopus' experience, divers were not classified among such mortal dangers as the eel or the grouper. It had therefore to form an opinion of us. It did so, and that opinion, apparently, was favorable.

This was very flattering to us, but it was also flattering to the octopus itself. It indicates a high level of understanding, which, for that matter, confirms what we learned from the octopus' behavior.

The most remarkable thing about the octopus, as I have already said, is its ability to grasp a problem that is presented and to find a solution to it by making proper use of its physiological and psychological equipment. This was made abundantly clear in the course of our experiments with the small octopuses of the Mediterranean, both at Riou and in Alicaster bay. Sometimes, we even had the impression that these experiments bore results far beyond our expectations.

It is sufficient to recall the incident with the lobster in the bottle to believe that an octopus can be as adroit as a vertebrate animal—as a monkey, for instance—in finding the proper motion and the proper means to get what it

Above. Bernard Delemotte observes an octopus' reactions in the open water.

Below. The octopus attempts to hide in a hole in the cliff.

Right. Raymond Coll has flushed out an octopus hiding among sea fans.

The *Espadon*, from which we worked while making our film on octopuses, offshore at Marseilles.

Right. The octopus, in addition to being able to change its color so as to blend with its environment, can also bristle—which is a supplementary means of camouflage.

wants. This dexterity is especially astounding in a mollusk.

We have had ample opportunity to observe that the curiosity and interest of the octopus is excited by human beings who approach it. "It is," affirms Falco, "about like a dolphin."

Obviously, the tricks that we can teach an octopus are less spectacular than those learned by the killer whales and the *bottle-nosed dolphin* in our marinelands. But it is not at all impossible to teach it to perform—as Joanne Duffy did in the undersea gardens of Seattle.

"They Know Me Very Well"

Mme. Mangold, who has spent twenty years breeding and observing octopuses at the Banyuls laboratory, has some interesting things to say about the reactions of the octopus to humans. "They know me very well," she reports. "There is no denying that a relationship develops between the octopus and the observer. But here we encounter a major obstacle. It is very difficult to interpret the responses observed in the course of an experiment, for the simple reason that we have even less affinity with octopuses than we do with mammals."

This is the same feeling that we experienced during our dives at Seattle, Riou, and Alicaster. Cephalopods live in another world. I mean not only that they live in the sea, which is now open to exploration by human beings, but also that they inhabit a world of sensations and perceptions that is not our

own. The evolutionary path which led cephalopods to a high degree of perfection is not that taken by the human race. It is nonetheless parallel to ours; and it may lead them farther still.

There will, no doubt, be objections from zoologists if I say that cephalopods are "intelligent." Scientists are always very reluctant to use that term, for, since we do not really know how to define intelligence in man, it is difficult to attribute intelligence to animals. Even so, one may take inventory of the physiological and nervous equipment of cephalopods and see what use they make of that equipment.

Kings of the Sea

Cephalopods, with the unusual means at their disposal, could have become the monarchs of the sea. And they were so, in fact, during the Primary and Secondary eras.

Octopuses and squids have exceptionally effective weapons. They have, first of all, their arms and their sucker disks, which serve many purposes—to touch, to grasp, and so forth. This gives them a great advantage over other marine animals, whether fish or mammals. A whale uses its tail as a weapon, and it uses its fins to support its offspring. But this is not the equal of the cephalopod's arms, which are prehensile and exploratory.

Octopuses could be not only the rulers of the sea, but also very dangerous creatures. In addition to their arms, they have a sharp beak and a supply of poison of greater or lesser effectiveness. They can both swim and crawl, and, as we have said, their eyes are highly developed.

The octopus' balance is maintained by two "receptors," the statocysts, which are located in the cephalic cartilage. This organ, which includes a partially calcified statolith, is analogous to the semicircular canals of vertebrates, which control their balance and their orientation. In the statocyst there is an acoustical "spot" and a semicircular crest to which the terminals of the acoustical nerve are connected. This nerve emerges from the arm mass, but originates in the cerebral ganglia (as in other mollusks). The presence of an acoustical nerve raises the question: Do octopuses hear? Most zoologists, including Mme. Mangold, who knows octopuses very well indeed, say that they cannot.

We ourselves can only put on record the results of our own experiences, which are perhaps worthy of being examined.

When the *Espadon,* in the course of our shooting, was moved from Hyères into Alicaster bay on one occasion, a diver went down even before the anchor had been dropped. He found our largest specimen—Octopissimus, as I had christened it—on the doorstep of its house, waiting to be fed. Falco and Genest, who are perceptive observers, have always believed that the octopus "heard the noise" of the ship's engines, which arrived every day at the same time. It is possible, however, that it was the shadow of the ship in the water, or that of the divers, which alerted Octopissimus to our arrival.

The octopus' tactile sense is particularly well developed, and the suction disks perceive both tactile and chemical sensations. They are fringed with extremely effective sensory organs—several thousand of them in every square centimeter of disk. Moreover, the flesh of the animal is sensitive to chemicals as well as to touch. It is totally deprived, however, of the ability to emit sounds—unlike many fish.*

The fact that the octopus is mute is compensated for by its pigmentation, which enables it, by means of color changes, to express itself and send out signals. They often assume a threatening posture—and frequently do so in the presence of divers. This has happened to Genest, among others, who has seen an octopus swell up, stand, and turn red at the sight of him. These are all ruses to intimidate an adversary; and the octopus used them against Genest in the same way as it would have against its natural enemies, the grouper and the eel.

The surprising thing is that, three days later, this same octopus, having become accustomed to Genest (who was bringing it food), abandoned its attempts to frighten him off. This was a change in comportment which implied the exercise of the octopus' memory and the rendering of a reasonable judgment.

168 Million Neurons

The nervous system of cephalopods, although it includes the ganglia typical of mollusks, is much more developed than that of other mollusks. Their "brain," protected·by a cartilaginous capsule which fulfills the same function as the braincase among vertebrates, is highly evolved and complex. About thirty anatomical lobes can be distinguished. According to J. Z. Young and M. J. Wells, the central nervous system of the octopus comprises over 168 million neurons.

The dimensions of the various lobes of the cephalopod brain differ from species to species. Mme. Mangold, in comparing eleven species of octopus and twenty-three species of decapods, observed that there was a correlation between the sizes of certain lobes and the species' various ways of life and means of habitation. Thus, it should be possible, from an examination of

---

*It should be noted that sounds emitted by squids have been recorded on tape; but it is not known which of their organs produce these sounds.

Above. An octopus takes on the color of the sea fans on which it rests.

Left. An octopus, unhappy at being thrown out of its house by Delemotte, shoots out an ink jet.

cerebral structures, to establish by deduction where an animal lives, and how it lives.

The optic lobes of decapods, for example, are enormous compared to those of octopods. And, among the decapods, they are even larger among the species inhabiting open waters, such as the *Loligo* or certain other squids of the open sea, than among the cuttlefish. The basal lobes, which control movement, are more developed among decapods and open-water octopods than among species which live on the bottom in coastal waters.

The octopods are the only ones possessed of a subfrontal lobe, which seems to play a part in the recognition of objects by tactile means.

A Scientific Advantage

There has been important scientific research on the nervous system of cephalopods, which will perhaps allow us some day to arrive at a better understanding of the human brain. This research began in 1936, when an

English specialist, J. Z. Young, discovered the presence, in squid, of giant nerve fibers. These fibers have a diameter from fifty to one hundred times greater than that of human nerve fibers. The long, thick axons which are found in the brain and periphery of cephalopods make possible the rapid conduction of information. In squid, nerve impulses can travel as fast as twenty yards per second, and this is almost the speed of nervous conduction in vertebrates. The size of these nerve fibers makes them ideal for physiological and electrophysiological research; and this, in turn, has resulted in the establishment of a new branch of cellular biology: cellular neurophysiology. Research in the field has been especially intensive in Britain and at the Oceanographic Museum of Monaco, where Dr. Arvanitaki and Dr. N. Chalanozitis have worked on the giant fiber of the cuttlefish.

There will be much to learn when we are able to do with the human brain what we can do with those of cephalopods or of sea slugs of the genus *Aplysia,** for instance. But, at the present time, human nerve cells are much too small to be investigated by the same techniques as can be applied to squid.

It is remarkable that, among all the mollusks, only the cephalopods go through a period of sleep analogous to that of mammals. The octopus sleeps every day. It remains immobile; there is a papillary contraction, and a noticeable slowing of respiratory activity. Squids also sleep; but, while the octopus' respiratory movements slow from 32 to 13 per minute, those of the squid drop from 45 to 32 per minute.

The Two Disks

It was my intention to complete, by laboratory experiments, the observations that we had made in the sea on our friend, the *Octopus vulgaris*. I therefore asked Dr. Geoffrey Sanders, of the University of London, who is a specialist in the study of learning and memory among octopuses, to join us at the laboratory of the Oceanographic Museum of Monaco. I also invited Andrew Packard, who for the past ten years has worked with octopuses at the Zoological Station of Naples.

I arrived at Monaco with *Calypso*. On board, we had a large number of octopuses which we had captured and installed in tanks. These, we now transferred into Museum jars.

*It was through electrophysiological research, similar to that which they had undertaken on cuttlefish, that Dr. and Mme. Chalazonitis discovered, in the course of experiments with *Aplysia*, that cell is not only an element of order, but also and simultaneously a high-frequency transmitter and receiver. When one cell speaks, the other cells listen. The brain is therefore the seat of a permanent electrical dialogue.

We began a series of experiments, all of which were filmed. Sanders very quickly taught an octopus to distinguish between black and white. When a black disk was lowered into the octopus' tank, it came out of its hole and put an arm out to the disk. As its reward, it received a piece of fish, which it took back into its hole.

When the octopus was presented with a white disk which it had never seen, it extended its arm—but, instead of food, received a slight electric shock. It returned to its hole rather sheepishly.

Sanders then showed it the black disk again, which the octopus immediately touched. It received its reward. Then, the white disk was lowered a second time. The octopus looked at it, hesitated, looked as though it would come forward—but then withdrew. It had understood.

Success or Failure

Many researchers have experimented in various ways with the behavior of cephalopods, with their aptitude for learning and remembering by distinguishing among sensations gathered through sight, touch, and the chemico-tactile sense. In addition, they have made cuts in the brains and nervous systems of cephalopods in order to study their effects upon the behavior of the animals. All of these tests indicate the extent to which cephalopods learn quickly and retain what they have learned.

M. J. Wells has demonstrated that the octopus is capable of distinguishing the size of objects, of choosing between complicated forms composed of lines and designs, and that it is capable of doing so even when in a stooped or vertical position. Wells noted that, regardless of the octopus' position, the black line of the pupil in the octopus' eye tended to remain horizontal. As we shall see, this tendency is even more pronounced in the case of the Nautilus, which moves while balancing its shell but keeps its eye at the horizontal.

Our friend Andrew Packard has recently recorded the case of an octopus able to distinguish between a vertical rectangle and a horizontal rectangle. It should also be noted that, once an octopus has acquired such knowledge, it does not forget it, but retains it at least for several weeks.

P. H. Schiller has reported octopuses capable of looking for a passage, moving down a corridor, and making detours to reach a crab which they had seen through a glass wall. On the whole, the octopuses were successful in their quest.

Other experiments have shown that blind octopuses could, by their sense of touch, perceive whether or not objects could be moved by them. It has also

One of the octopuses living among the ancient amphorae on the floor of the sea off the coast of Marseilles.

An octopus has built a "house" by stacking up bottles at the entry to its hole.

Left. Captain Cousteau and Geoffrey Sanders in front of the octopus tank at the Oceanographic Museum of Monaco.

Right. Captain Cousteau and the English biologists, Geoffrey Sanders and Andrew Packard, preparing to experiment in order to determine the octopus' ability to remember.

been demonstrated that the senses of taste and smell, as well as the chemico-tactile sense, are very important to cephalopods who live on the bottom. The result, however, is paradoxical. Man is too poorly endowed with comparable senses to be able to interpret correctly the reactions of the animals with which he is experimenting.

We should not use such experiments as a foundation on which to build illusions. We have still studied very little about the behavior of the octopus—much less, for example, than that of the dolphin, whom man has now trained to play a role in his wars. Still, it is useful to mention the research taking place, little as it may be, in order to give some idea of the extraordinary potential of cephalopods in exploring and knowing their environment and adapting their behavior to it.

Cephalopods, despite their remarkable development, have ventured neither into fresh water nor onto land. They are, however, capable of living out of the water. We have often seen octopuses, brought aboard *Calypso* for observation or dissection, survive in the open air for a more or less extended period—especially if their bodies were kept moist. Occasionally, this period ran to one or even two hours. They seem more vulnerable to sun and heat than to asphyxiation.

There are many witnesses who maintain that octopuses have climbed onto beaches to hunt for crabs among the rocks. One such case was reported by a German zoologist from the laboratory at Naples. We ourselves have seen how easily and quickly an escaped octopus was able to scurry across

Calypso's rear deck to throw itself into the water. I tend to believe, however, that these are exceptional cases, motivated by either hunger or fear.

In his excellent work, *Brain and Behaviour in Cephalopods*, M. J. Wells devotes a chapter to what he calls "The Downfall of the Cephalopods." He begins by pointing out the perfection of their senses, which, he says, approaches, and sometimes equals, that of vertebrates. Where, then, is the element of downfall? For Mr. Wells, it consists in a "historic" defect of cephalopods which has its origin, among other factors, in a peculiarity of cephalopod blood: it is not red, like that of mammals, but "hyalin," or blue-green. Its volume is considerable, and it is driven through the cephalopod's body by a powerful heart. But the respiratory pigmentation which fixes oxygen in the blood is not the same as the hemoglobin which gives its color to human blood. There is no iron in its composition, but only copper: hemocyanin. And copper is not as effective as iron in carrying oxygen. Among cephalopods, the total capacity for absorbing oxygen runs from 3.1 per cent to 4.5 per cent, while, among fishes whose respiratory pigment is hemoglobin, it is 10 per cent to 20 per cent.

This explains the phenomenon of "breathlessness" which we often noted among the giant octopuses of Seattle and the octopuses of Riou when we forced them to swim for any distance.

Following page. A typical scene on the floor of the Mediterranean at about 125 feet: algae and red coral.

Two divers suiting up aboard the *Espadon*. Yvan Giacoletto is facing the camera.

Three Years of Life

If, in spite of all its gifts, its highly developed nervous cells, its ability to remember and to judge, the octopus is not the ruler of the sea, it is perhaps because, in addition to the composition of their blood, they die too young.

The longevity of the octopus—about which not much is known—seems not to exceed three years. That is long enough, certainly, for the octopus to be able to learn what it must know about its environment. It is fascinating to speculate, however, on what the octopus could be if it lived longer. Its increased experience might then make of it a sage of the sea, as clever as it is formidable.

It seems likely that some specimens of *Octopus dofleini* at Seattle live beyond the three-year limit and live to five or six years, or even longer. But these added years do not seem to confer on them any special qualities. They are, like their younger confreres, rather lazy and easily tired. But we will have to wait for the results of a course of training attempted by Jerry Brown, with one of these giant octopuses, before we can know whether experience and age have an unusual effect upon behavior.

It seems that many cephalopods die after having borne young. This is the case at least with small male and female squids, such as the *Loligo opalescens*, whose story we will tell further on in this book. It is also the case with most female octopuses, who exhaust themselves by guarding their eggs during the entire period of incubation.

The female cuttlefish, on the other hand, does not watch over her eggs as

Equipment used by Professor Chalazonitis, in the neurophysiological laboratory of the Oceanographic Museum of Monaco, to record electrical activity in the giant axon of cephalopods.

does the female octopus. After having deposited them, she loses all interest.* It may be this which explains the fact that cuttlefish live longer than octopuses and reach the age of four or five years. We must also take into account that cephalopods are susceptible to a large number of dangerous parasites, which invade their gills and their intestines. Most prominent among these are the dicyemids—worms visible only through a microscope, and whose life cycle is very complicated. This also is an area in which we are very much

*According to a recent thesis by M. Richard, the female dies after giving birth, and the male then guards the eggs.

A small tube has been inserted into the giant nerve fiber of a cephalopod. The fiber, though isolated, is alive.

in the dark. It is possible that, if we were to rid an octopus of its parasites, it would live longer.

Putting aside such considerations, we can say that, for invertebrates, the anatomical equipment of the octopods and decapods is remarkable. Two gills (except for the Nautilus, which has four) take care of the circulation of gases, while respiratory activity, handled by the mantle, assures the renewal of the water in the cephalopod's body cavity.

This respiratory system is similar to that activated by the gills of fish, and owes nothing to the motion of cilia by which invertebrates stir up the water and thus take in oxygen and food. According to Pierre Grassé, it is a question of "the pure effect of ecological convergence"—that is, one which has occurred because of the similarity of environment common to both fish and octopus. Be that as it may, the fact remains that, in respiration as in vision, cephalopods have attained "solutions" which are almost equal in their effectiveness to those of vertebrates.

Left. An octopus moving in the open water is strikingly graceful.

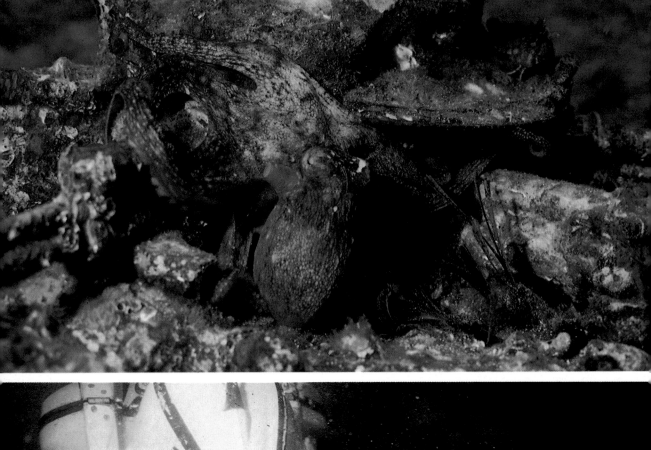

SEVEN

A Quick-Change Artist

After many hours of diving and long shooting sessions both in the Mediterranean and the Pacific, we feel that we are well acquainted with the marvelous array of defensive weapons which the octopus is able to deploy and which allow it to survive.

The octopus is the chameleon of the sea. Or rather, the Proteus of the sea—the modern-day embodiment of the mythological hero who escaped his enemies by constantly changing his form. Indeed, the sudden changes of color and form by means of which cephalopods attempt to throw their enemies off the track are called "protean manifestation." For cephalopods are excellent actors, with vast repertories, and they are able to play many roles by

Above left. An octopus on a wrecked aircraft engine, off the coast of Marseilles, takes on the color of the engine.

Below left. To determine the extent of the octopus' color-changing ability, we placed a specimen on a white plate at the bottom.

making use of strategems which, on dry land, are usually found only in the theater: disguises, gestures, mime, poses and posturing.

The octopuses we encountered displayed all these tricks in abundance for our divers, just as they do for eels and groupers. Being without the natural protection of shells, they find safety only in flight or in disguises. They are undoubtedly the champions of hide-and-seek.

The most common reaction, and the most obvious, is a change in form. At Alicaster and at Riou, whenever we surprised an octopus in its house, its first move was to withdraw as far as possible into its hole and to disappear into the darkness by making itself as small as possible. At that point, there was nothing that we could do. If we had tried to make it come out by force, the only result would have been a painful struggle, in the course of which the octopus might have been injured.

A Display of Colors

If the octopus' hiding place is not deep enough for the animal to be able to disappear altogether or to withdraw beyond reach, and if one tries to force it to come out, its body turns pale. Two black circles form around its eyes—a sign of anxiety. Then the octopus rises, draws the tips of its arms under its body and turns outward its rows of sucker disks with their white spots. These spots are even more visible than usual because, by then, the arms themselves have become darker and have taken on a reddish-black hue. It is almost impossible to do anything with an octopus in this position. Its sucker disks have been mobilized as an impenetrable line of defense.

The muscular system of the octopus gives it great suppleness and allows it a wide choice of postures. The muscle fibers are arranged in three spatial dimensions. Not only do these powerful muscles make it possible for the arms to assume any position or to draw together and take on all the rigidity of protective armor, but also the subcutaneous muscles, which control the octopus' interbrachial membrane, come into play. The sucker disks, which are controlled by three different muscles, are able to act independently. This whole prehensile aggregate constitutes an extremely effective means of defense.

There is also another defense mechanism which may be called a display of colors, and which some specialists designate as "the cloud passage." This consists in waves of dark coloration which, starting at the octopus' head, run through its body, and, when the animal stands erect, reach even the base of its arms.

If a diver holds out a piece of crab or fish to attract the octopus, it comes forward slowly and cautiously. But it retains its color and it bristles. One can sense that it is torn between hunger and fear—the psychological conflict which plays so large a part in the life and behavior of octopuses.

One day, Genest offered a crab to an octopus at Alicaster. The octopus took it—but then Genest pretended that he wanted to take it back. The animal reared up on its legs, puffed up its mantle to make itself appear as large as possible, and turned red. It was a whole courageous display of tactics, intended to intimidate an adversary, the size of which the octopus, thanks to its excellent vision, was certainly aware.

We have observed that octopuses, when frightened, move in open water by means of jet propulsion, with their arms folded up near their bodies in the form of spirals and semicircles. It is as though the animal is attempting to protect its arms from the teeth of, say, a grouper; and this method of swimming, with its arms withdrawn, is probably intended to present as small a target as possible to an enemy. It also happens that an octopus, when disturbed, will hold its arms over its head to protect itself.

If, however, an octopus is not being pursued, it lets its arms hang loose in its wake, and it then takes on the appearance of a perfectly hydrodynamic form. When it is not afraid, it takes on the brownish tint which is its usual color. Having reached its destination, the octopus folds out like a parachute. Or rather, it takes on the form of a parachute and comes to rest gently on a rock. It then shows the various colors of things present on the rock—algae, concretions, fixed animals—which may run from greenish-black to dark red. But if the octopus settles on sand, it becomes much lighter, sometimes almost white.

Michel Deloire has noticed that small octopuses change color more rapidly and more vividly than large octopuses. It may be that small octopuses are more easily frightened or react more strongly than large octopuses. In any case, it is certain that the former bristle much more noticeably than the latter.

An Exercise in Invisibility

The most important weapon of many cephalopods is homochromatism, the mimetic quality which enables them to take on the basic color of the object on which they are resting. This ability has developed to such a degree that it is extremely difficult for a diver who has no experience with cephalopods to detect an animal. Moreover, the animal thus concealed remains perfectly motionless so as not to betray its presence.

At Marseilles, where our team began shooting the film on octopuses, most of our divers reported that there were no octopuses in the area; or, that

Following page. In the course of a fight, both octopuses change color, with the loser turning pale.

if there had been some, they were no longer there. In fact, the divers were swimming right past the octopuses, who were so well camouflaged as to be practically invisible. Using the camera, and taking in a very large area, we were able to discover only a single pair of eyes. The owner's body was wholly blended into its surroundings.

Albert Falco, on the other hand, had been finding octopuses since his childhood, and he was quite skilled at discovering our invisible friends.

At Riou and Porquerolles, we performed several experiments to test this amazing ability of the octopus to take on the color of the bottom or of the object on which it rests. On one occasion, we let down into the water some plates of white plastic and put an octopus on one of them. It became pure white almost immediately.

It was not with the octopus, however, that we obtained the most spectacular results, but with the cuttlefish. In order to make the test more complex, we placed several plates on the bottom, on which there were geometric designs: straight black lines on one plate; lozenges on another; and a check pattern on the third. The cuttlefish reproduced exactly on its body the lines and squares—except if the squares were larger than 3.75 inches. We were not able to establish whether this rapid mimetic exercise, which we compelled the cuttlefish to endure, induced any unusual fatigue.

It did, however, elicit the admiration of our entire team.

"In the water," said Michel Deloire, "it is a beautiful and graceful animal. You can't see it without liking it. It is especially striking when it takes on the shape of a delta and folds back its arms to glide. It is able to change not only its color, but also its rhythm and speed according to the terrain. When the bottom is flat, it moves by means of water jets. If it is on rocks, it uses all its arms; but, on a sandy bottom, it keeps two or three of them folded."

Michel shot several sequences to show the metamorphoses of his favorite animal. On one occasion, he followed a specimen for ten minutes, as it passed over rocks covered by seaweed, seaweed on a sandy bottom, and sand in the open water. Each time, it changed its speed, form and color.

Chromatophores

The protean qualities of cephalopods do not seem completely dependent upon sight. So far as one can tell, it is not necessary for an octopus actually to see the colors of its environment for it to be able to reproduce them. A blind specimen, for example, has no difficulty in taking on the colors of the bottom on which it is resting, but blindness has other behavioral effects. The body of an octopus which has just died is able, for a certain amount of time, to change its color according to its environment. We have filmed this phenomenon. It seems sufficient that the chromatophores in the body remain functional.

The executive agents of these color changes are the chromatophores, the color cells. An octopus has two different kinds of chromatophores, which produce various colors according to their degree of expansion, from reddish brown in the darker colors to red and pale yellow-orange for the lighter ones.* These elements of color are reinforced by reflectors, the iridocytes, which produce greens and blues by refraction, and white by reflection.

This delicate and balanced system is as vast as it is complex. An octopus, at birth, has only seventy chromatophores; but, by the time it is an adult, it will have one or two million of them. On the upper surface of an adult octopus' body, where they exist in greater abundance, there are between one and two hundred chromatophores per square millimeter. These chromatophores do not grow as the animal grows; their size remains constant.

Each chromatophore is attached by branches to smooth muscle fibers. These fibers contract simultaneously and "pull" the membrane of the color cell so that it stretches to fifteen or twenty times its normal diameter. The pigments are then exposed and provide a dominant color. The more the muscles contract, the more the cells are dilated. When the muscle relaxes, the chromatophore contracts and therefore shows a minimum of color. This entire process presupposes an exceptional elasticity in the chromatophoric membrane, since its volume may be increased from two to sixty times. Various stimuli determine the expansion or contraction of the chromatophores. The most important of these seems to be light.

The octopus, regardless of the side of its body on which it rests, is always paler in color on the part of its body in contact with the support than on the upper part. This, however, is not a matter of light, but of contact. It is known that the sucker disks, which contain the tactile organs, also play a large part in the action of the chromatophores.

Chemical substances also contribute to variations in color. Tyramine, related to adrenalin, and betaine, related to acetylcholine, act on the nerve influx and on the muscle fibers which control the chromatophores.

*Among cuttlefish, the chromatophores seem to be arranged in three layers: an upper layer of bright yellow pigments; an intermediate layer of red-orange; and a deep layer of dark colors (brown to black). The interplay of these three layers allows the production of all colors, as one layer covers the others or retracts to expose them.

Following page. An octopus, pursued by Bernard Delemotte, is beginning to be afraid and to change color.

Tyramine is stored in the posterior salivary glands. If these glands are removed, the complex mechanism of the chromatophores comes to a halt. The ability of most cephalopods to change color and disguise themselves, therefore, is under a double control: one nervous, and the other humoral.

Each chromatophore has several branches of nerve fibers which control an entire range of expansion and of combinations among groups of chromatophores. The cellular bodies of these nerve fibers—approximately 150,000 of them in each adult—are situated in the lower regions of the brain. They are called the "subesophageal mass."

The roughness of the octopus' skin is due to highly developed papilla on the head and on the mantle. Iridocytes are found in large quantities in such places. These iridocytes are very small cells containing a series of reflecting plates arranged in chevrons. The plates are composed of microcrystals of guanine. (Guanine is a substance found also in fish which gives a silvery color to their stomachs and, sometimes, to their bladders.) The guanine plates act like tiny mirrors, refracting light into iridescent colors.

It would be very interesting to know exactly the workings of the cephalopods' mechanism for producing changes in color and appearance. An English researcher, B. B. Boycott, has observed the effects of electrical stimulation upon the brain centers of the cuttlefish. When such stimuli were applied to the lower chromatophoric lobe, they first produced a uniform darkening, and then darkening with erection of the papillae on the opposite side. Stimulation of the upper lobes resulted in whitening; and that of the optic lobes produced spots. There is obviously a hierarchy in the nervous control of these manifestations. But, whether they are simple or complex, they are controlled by the subesophageal mass.

The centers of the pedal lobes control the contraction of the chromatophores situated respectively on the head and arms and on the mantle. According to Grassé, the subesophageal mass is primarily a motor center. In addition, three lobes of the "brain" control the activity of the head and arms, the activity of the mantle and the funnel, and the expansion of the chromatophores.*

The Devils

It has been our experience that octopuses are the animals least capable of hiding their emotions. The problem is to learn how to interpret the signs by

---

*The brain, so far as control of the chromatophores is concerned, seems to depend upon the presence of tyramine and histamin in the blood. When these substances are present in larger than normal quantities, there is a dilation of the chromatophores, but through the intermediary of the nerve centers.

which they express those emotions. Some of these signals are clear enough: they are intended to inspire terror. This is the demoniac display—What J. Z. Young calls the "dymantic display."

The purpose of this display, which occurs with great suddenness, is to intimidate an adversary; and it is indeed an impressive sight. Here is a description based upon our own observation of this phenomenon: "The arms curve out to their maximum extent, the mantle takes on the shape of a bell. The larger part of the body is pale, and it is edged with dark red or brown where the bases of the sucker disks are visible. Does the octopus really intend to offer a terrifying spectacle? It is difficult to say; for whatever our conclusions they will be based upon human feelings—feelings too human perhaps to attribute to a cephalopod.

"Two great, dark eyes shine. The pupils are dilated, and form a thick black bar. The body, the arms and the head are flattened; the eyes stare fixedly toward the front. If the octopus is outside its lair, it shoots powerful jets of water toward its adversary while balancing itself on its fourth pair of arms, so as always to keep its terrifying mask turned toward the enemy. If the octopus' excitement increases, or if it begins suddenly, the second pair of arms are thrown out to the side and toward the front, and then quickly withdrawn."

There is another sort of display, quite flamboyant, put on by an octopus, the purpose of which is not to frighten its enemies, but to make its body's shape indistinguishable by integrating it totally into its environment. This display calls for every bit of talent the animal possesses, and it becomes truly protean. The octopus is covered with spots, specks, and erect pimples. The body is flattened or compressed, or rolls up into a ball, depending upon circumstances, and is immobile and extraordinarily elongated. The black bar of the pupil grows large. White spots appear on the arms. Alternating bands of light and dark are seen on the body, and the edges of the mantle curl in places in order to give the octopus the appearance of discontinuity.

Everything about this display is designed to confuse the eye of the beholder. The white spots are supposed to distract the enemy's attention. Even the diver is perplexed by this living kaleidescope, and his eyes have as much difficulty in making out its contours as his hands would have in grasping that elastic body. The octopus, as much by its structure as by its slippery flesh, is a creature designed for flight.

It is not difficult to understand why. The octopus has lost the protective shell which is retained only by its more primitive cousins, the Nautilus and the Ammonite. But its ability to disguise itself is used not only to protect itself, but also to take its prey by surprise. "We usually think," write Andrew Packard and Geoffrey Sanders, "that the octopus adapts to its environment

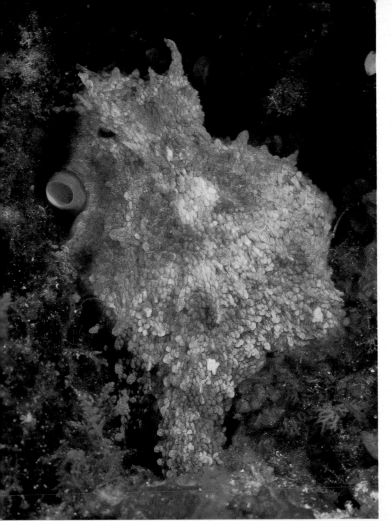

Left. Bristling and rather amorphous, this octopus is trying to blend with the rock on which it is resting.

Below. This specimen has taken on the greenish hue of the bottom.

Right. Jean-Pierre Genest has removed an octopus from a sea fan; and it immediately takes on another color.

by a sort of reflex, by virtue of which it reproduces what it sees. . .But there is no consistency of reflex in the appearance of different specimens in the same surroundings. . .Their repertoire is preprogrammed, with the more complex programs being stored in the most highly developed anatomical centers."

The role that a cephalopod may adopt in any given circumstance, therefore, depends upon the choice of the animal itself. Even so, there is a certain appearance of the octopus that we could call "normal," in that it is the appearance most generally presented, and that to which the octopus returns, as to a starting point, after a sudden series of color changes. In this condition, the octopus' skin is finely speckled with dark spots. The over-all color—though there are variations—goes from red to brown and even to gray. The papillae, though visible, barely protrude.

Emotions from A to Z

The cuttlefish takes two-thirds of a second for the whole cycle of expansion and contraction of its chromatophores. But, even though this phenomenon has been closely timed, no one has yet taken inventory of the various disguises of which a cephalopod may make use according to circumstances.

First among these, as I have mentioned, is homochromatism, by virtue of which the animal renders itself invisible by taking on the spots and colors of the bottom. This behavior may be observed not only in individual specimens, but in groups of cuttlefish which, over the same bottom, take on identical colors.

The ordinary appearance of cuttlefish, characterized by stripes, gives to its body an aspect of fuzziness or imprecision; a predator, therefore, cannot easily make out its form.

The cuttlefish also has a hunting costume. It attracts the attention of its intended victim to a particular part of its motionless body—the head, for example—and camouflages the rest of it.

Like the octopus, the cuttlefish has a battle uniform of brilliant hues, which it complements by swelling up in a posture of intimidation. Emotions, too, are expressed by changes in appearance. Anxiety is manifested by black circles around the eyes. When danger is perceived, two dark spots appear on the cuttlefish's back. And, finally, there is a special apparel for mating, as we shall see in a later chapter.

During our very first Aqua-lung dives, Frédéric Dumas, who has always had a predilection for octopuses, went looking for them in their holes. It was the first time that man and octopus met face to face in the sea and observed each other. I would guess that the octopus' astonishment was about equal to that of Dumas'. But the octopus, unlike the human, seemed to resent the confrontation. There is a photograph showing it squirting a jet of ink directly onto Dumas' mask.

It has often been said that this black ink is dangerous to the eyes. This is certainly true with respect to the ink of the giant squids of the Humboldt Current. Michel Lerner, who hunted these animals off the Peruvian coast, reports that he was obliged to take special precautions against their ink. But these were animals whose bodies were ten feet long and who weighed 125 pounds. We did not run the same risks with our *Octopus vulgaris* in the Mediterranean.

Our experiences with octopus ink were always generally the same, whether at Riou or Alicaster; it was as though they followed a set program. One example therefore tells almost all that there is to know. On one occasion, Dumas succeeded in luring an octopus into the open water. He then allowed it to move away, by jet propulsion, to a distance of twelve or fifteen feet. The octopus settled on the bottom and immediately took on its color so perfectly as to be almost invisible. But Dumas' eyes had followed the animal, and he now prodded it and forced it to move. The octopus was angry, or frightened, and released its ink.

This ink is a sort of undersea cloud or fog. The octopus does not hide behind it, as is generally believed, but uses it to distract a pursuer while making its escape. The whole process is very quick. In a couple of seconds, thanks to the cloud of ink, the octopus has fled—but, at the same time, it has also changed its color in an attempt further to confuse its enemy.

The octopus can repeat this maneuver several times, depending upon the volume of the first jet of ink. Some young, small octopuses are able to emit several small clouds of a very black ink. Large octopuses make use of this means of defense less frequently than small ones. It may be that they are less easily frightened.

The ink is contained in an organ peculiar to cephalopods, the ink sac, which is located near the rectum. The ink belongs to the melanin group and is produced by alveoli in the form of melanin grains. These grains are suspended in a liquid and are extremely powerful. It takes only a few milligrams of melanin to form a protective cloud in the sea.

Our team filmed a repeat of Dumas' performance. For twenty minutes, they followed the movement of an octopus across Alicaster bay and were treated to an extraordinary festival of color. At every opportunity, the octopus stopped, shot out a spurt of ink, and changed its hue. The divers would then prod it on, and it would change once more. It was a remarkable demonstration of the mimetic art. Six or seven divers surrounded the octopus and

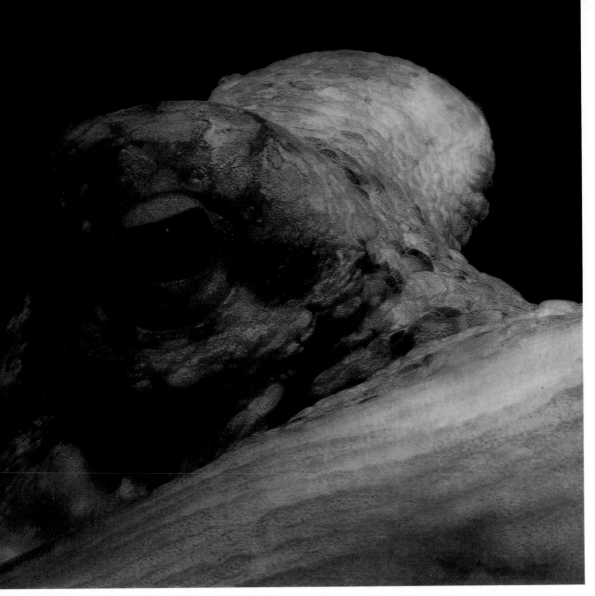

Close-up of the eye of an octopus.

forced it to move, but it was allowed to go wherever it wished. It rested on rocky bottoms, on sand, and among seaweed. Once it had exhausted its supply of ink, which it did rather quickly, it made use only of its chromatophores.

This entire scene was a special treat for everyone who witnessed it. It was at once a ballet, in which the octopus displayed all of its suppleness and grace, and a display of living color. The only problem was that the performance was too short, and gave the impression that, although it was a masterpiece of its kind, it was a hurried masterpiece.

The octopus who starred in this film was familiar to the divers. It appeared to be less sedentary than the others, and was accustomed to the open water. We ran into it every two or three days.

An octopus hides in a patch of posidonia.

A Crown

Cephalopods offer the most remarkable example in the animal kingdom of bioluminescence; and, among the cephalopods, the squids—especially those who live in deep water—are the most gifted in this respect. It would seem that no true octopus is luminous, even though Darwin records having observed one.

Many decapods remain deep in the water during the day and rise to the surface during the night. This habit has made it possible to observe them. Here is a description of one of them by Professor Carl Chun: "One would think that the body was adorned with a diadem of brilliant gems. The middle organs of the eyes shone with ultramarine blue, the lateral ones with a pearly sheen. Those towards the front of the lower surface of the body gave out a ruby-red light, while those behind were snow-white or pearly, except the middle one, which was sky blue. It was a glorious spectacle."

The luminescence of cephalopods has three different sources. It is caused by bacteria, by a secretion, and by special organs called "photophores."

A cuttlefish, *Sepiola birostrata,* has glands located near its siphon which contain luminous bacteria, and it gives off a pale blue light. The common cuttlefish is also illuminated by bacteria, of which five species have been detected. Even the "bones" of the cuttlefish may have a certain luminosity.

A small squid which lives in deep water, the *Heteroteuthis dispar,* produces light by secretion. This species is occasionally caught along the coasts of southern Italy—especially in the Straits of Messina—to which the current brings many forms of bathypelagic life. This particular squid, which was described by Aristotle, has a gland situated near its ink sac. This gland produces a luminous mucus. The gland is voided, when the squid is frightened, by means of a muscular contraction. Oxygen in the water causes the mucus to dissolve, and it shines in the form of tiny points of gray-green light. This luminescence is due to the presence of luciferin. The secretion does not entirely replace the squid's ink, but it plays a similar role. It serves to distract the attention of an enemy, which is attracted by the light, while the squid escapes in another direction.

Finally, luminescence in cephalopods may be produced by special organs, the photophores These are also found in a small squid, the *Lycoteuthis diadema,* which contains twenty-two such organs of ten different varieties.

Photophores—the structure of which varies from one species to the other—are as complex as the eyes of cephalopods. They contain lenses, mirrors, color screens, and even eyelids. There are photophores whose light is glandular; or, it may also have its origin in certain luminescent bacteria stored by the cephalopods. In the Bay of Villefranche, a squid was once observed giving off luminous red clouds, which must have been a rather exotic display of fireworks.

The field of bioluminescence is vast and little known. In the Pacific, two squids of the same species were observed, one of which was covered with photophores and the other of which was entirely devoid of them. This may be due to a difference in sex—but no one knows. Even in individual specimens there are apparent anomalies: certain cephalopods have a string of lights around one eye and nothing around the other. This is the case with the *Histioteuthis,* whose right eye is surrounded by photophores, and whose left eye not only has no photophores, but is much larger than the other.

Photophores may be found on any part of a squid's body—the head, the eyes, the mantle, the arms and tentacles, the siphon, the fins, or the body cavity. Louis Joubin, who, in 1893-1894 conducted the first histological study of the *Histioteuthis ruppelli* caught at Nice, counted, on the body of this squid, two hundred luminous organs. It may also happen that a single specimen may have two or three, or even more, different kinds of photophores.

In a species of deep-water squid, the *Watasenia scintillans,* the organs on the arms light at thirty-second intervals, and all three organs may be lighted.

We may say that the gift of light conferred by nature on squids exceeds that of any other luminescent animal, such as certain species of worms and crustaceans. There is such a diversity of means and of manifestations among squids that we are unable even to measure its extent.

What is the purpose of such a diversity of lights? Do they serve the squid as a means of defense, or are they used to attract prey? Do they serve as a means of identification among individuals of the same species, or do they lure members of the opposite sex during the mating season? Can we speak of these lights as signals, or even language, or are they merely camouflage—if indeed it is not possible for them to be both at once.

We may excuse our inability to answer such questions by citing one of the most eminent specialists in the field, Dr. E. Newton Harvey: "The embryology and the development of luminous organs belong to a field of which almost nothing is known. They will remain mysteries until we succeed in perserving in captivity some specimens of deep-water squid."*

*E. Newton Harvey, *Bioluminescence.* Academic Press, New York, 1952.

EIGHT

Love with Many Arms

In discussing the love life of the octopus, we touch upon one of the most mysterious aspects of cephalopodic existence.

In *Octopus vulgaris,* sexual maturity is attained relatively late, in the second half of the animal's life span. Males mature more rapidly than females and reach a greater size.

Both at Riou and in Alicaster bay, we attempted to observe the mating of the *Octopus vulgaris,* and found that it was almost impossible to follow, in the open water, the whole mating process, which is preceded by a complicated and lengthy ritual. We did succeed, however, in taking a few representative shots showing the male and female together, caressing one another and showing every sign of attraction. This, however, may not have been a part of the actual mating, but a sort of prenuptial experiment.

In order to get a clearer idea of the mating process, I decided to film as

Left. An octopus has come to rest on Genest's mask.

much as I could of it at the aquarium of the Oceanographic Museum of Monaco.

There, matters were more simple. For an octopus in the ocean, finding a consenting adult female is a matter of pure chance. In the laboratory, however, we took it upon ourselves to provide our male specimen with an appropriate partner, which we placed in his tank. We did not have to wait long for the desired result.

It was the female who made the first advances. These took the form of a rather strange ritual. She began by undertaking, within sight of the male, a thorough cleaning of her sucker disks. This, apparently, was a signal of her intentions. The male responded by showing his own sucker disks to the female, of which one was larger than the others. (This, as we have already noted, is a distinguishing characteristic of male octopuses.) He then raised his arms and extended them toward the female. These, obviously, are signs, language of a sort, through which the two specimens invite—or try to invite—one another. At the same time, the male's eyes took on a new brightness, and the rings around them darkened. This reaction seems to be indicative of amorous intentions; but it also indicates other emotions, as we have seen.

The Embrace

With these preliminaries out of the way, the male put forward the third arm to the right of his head. This arm differs from the others anatomically. Its tip widens into the shape of a spatula, and there is a groove running from one end of it to the other. This is the hectocotylus, or hectocotylized arm, which is the male octopus' copulatory organ. It is used first to caress the body of the female, and then to penetrate her body cavity.

Once penetration has been achieved, the groove of the hectocotylus is used to transmit the octopus' spermatophores* to the female, who receives them into her oviduct, where they are stored in a gland.

This, of course, is an extremely simplified description of a very complex process. An American zoologist, Gilman Drew, gives us an idea of what is involved in this process when he describes "the nervous mechanism that sees to it that each secretion (of spermatophores) is started and stopped at the proper time, to make the whole a complete, well-formed, complicated machine."

The hectocotylus remains in the female for a certain length of time, dur-

---

*All species of octopus have very large spermatophores. The largest of all are those of the *Octopus dofleini*—the giant octopus of Seattle—which are 43 inches long. In many species, they are as long as the octopus' mantle. The *Octopus vulgaris* and the *Eledone* produce over a hundred spermatophores.

ing which it undergoes a series of spasms apparently intended to convey the spermatophores. The actual mating usually lasts about one hour—although it may, on occasion, extend to several hours with discharge of spermatophores occurring at ten-minute intervals. According to some authorities, it is not unknown for the mating of the common octopus to last up to twenty-four hours. It happens, rarely, that the female, at the critical moment, attempts to withdraw from the male's embrace. The latter then seizes her by the head or the mantle and holds her still until he achieves penetration. Most often, however—at least in the case of *Octopus vulgaris*—mating takes place at arm's length, so to speak.

During the mating at the museum of Monaco, it was obvious that the octopuses were in a state of excitement, with the male changing his color. Our friend Andrew Packard, who was present, had the impression that both male and female experienced a certain satisfaction. They were oblivious to the presence of humans, to the noise of the cameras and the glare of the lights. They were, to all appearances, totally absorbed in one another.

Once the mating was completed, the female pushed away the male as though to indicate that, from that moment, her sole preoccupation would be the care of her young. That is, in fact, precisely what happens. The female is fertile only once in her lifetime. The male, however, may mate with other females during the mating season, if he has the opportunity.

The female lays her eggs after an interval of time which varies according to the temperature of the water and to the season of the year. It may be as little as three weeks, or as much as two months after fertilization.

Certain species of octopus lay large eggs, and the period of "incubation" for these is longer. The *Octopus bimaculoides* requires four months. And it is likely that among deep-water species—*Bathypolypus* and *Benthoctopus*—the period is of even longer duration.

There is an oviductal gland among certain species of octopods which provides both the stalks for the eggs and the mucus by which the eggs are attached to one another. This is the case with *Octopus vulgaris*. But this duct has yet another function. It serves as a storage place for spermatozoids, which fertilize the female's eggs as they are released and pass into the gland.

We were able, as I intended, to observe the mating of octopuses at Monaco. The female octopus, however, was a specimen which we had taken from the sea for that purpose, and I found it painful to think that she, and her young, would spend their short lives in captivity. Moreover, it seemed to me that incubation would more likely be successful in the sea, in the natural environment of the octopus. I therefore asked the divers to return the female to the sea, to her own house, from which we had taken her.

Above. Raymond Coll has turned around an octopus. It is a male, as can be seen from its two large sucker disks.

Above right. The preliminaries to mating: the male extends his arms toward the female to caress her.

Middle right. The female seems willing.

Below right. The male has succeeded in immoblizing the female. Copulation may take place several times successively.

A Courageous Mother

The octopus easily accepted the restoration of her freedom and set to work fulfilling her maternal duties. From the ceiling of her cave, she suspended whitish cylinders, about four inches long, containing tens of thousands of eggs. Her whole life now centered around these cylinders. She protected them against predators, cleaned them by rubbing them with her arms, and aerated them by shooting out jets of water from her funnel. She fortified her house against attack by piling up stones at its door. And, in guarding her eggs, she assumed a characteristically defensive posture, in tulip form, with her arms folded upward. Even in this position, she kept her funnel toward the eggs, so that they could be aerated from time to time.

The eggs of *Octopus vulgaris* are of small size.* They are connected by a stalk around a central filament, and form clusters of varying density. The length of these clusters depends, apparently, on the height of the ceiling in the mother's lair.

Daily visits by our divers revealed that the eggs were slowly developing. They were taking on a brownish tint and would become dark brown when ready to hatch. We spent most of October in shooting film of the mother octopus. This did not seem to disturb her, and she was content to let us do what we wished. We could see her arms placed protectively around her eggs, behind her wall of stones. But we would also see one of her eyes watching every move we made. We were able to get shots of her "blowing" out of her house some debris that had made its way inside. Genest tried to feed her bits of crab and lobster, but she would not accept his gifts. Most females will not eat after they have laid their eggs. One opinion is that they refuse food instinctively, because the debris from food would pollute the water in their houses and affect their eggs.

When Genest tried to force food upon her, she charged him in a rather pathetic effort to chase him away. She would die of exhaustion before long, but she simply would not eat. Her sole care was to protect her eggs. No one has ever reported that a female octopus left her eggs unprotected. Her courage, however, did not wane with her strength. If Genest ventured too close to her house, she attacked him bravely. She also attacked another octopus which Genest placed outside her door, and which promptly disappeared among the rocks.

Some females remain in their holes after the eggs have hatched. We have occasionally found their corpses. Those who do not die immediately

---

*Very little, if anything, is known about the eggs of most species of cephalopods which do not live in coastal zones. Comparative terms are therefore somewhat misleading.

In the Monaco aquarium, an instance of love at arm's length: the male extends his hectocotylus toward his partner.

after the hatching do not have the strength to go far. It also happens that females die during the period of "incubation."

Toward the end of this period, whenever there was even a weak current, one of the strings of eggs would be detached and swept out into the open water, carrying thousands of unhatched octopuses with it. A number of fish stationed themselves near the entry of the octopus' hole in the hope of obtaining a meal of eggs or of newly hatched octopuses.

200,000 Births

We have a special camera which was used for the first time at the hatching of the eggs. Perfected by the CEMA of Marseilles, it is called a "plankton camera" and allows us to film underwater scenes on a greatly magnified scale. It was because of this new equipment that Michael Deloire was able to film the birth of the infant octopuses.

There were about fifty bunches of eggs hanging from the ceiling of the

The female always returns to her eggs.

hole, and each bunch contained up to 4,000 embryos. In the film, one can see
the large eyes and the swollen mantle of each tiny octopus. At the proper
moment, they tear through the tissue surrounding them and emerge into the
water. Each of them is about two millimeters long (1/12 of an inch), and, at
the entrance of the hole, they resemble a small cloud hovering over the bottom. On their bodies, one can make out five chromatophores, which are al-

Left. Jean-Pierre Genest tries to make the female come out of her hole.

ready changing in intensity as a prelude to a life of camouflage.

Not all of the eggs hatch at once, for they have not all been laid at the same time. The laying of eggs is a long and complicated operation; and, because of this, the subsequent hatching can stretch out over seven or eight days.

The newborn octopuses, when they leave their mother's house, begin a dangerous journey. Very few of them will survive. The first threat is from the fish gathered around the entry to the hole, who take a terrible toll. Of the 200,000 octopuses who have just emerged from their eggs, only one or two will survive to become adults. The others will become a link in the food chain of the sea.

Immediately after their birth, the octopuses begin a wandering life which lasts about one month, during which they are carried to and fro in the open water by currents. This is the most dangerous stage of their existence, for they are then at the mercy of every fish. At the end of this time, they go into shallow water, where they are able to find shelter.

The weight of young octopuses increases by 20 per cent every day—an almost incredible rate of growth. At the time of hatching, they are able to produce spurts of ink as though they were adults.

The Art of Loving

The mating of octopuses is generally peaceful. It is rare that a female refuses to respond and that the male must use force.

Among the *Eledones*, mating is quite different from what it is among specimens of *Octopus vulgaris*. Mme. Mangold describes it as follows: "The male approaches the female from above and seizes her by the head with his dorsal arms. His interbrachial membrane covers the female's mantle almost entirely. The female *Eledone* raises her dorsal arms over the male and holds him by the head. The ventral and lateral arms of the male are rolled up, and the hectocotylus is introduced into the female's body cavity from the right side."

Among cuttlefish, mating is somewhat more ceremonious. During the mating season, the male takes on a special coloration. At the approach of any individual of the same species, he covers himself with alternating stripes of red brown, pale yellow, and white.

The hectocotylus of the cuttlefish is not the third arm to the left of its head, as in the octopus, but the fourth. This also is modified during the mating season. Its ventral side becomes larger, and its sucker disks become smaller. The entire arm is covered with well-defined stripes of black and white, which the cuttlefish displays prominently. Other male cuttlefish, when

This is the plankton camera made by CEMA from Armand Davso's design. With it, we were able to photograph the baby octopuses at the time of their birth.

they see this display, take on the same colors. The females, however, do not change their color.

It seems that the changes in the male cuttlefish are designed not so much to attract the female as to intimidate other males. However, when two male rivals meet, they do not fight. They simply swim side by side until the smaller and weaker of the two withdraws from the competition.

The nuptial ceremony is especially complicated among cuttlefish. The female, during the mating season, is luminescent. "The wedding dress glistens," writes Professor Raymond Vaissière, "like true nuptial apparel, with

A female in her hole defends her eggs.

silvered damask set off by black stripes. The male's colors are rather more somber. The female gives the impression of being in continual vibration. Waves of russet color move from the head to the opposite extremity. The edge of the mantle is a delicate fin, undulating gently and holding the animal perfectly stable."

If one can observe the mating at night, one discovers that both the male and female are luminous—the male more so than the female. And his fourth arm, the hectocotylus, is particularly brilliant, with luminescent flecks of silver with green lights.

The pair swim close together, the male following exactly the movements of the female. If another male approaches, the first male places himself between the newcomer and the female, facing the latter.

Strings of eggs hang from the roof of the cave. They may contain as many as 250,000 embryos.

The sexual act begins with tenderness: the male and female juxtapose their mouths and entwine their arms. Cuttlefish always adopt the head-to-head position, and the male deposits the spermatophores on a groove surrounding the female's mouth, which is the female's sperm receptacle. Other decapods, however, use mating methods that are more or less aggressive in nature. The male squid of Terra Nova, the *Illex illecebrosus,* for example, attacks the female from the underside and holds her around the mantle while he places his spermatophores in her body cavity. This is the head-to-mantle position. In other cases—among the *Sepiola* for example—the male turns the female onto her back and then deposits the spermatophores in the body cavity. In every case, however, arms other than the hectocotylus are used to hold the female. The hectocotylus is used solely to transmit the spermatophores.

Mating may be repeated several times in one day. In general, the male and female remain together for some time after mating, until the eggs are laid. Then the male leaves in search of another female.

The behavior of the female squid also merits attention, for, without leaving ourselves open to the charge of anthropomorphism, we can say that she shows certain signs of emotion when being pursued by a male. Sometimes, either out of fear or flirtatiousness, she flees. But, if she is willing to accept the male, she does not hide her feelings. Water is shot rapidly through her funnel, and she flutters her fins. The male who has chosen her appears, momentarily at least, to lose interest in other females and pursues only the one that he has chosen. Frequent changes in color testify to the fervor of his devotion.

It appears that mating among cephalopods is not lacking in imaginative methods. The strangest method is perhaps that of the argonauts, who are octopods. The male's hectocotylus, carrying a single spermatophore, detaches itself from the male and enters the body cavity of the female.

This singular method of fertilization caused a great deal of confusion in earlier times. For many years, zoologists knew only the female argonaut. They had never been able to find a male of the species. Then, in 1827, an Italian naturalist discovered, on a female argonaut, a strange creature which he took to be sort of a parastic worm. Georges Cuvier, the French naturalist, was of the same opinion, and he gave to this unknown species the name of *Hectocotylus,* which means " arm of a hundred disks." It was not until the middle of the nineteenth century that Cuvier's error was rectified and the hectocotylus identified for what it was: the third arm of the male argonaut. Examination under the microscope revealed the presence of chromatophores and of sucker disks remarkably similar to those of the argonaut. Finally, in 1853, specimens of the male argonaut were found near Sicily, and the mystery was completely solved.

The error of scientists up until that time is understandable. Nature, it seems, has outdone herself in the complexity of the reproductive mechanism among argonauts. The female, for one thing, is twenty times larger than the male. The latter rarely measures more than one-half inch, but its hectocotylus, which is enclosed in a sac, may be almost five inches long. This organ, which has between fifty and a hundred sucker disks, bursts the sac in which it is carried, detaches itself from the argonaut's body, carrying with it the spermatophore. Once it is free, it is able to swim and wiggle in the water for several hours, until it succeeds in penetrating the body cavity of the female.

It happens occasionally that the female carries the male in what used to be called her shell. The reason is not that the male is a parasite, but that his sexual member, when it is freed within that shell, has a much greater chance of reaching its goal.

Genest with a string of eggs.

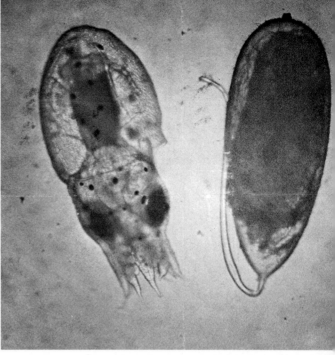

Two octopus eggs photographed with the plankton camer
The embryos can be distinguished.

Octopus embryos photographed by the plankton camera.

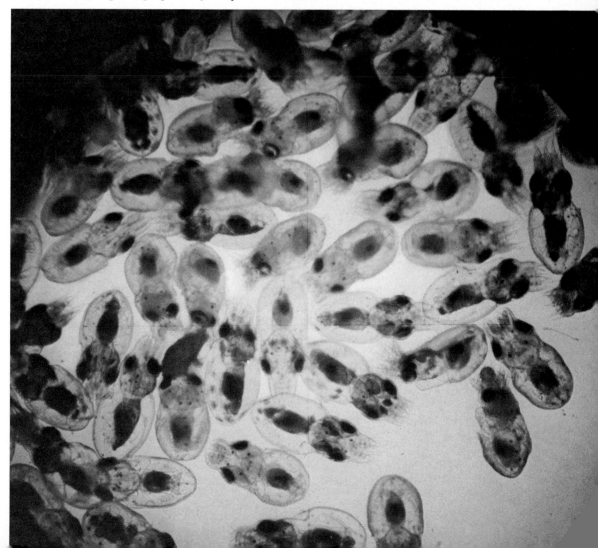

Aboard *Calypso*, Captain Cousteau and Andrew Packard watch octopuses in a tank.

Fertilization by means of a detachable or autonomous member is not the privilege solely of argonauts. The same phenomenon is found among the *Ocythoë* and the *Tremoctopus,* species of octopus. The length of the hectocotylus varies; but the Museum of Natural History in Paris has on display an example of such an organ from an *Ocythoë,* found at Nice, measuring over ten inches in length.

The nautilus, on the other hand, has no hectocotylus in the proper sense of that term. In this case, four of its small arms are transformed into a conical organ, the spadix, which assumes the role of the hectocotylus.

Irresponsible Mothers

The females among cuttlefish, squids, and decapods are, to all appearances, bad mothers in most cases. They do not watch over their eggs, or defend them against predators, or show any interest in the fate of their young.

The cuttlefish at least has an excuse. Her eggs, which are brown, are considered inedible by fish because of either their taste or their smell. None-

Calypso approaches the Oceanographic Museum of Monaco, where our specimens will be placed into tanks.

theless, the young cuttlefish, as soon as they are hatched—transparent, and with enormous eyes—are readily eaten by predators.

The best mother seems to be the argonaut. She carries her eggs with her until they are hatched, in her thin floating shell which she secretes and which she supports with her two rear arms.

The female *Tremoctopus* attaches her eggs to the base of her dorsal arms, where they are held in place by sucker disks.

In the case of the *Ocythoë,* however, the eggs develop entirely within the mother's body, in the oviduct.

There is obviously a wide variety of ways in which cephalopods lay their eggs and dispose of them. The simplest method perhaps is that adopted by the female of the squid *Vampyroteuthis infernalis,* a strange animal known of for only a short time, who releases her eggs one by one and allows them to float away.

A species of small squid, the *Loligo,* as we shall see in the next chapter, attaches its eggs to any irregularity on the bottom, so that there are aggregates of egg bunches held down by filaments. After doing this, however, both the male and the female die.

The common cuttlefish (*Sepia officinalis*) also anchors her eggs, but usually to a support which has branches—such as the branches of a sea fan. These eggs resemble a bunch of grapes. It happens frequently that several females will pool their eggs.

So far as deep-water squids are concerned, we have very little information. It is thought that their eggs are attached to a gelatinous belt which floats freely in the water. It was apparently this sort of belt that I found in the Indian Ocean, after spotting it, floating in the water, from *Calypso*'s bridge.*

Both baby octopuses and baby cuttlefish may be classified as larvae, since they have transitory cutaneous organs: the Kölliker canals. (The newborn cuttlefish, however, unlike the octopus, looks very much like a miniature version of the adult.) The cuttlefish, like the octopus, spends the first month of its life being carried by the currents. At the end of that time, it is ready to begin adult life and it settles to the bottom and seeks shelter.

In certain species, the larvae are so different from the adults that naturalists have mistaken them for distinct species. This is the case of the larvae of *Chiroteuthis veranyi,* who were christened *Doratopsis vermicularis.*

The larva of *Vampyroteuthis infernalis,* which is peculiar in many ways, has a pair of temporary fins. These are replaced by others when it reaches adulthood.

*See Chapter One.

NINE

The Night of the Squids

In April 1969, the whole of *Calypso*'s team was occupied with the study of gray whales.* We were following their migration from San Diego to the lagoons of Baja California. The work was exhausting. We were obliged to follow, in our Zodiacs, these gigantic and surprisingly clever cetaceans. Often, our divers and cameramen attempted to grab and hold onto the dorsal fin of a whale, but what usually happened was that the whale would dive and disappear even before we could film or photograph it. It also happened that, with a flick of its tail or a stroke of its flipper, it overturned the Zodiac and sent all its occupants, as well as its engine and all the equipment aboard, into the water. We had, to put it mildly, a few adventures while in pursuit of the gray whale.

Every night, the team would meet in the wardroom. The cameramen and the divers, exhausted, could hardly move their arms, and no one could think

*See *The Whale: Mighty Monarch of the Sea*, by Jacques-Yves Cousteau and Philippe Diolé. Doubleday, New York, and Cassell, London, 1972.

Above. Off Catalina Island, *Calypso*'s team watches a huge mass of squids lighted by our floods.

Left. An ocean sunfish, surrounded by squids.

Above right. Squids gathered for mating.

Below right. A blue shark gets ready to launch into the squids.

of anything but getting to bed. We ate mechanically and without hunger.

On April 12, *Calypso* was anchored along the western coast of Baja California, off the island of Santa Catalina, in water 120 feet deep. Suddenly, the siren sounded— as it does whenever one of our engines overheats. Our maintenance officer rushed below. Almost immediately, the electricity went off. The water pumps were no longer working. We were in darkness. Our emergency lighting system was activated.

By then, we were out on *Calypso*'s deck, and what we saw made us forget about lights and water pumps. The sea around us, which only a few moments before had been almost completely calm, seemed now to be boiling. *Calypso* was surrounded by millions of animals thrashing about in the water. Obviously, tired as everyone was, it was necessary to find out what was happening. Bernard Chauvelin and Jacques Delcoutère suited up immediately and dived. It was as though they had plunged into a kettle of squid. Everywhere around them, there were animals in motion, most of them not more than four inches long, some of them red and others golden.

At the request of René Robino, our maintenance engineer, Chauvelin and Delcoutère went down to inspect the screens over the intakes of our water pump. As René suspected, they were blocked—but blocked by the gelatinous bodies of squids; about two and a half pounds of soft flesh. The two divers pulled them away from the screens by the handful. But, as soon as the pump was started again, more squids took the place of those which had been removed. Once more the pump stopped. We had to improvise large baskets, made of metal wire, which we fastened over the intake openings. Then we appointed a clean-up team, which was to clear away the squids every two hours.

By then, I had decided that we could not afford to let this opportunity pass. We would have to take advantage of this extraordinary spectacle in the sea by filming it. As soon as electricity had been restored, I had all of our underwater lighting apparatus hooked up. The cameras were made ready. And my son Philippe joined Chauvelin and Delcoutère in the nocturnal squid bath surrounding *Calypso*.

A Living Tide

It was the first time that we had seen squids along the California coast. Now, however, they were a veritable living tide, hundreds of thousands of tiny diaphanous ghosts in the midst of which submerged floodlights traced patterns of gold in the black water.

Albert Falco, our chief diver, took advantage of the occasion to test his new tight-beam floodlights in underwater shots.

I had all of *Calypso*'s lighting equipment turned on and aimed out at the water. It was an unbelievable sight. We were in the middle of an almost solid layer, several yards thick, of writhing, squirming creatures who darted to and fro by expelling water from their funnels, like a vast fleet of minute jets. Or rather, like a giant puree of hyperactive microbes, magnified millions of times.

The Sharks

In the midst of this mass of squids, there were sharks cutting wide swathes which were quickly closed again. Their great jaws wide open, they were gulping down squids as fast as they could fill their mouths, and then stopping for a second to swallow their prey before beginning again. We could see them shaking their heads and twisting their bodies in an effort to swallow more quickly.

To Philippe and his two companions, who were in the water watching the sharks in the midst of the cloud of squids, the scene was, to say the least, disconcerting. Philippe recalled* later that "I was certain the sharks would not attack us; at least not immediately. Those around us were eating squids as fast as they could. It was an effortless hunt, with a superabundance of game. There was every chance that the sharks would be too busy to bother about us."

The mass of squids was so dense, however, that, beneath the surface, it was impossible for the divers to see for more than two feet ahead of them. Squids were stuck to their arms, hands, masks, and to the divers' lights. There were several face-to-face encounters with sharks, but, in each instance, the shark turned away. As Philippe had suspected, they were too busy with squids to be concerned about humans.

These were "blue sharks," although their undersides appeared very white in the glare of our underwater lights.

*See *The Shark*, by Jacques-Yves Cousteau and Philippe Cousteau, Doubleday, New York, and Cassell, London, 1970.

Following page. Squids often mate in groups of three or four.

This great gathering of squids was nothing less than a lovers' rendezvous. Seen from beneath the surface, its purpose was obvious; and this made it all the more fantastic. The animals were in pairs and were swimming with their tentacles interwined. Their bodies were translucent, but wavy and colored in the light of our lamps. They were dancing, face to face. They were searching for partners. And they were embracing, by groups and by clusters of five or six individual specimens.

In certain of these groups, nothing could be seen except a writhing mass of arms and tentacles. There were also isolated individuals searching frantically for partners and attaching themselves to any other squid, male or female; then, separating and swimming away rapidly, the victims of a blinding frenzy. They were bright red in the middle of a golden field of intertwined bodies. In their excitement, they ran into our lights and cameras, making it impossible to do any shooting. We had to stop, turn out the lights, and wait until they went away.

Now in the limited visibility of the water, the divers could no longer see the sharks in their vicinity. They could, however, sense that they were becoming more nervous and more aggressive, and more aware of the presence of the divers among them.

"The sharks," Philippe said, "were beginning to notice us. They nudged us with their heads and brushed against our equipment. One of them charged and smacked into our camera. It turned away for a moment, but then came back. It was obviously time for us to leave."

I know from my own experiences in the Red Sea that, while sharks always give warning of their intentions, a diver must know how to interpret those warnings. Happily, Philippe had participated in all our previous dives among sharks, and he knew more about the behavior of sharks than anyone else. He therefore gave the signal to return to *Calypso* at the proper time.

Nonetheless, I did not give up my resolution to learn more about this nightmarish gathering of squids. And we had a way of knowing what was happening beneath the surface of the water, and even of filming it, without placing any of our divers in danger.

At 4:15 A.M., the minisub SP-350 was in the water. Falco, who was at the controls, told us by telephone that everything was going well and that he was preparing to submerge.

The Minisub Breaks Down

Jacques Delcoutère then disconnected the telephone and the safety line. The minisub dived, and we could see two headlights shining like two golden beams in the boiling water.

Albert Falco, *Calypso*'s chief diver, pilots the SP-350 diving saucer.

At 100 feet below the surface, Falco leveled the minisub above the bottom and began to describe, by ultrasonic telephone, what he saw through the portholes of his vehicle. But he stopped short to announce that the minisub's engine had just stopped.

Jacques Roux—whom we call Gaston—our electrical engineer, advised Falco to shut off all electrical equipment in the minisub. It was not really a dangerous situation. The minisub has an independent supply of oxygen good for twenty-four hours, and Falco would be able to stay in contact with *Calypso* by means of the ultrasonic telephone.

Falco next informed us that, in order to be able to rise to the surface, he intended to jettison the minisub's ballast: a fifty-pound weight of cast iron. A launch was put into the water and went to the spot where it was expected that Falco would surface. Shortly, we saw the top of the minisub in the light of our floods, and Delcoutère was already manning the hoist. There was nothing more to do except to bring the SP-350 aboard.

Bringing such a vehicle aboard is not a secret operation. The launch's engine, the shouts of the divers, the camera's flashbulbs—all this should have frightened off the squids. Instead, it had the contrary effect. The squids seemed oblivious to what was happening, and they continued to flow around *Calypso*; and not only around *Calypso*, but also on the hull of the minisub that now rested on *Calypso*'s deck. André Laban lifted up a cluster of five or six squids still united in a single act of love. We also discovered, on one of the minisub's portholes, a number of gelatinous balls containing squid eggs. We had, by accident, dropped anchor in the middle of the mating grounds of the squids.

The minisub was quickly repaired. The trouble had been caused by squids, who had been drawn into the vehicle's intake pipe. Their bodies had blocked the pipe, and the motor had overheated to the point where the circuit breakers were thrown.

I was aware that, in this rendezvous of squids, there were the makings of a film as unusual as it was unexpected. It seemed to me especially remarkable that these little cephalopods, which one hardly ever sees except at depths of between 350 and 1,000 feet, and which are usually very timid, were suddenly so obsessed with mating that they allowed themselves to be touched, and even captured, by our divers. Philippe and his companions had brought aboard a great many specimens, which we had immediately placed in an aquarium. But the cook, without telling anyone, had fished them out with a strainer so as to prepare them *alla Romana* for lunch the next day.

We had all learned long before to bend to the whims of the sea. When the sea wishes to share its secrets, it does so, and we must plan our own affairs accordingly. In this light, the observation of gray whales lost its importance, at least for the moment. We must always be ready to change our plans in order to profit from an opportunity. I therefore decided to film, for the first time in open water, the complete mating cycle of the squids. And *Calypso* would remain where she was as long as was necessary.

I called a meeting of the team's leaders—Falco, Delemotte, and Yves Omer—to decide on a program of shooting that would run twenty-four hours a day so as to cover all phases of the cycle. Then, the cameras and diving equipment were checked out thoroughly. For this was to be an exceptional undertaking. A scientific record would be compiled, for use of biologists, on the mating habits of *Loligo opalescens*, the squid of the western coast of North America.

The Alimentary Chain of the Sea

The subject of this record was not without some importance. Squids provide food for many species of marine life, and experts are alarmed at the lessening of their numbers in certain areas which were once excellent fishing grounds. Marine animals, especially, thrive on squids, which are an essential link in the alimentary chain of the sea.

Thanks to the underwater television camera that we were using, we could see that the sharks were not the only animals devouring squids. There were also pilot whales, porpoises, fifty-ton sperm whales, and even moonfish taking advantage of this windfall.

The SP-350 is taken out of the see at dusk.

Many species of fish also eat squids, from salmon to swordfish. Even birds—auks and terns, for example—claim a share. And, finally, man eats squid in great numbers. In the waters of Japan, each year between 500,000 and 700,000 tons of a certain species, *Todarodes pacificus*, are caught. The Japanese are even beginning to breed squids in underwater "ranches" in the sea.

The uncontrolled fishing of squids may cause an irreversible disequilibrium in marine life. I could not help imagining what disastrous consequences the use of a net might have had at the spot where *Calypso* was anchored during the mating of these animals.

During our second night with the squids, they rose, as they had the preceding night, to the waters near the surface. The nuptial dances, however, seemed fewer than before, and there was a corresponding increase in actual matings. This announced the beginning of seventy-two consecutive hours of violence, fecundation, and agony.

Sixteen Hours of Shooting in the Water

I asked the divers to try to film couples separately, within a wide frame. This was a difficult task. One might as well have tried to film two snowflakes in a blizzard. Meanwhile, our television team was keeping continuous watch over the progress of the mating of the squids.

At nine o'clock at night, the operation began. The divers were about to undertake sixteen hours of shooting in the midst of a sea of love-crazed cephalopods. Before it was over, the divers had used over a mile of film and had emptied thirty-six bottles of compressed air. In the dark sea, lighted by our floods, they were witnesses to one of nature's great dramas.

The English call these squids "sea arrows," possibly because they swim quite rapidly. They move backward, by jet propulsion. This method of locomotion plays a much more important part in their lives than in that of the octopus. They have, for that matter, a perfect hydrodynamic shape. When they wish to remain more or less stationary, the squids use the two fins which are located one on each side of their bodies.

It seemed that there were as many males as females among the squids, but, in the general confusion which we witnessed, sexual contacts were dictated by opportunity. Polygamy seemed the rule and threesomes were quite frequent. Male squids, in their erotic frenzy, attacked other male squids—which elicited violent, and presumably indignant, reactions.

The Females Lay Their Eggs

In the course of the mating, changes in color and in the intensity of color were so frequent and radical as to be unbelievable. The normal hues of squids are rather delicate, iridescent, and diaphanous. But, in the throes of desire, the males were purple. At the summit of excitement, their heads and tentacles were surrounded by waves and stripes of red and maroon as long as they were embracing females.

Gradually and slowly, the squids began to sink toward the bottom of the sea. The females were depositing the gelatinous capsules which contained their eggs. For three days, each of them would lay between ten and twenty cylindrical capsules, each containing a hundred eggs. But the females did not simply lay the eggs and then abandon them to their fate. In order to prevent them from being washed away by the current and into less temperate waters, the females took great pains to attach each capsule to algae, or to some irregularity on the bottom, by means of a viscous filament. Most of them carefully arranged their eggs in bunches resembling chrysanthemums.

Even while engaged in these maternal tasks, female squids were not safe from assault by males. The males were still emitting their semen into the water, near the bunches of eggs; and the walls of the capsules were soft enough for the spermatozoids to penetrate and fertilize the eggs. This, however, is not the ordinary means of fertilization. Most often, the spermatophores are deposited on the female herself.

An Aggressive Shark

Our divers filmed these scenes with such concentration that they forgot there were sharks in the vicinity. Nonetheless, these predators were present in great numbers, attracted no doubt by the frantic movement of the squids as they are by the distress signals of wounded fish.

Blue sharks are known both for their limited intelligence and their unpredictability. The divers had therefore taken down with them a defense weapon: a shark stick, which is nothing more than a piece of wood with a few sharp points at one end of it. Then, with professional calm, and ignoring the danger of an attack, they had set up their cameras and lights and proceeded to the work at hand.

The "sea arrows," thanks to their system of jet propulsion, are among the fastest swimmers in the sea, and, given their small size, they are not an easy prey. But, at this particular moment, blinded by their sexual obsession, they were particularly vulnerable. The irony of it was that they were being devoured by sharks during the single opportunity given them to create life.

There was a ten-foot shark swimming among them, its mouth open—when it caught sight of Yves Omer's legs. Fortunately, Yves was able to see the shark moving to the attack and quickly pulled himself up *Calypso*'s ladder. The incident reminded us, however, that we were fragile strangers in a domain where the shark is king.

Raymond Ammadio, our chef, was not concerned with sharks. His sole preoccupation was with the hundred ways in which to prepare squids. We ate them for two weeks: squids *à l'espagnole, alla bolognese, alla Romana*, and *à la casserole*.

André Laban was the only one who shared Raymond's enthusiasm for squids. Someone had told him that a diet of fresh squids would make hair grow.

The Lesson of Love

When it came time to shoot the scientific part of our film—the most interesting part—we invited aboard *Calypso* a specialist in invertebrate life forms, Miss June Lindstedt. Miss Lindstedt is a zoologist associated with the Laboratory of Marine Biology of the University of Southern California. She was interested in our work, and she kindly accepted our request for her help.

By using a special camera, we were able to record the mating of the *Loligo opalescens*. The males seize the females from underneath, to the side. The action is extremely rapid, but our photographs allow us to make out the details: the male holds the female while the tip of his hectocotylus slides under her mantle and reaches the oviduct. He is able to repeat this operation several times before relaxing his embrace.

It was less than seventy-two hours since the gathering of squids had become an orgy in the sea, and already our divers were reporting signs of fatigue among the squids. Many squids, who had come from far off and had shown themselves full of strength and vigor, were now resting on algae, drooping and limp. Yet, other squids were still active and aggressive twenty-four hours later. They interrupted their sexual assaults only to devour exhausted females.

Miss Lindstedt, who has specialized in the *Loligo opalescens*, pointed out to us that there are three distinct and successive distributions of spermatozoids. The first takes place when the male penetrates the female and places spermatophores in her body cavity. The second distribution occurs when the eggs are laid, at which time the female disposes of the spermatozoids stored by her. And the third, as we have seen, takes place when the male

Bunches of squid eggs on the ocean floor look like dahlias.

emits semen into the water near the eggs attached to the bottom. Nature has taken extraordinary precautions to assure the survival of *Loligo opalescens*.

The eggs of the squid are developed in the ovary, and when they cross the oviduct, a protective envelope is formed among them. The entire mass is then expelled through the funnel, with considerable effort on the part of the female. The first thing to emerge from the funnel is a filament—a sort of anchor line. But, once the capsule of eggs is entirely free of the funnel, it rocks back and forth until the female is able to seize the end of the filament with her arms. The filament is then used to anchor the capsule to the ocean bottom.

We have observed that the laying of eggs lasts three or four days.

A Field of Death

April 16. Many females no longer have the strength to complete their work, to expel the last of the capsules containing their eggs. Others, exhausted by having given life, are on the point of death. Some, still alive, are locked in the embrace of males who are in agony and who will take the females with them into oblivion. The long night of the squids is about to end.

Our two minisubs are lowered into the water together. Albert Falco and I, using these vehicles, discover thousands of egg capsules and innumerable corpses. On the bottom, nothing moves, other than one last squid which is barely alive. Twenty million pale cadavers cover the flat sandy floor of the ocean.

The rendezvous of the squids has been with both love and death. But we will have the opportunity to see life reborn. In one month, the eggs will hatch, and the new squids will emerge.

Seven Billion Embryos

April 18. This morning, a school of pilot whales arrived to feast on squids, but they were disappointed. There was not a single squid alive. The whales therefore returned to deep water in search of other food.

I asked the divers to reconnoiter the bottom in order to determine the extent of the area over which the squids' eggs were spread. On the basis of this information, we may be able to estimate the size of the generation that is to be born here.

Bernard Delemotte and Louis Prezelin were surprised to discover, in this field of death, a female still living. She was trying bravely to eject her egg capsules. Delemotte helped her. It is not often that one can play midwife to a squid.

Today, over the bottom, we saw large gray rays devouring either the dead squids or their eggs. The rays' wings have suddenly taken on a sinister aspect; they remind one somehow of the angel of death.

The divers go down every day to inspect the immense nest below us; an incubator in which seven billion embryos are alive. This is the approximate figure at which we have arrived.

From day to day, the eggs have changed color. In the light of our lamps, we saw them becoming darker and darker. But this brownish color is due to tiny mushroomlike growths that have covered the egg capsules. This layer has a very bad taste. Moreover, the capsules themselves have grown harder. Very few predators are now tempted to attack them. Only the starfish, whose stomach is proof against anything, eats squid embryos. Even so, the capsules are tough, and it takes the starfish three or four days to digest them. It therefore attacks them only when there is nothing else to eat.

I have decided to dissect one of these capsules in order to examine it under the microscope. It is so elastic that it is difficult to cut, even with a scalpel.

From the gelatinous mass I take a single transparent chorion. It is almost an individual aquarium, constituting the ideal environment which responds to all the needs of the embryo. The color of the tiny form already has a sparkle that is discernible with the naked eye. Under a powerful lens, one can see a perfectly formed squid palpitating with a life force that has come down to it from ancestors whose origins go back 200 million years.

Under such a lens, the skin of the embryo seems already pigmented in a fashion reminiscent of a mosaic.

Thanks to Miss June Lindstedt, we have been able to follow, and to film in the laboratory, by using a high-powered instrument, the entire embryonic development of *Loligo opalescens*.

Within the capsule, the eggs are tightly packed; but in each egg there is sufficient place for the embryo's movements and growth. One can already distinguish three swellings in the embryo. One will become the mantle and most of the internal organs. The arms are already visible under two lateral swellings. Another will become the eyes and a part of the brain. The central mass is the yellow exterior sack of the embryo—the yoke of the egg. One can even make out the sucker disks on the arms; and the eyes are already completely formed.

In order to emerge from the egg, the embryo makes use of a special organ situated between its two fins. It is shaped like a two-pronged fork and secretes enzymes which dissolve a part of the membrane of the chorion. At the same time, this organ, activated by vibrations, perforates the wall of the embryo's cell. The embryo then leaves through the breach, using for the first time its jet propulsion to emerge from the egg.

Upon hatching, the baby squid measures 1/10 of one inch in length. It immediately manifests great activity. Strangely enough, it happens that its first act is to shoot out a jet of ink.

Appropriately, it is Yves Omer who filmed this beginning of life for a new generation, as he had filmed the death of the old in these same waters.

The Place of Death in the Sea

The great sacrifice and suffering which accompanies the creation of life in the sea leaves us bewildered. Our experiences during the month we spent at Catalina have given us some idea of the place that death occupies in the

A diver holding a "shark stick." There is a shark in the background.

Right. The diving saucer lights up the corpses of thousands of squids lying on the bottom.

history of a species.

Twenty per cent of each generation of squids dies before hatching, mostly because of changes in the environment. Fifty per cent of newborn squids are devoured by predators during the first week of their life. Those who survive are the sole hope of the species.

These survivors carry in their being an instinct, blind and irresistible, which pushes them to multiply in every ocean of the world. Like every life form, including man, squids aim at nothing less than the conquest of the planet.

May 18. It is now over a month that we have been working off Catalina. I have sent the divers down for a final inspection of the area in which the eggs were laid. They report that visibility is excellent, and that biological activity is negligible. Where the squids had assembled by the millions, where they mated, and where a new generation was born, there is now nothing left. Everything has disappeared. Where, only a few hours ago, the infant squids first emerged into the water, there now remains only an eternally mute witness, the sea.

We were not yet entirely free of the squids. During this same expedition, a few days later, *Calypso*'s sonar several times registered unidentified echoes.

I think that these "echoes" are probably migrating squids.

At nine hundred feet, from the minisub, I see young squids only two or three inches long. Blinded by my lights, they stick their heads into the mud on the bottom and then bounce up and begin that strange movement to and fro.

I remember, too, the night when *Calypso* dropped anchor so that we might make a nocturnal dive. The sea was smooth as a mirror. There was no moon, and the sky was dark. Suddenly, within a radius of a couple of miles, we saw tiny creatures spring out of the water and fall back with a splash. The creatures were our squids. For a moment, one would have thought it was raining on the sea.

Thus, from month to month, from expedition to expedition, we are engaged in establishing new ties with marine animals. We are learning to know them better, and we are overcome with admiration at their prodigious detours by means of which they maintain that improbable phenomenon: life.

TEN

Giants of the Deep

On at least one occasion, I encountered one of those unknown and utterly fantastic cephalopods which are said to live in the deepest parts of the sea.

It was during one of *Calypso*'s expeditions in the Indian Ocean. I had gone down in the minisub SP-350 to inspect two DSLs—sonic layers registered by our sounding equipment at 100 and 150 fathoms. I supposed that these were nothing more than layers of food—plankton, for example—for the marine animals, such as whales, who were plentiful in that area.* And, in fact, between 160 feet and 500 feet, I found a cloud of plankton. At about 1,000 feet, I jettisoned my ballast and began to rise.

When I had reached 800 feet, I saw, through a porthole, a very large cephalopod, only a few yards from the minisub, watching the vehicle as it moved slowly past. I could not take my eyes from that mass of flesh, though it seemed not at all disturbed by the presence of the minisub. It was an un-

*See *The Whale: Mighty Monarch of the Sea*, by Jacques-Yves Cousteau and Philippe Diolé. Doubleday, New York, and Cassell, London, 1972.

earthly sight, at once astonishing and terrifying. Was it sleeping? Or thinking? Or merely watching? I had no idea. It was there, nonetheless, enormous, alive, its huge eyes fixed on me. Then, suddenly, it was gone. I did not even see it move, though I am sure that an animal of that size is able to move with extreme rapidity by means of water jets from its funnel. The impression it made was one of size and power. I can understand how formidable a giant squid must be.

I wonder how many of us there are in the world who have ever seen such an animal; who have exchanged looks with those great, unblinking eyes, which resemble nothing I had ever seen before.

Such an encounter can only be the result of chance. The odds are very much against it, obviously. For in all my dives, both in the minisub and (less frequently) in bathyspheres, I had never before, and never since, seen a cephalopod of such size.

Undoubtedly, there are giants in the depths of the oceans, but the sea is so vast that we have had practically no experience with them and know very little about them. The best reports we have, and the most dependable, go back to the end of the nineteenth century; to Albert I of Monaco, an expert oceanographer with a record of many important contributions to science.

The Revelations of a Cachalot

The best way to do justice to Prince Albert is to reproduce his *Observations on Cephalopods*, as edited by Louis Joubin, which record the results of his expeditions with the *Princesse Alice* from 1891 to 1897.* Very little more is known today than what Prince Albert learned three-quarters of a century ago.

Albert's experience with cephalopods began on July 18, 1895, when a cachalot, captured off the Azores, regurgitated deep-water specimens of very large size. It is worth noting that these specimens belonged to genuses and species which remain unknown to this day. Prince Albert himself recorded the capture of the cachalot, which measured forty-six feet in length. He tells first how he sighted fishing boats in pursuit of a school of these whales. The *Princesse Alice* maintained a distance of a mile and a half from the boats, and

---

Remarques sur les Céphalopodes, ed. Louis Joubin, fascicule xvii. Monaco, n.d.

Right. A squid caught by Prince Albert of Monaco and reproduced in his own work on cephalopods, fas. 17: *Entomopsis aliceijoubin*.

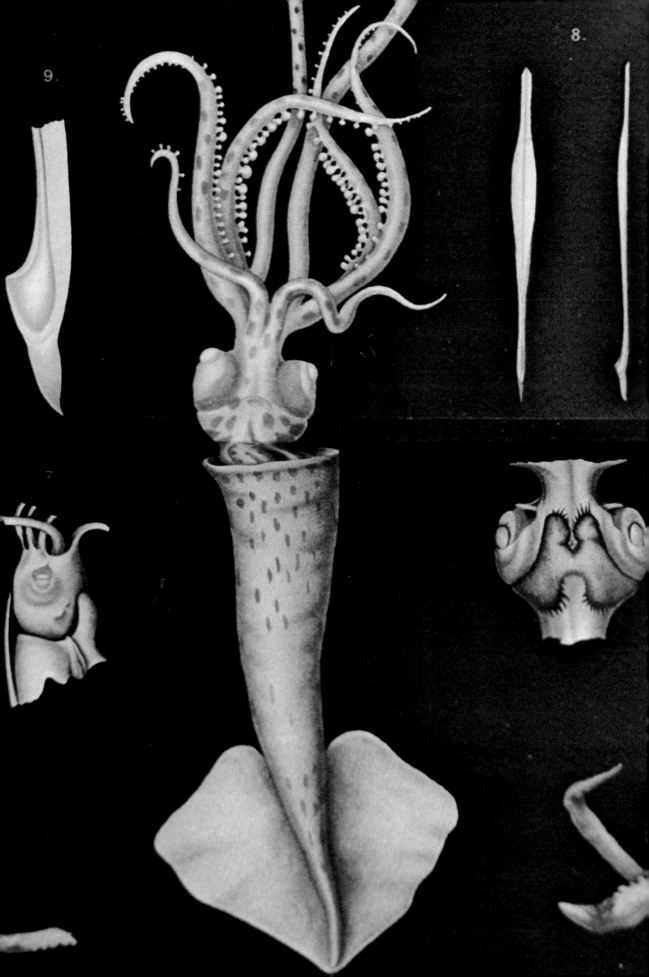

witnessed the first stages of the chase. When the *coup de grace* had been given to this particular specimen, Albert ordered his yacht to move in closer, since there was no longer any danger of frightening the whales. He was thus able to observe closely what followed:

"By the time I reached the spot, the second group of whalers had already moved eastward in pursuit of the school, which had fled in that direction. The wounded whale, however, was now quiet after the wild ride on which it had taken its pursuers' boat. When I arrived, it had just been given the mortal blow. Shortly afterward, the spout rose from its blowhole and the vaporized water which it threw into the air was tinted pink, and then took on a red color. Soon, the water itself was red with the blood of the whale.

"The giant alongside us was in its final agony. Its enormous dark body, which seemed to be sleeping submerged in the sea, sometimes stirred heavily, and its great tail struck the water violently, causing the red color to change momentarily as it was replaced by white foam.

"The persons aboard my ship were grouped on the forward deck, standing on the trunks, and some had even climbed up the masts so as to see what was happening. They were all struck dumb by the sight. I myself, affected to the marrow of my bones by the grandeur of this spectacle, watched it as attentively as I would have watched a vision that might vanish at any moment. I was greatly moved by the obvious suffering of the giant, which, in every way, seemed more intense than that of lesser beings. I pitied this great creature of the sea which had, perhaps for centuries, traveled in every sea and to every depth without fear, which had survived a thousand storms only to fall, finally, to the spear of a pygmy.

"All this spilling of blood, and the wounded body of the whale itself, seemed to me a disaster. It was like the fall of a great tree, or the sinking of a ship.

"Suddenly, the cachalot ceased thrashing about and, as though our proximity had revived it, it made straight for us at great speed. I had sufficient presence of mind to wonder what would happen if, either willingly or perhaps in the throes of a convulsion, the whale should swim into the side of the ship. But, when it was about sixty feet from us, the animal disappeared beneath the surface. For an eternity of ten seconds I wondered: Would it smash the keel of the ship, or the rudder or propeller, with its back or with one stroke of its tail? Then, we saw the whale appear on the other side of the ship. It was no longer moving. The whalers came nearer to harpoon it once more, and death entered into all its parts while the spectators watched in breathless silence.

"The ship was now afloat in a hectare of reddish water, through which ran rivulets of deeper hue as blood poured from the animal. The more intense color was dissipated, then blended into various tints, as clouds coming down from the mountains are confounded with fog on the plains.

"The whale's gigantic head was alongside our stern, and its lower jaw, hanging loose now that the muscles had relaxed, was moved by the action of the waves. I could see the mouth, like a yawning cavern. And I saw it vomit out, one after another, the bodies of several cephalopods—octopuses or squids—of colossal size. These, apparently, were the fruits of the whale's final plunge to the depths, following which it had been harpooned on the surface; a recent meal which had as yet hardly been affected by digestion.

"I knew the value to science of these cadavers from the deep, of creatures whose strength had hitherto enabled them to defy capture, and the existence of which we suspected only through stories of adventure regarded as fables.

"We immediately sent out a launch to recuperate these bodies; but their density was dragging them below the surface, and we were afraid that they would disappear completely before they could be reached. I therefore ordered the ship's engines reversed, so that we moved backward slowly toward where these corpses were, about thirty feet from our stern. My idea was that the motion of the propellors would bring the bodies back to the surface. That is what actually happened, and the men in the boat were able to reach them with their nets."

Unknown Species

"After my return to port, the five octopuses and squids which had been obtained in this unexpected way were turned over for investigation to M. Joubin, professor of the Faculty of Rennes. These specimens were completely unknown, with respect to both genus and species; and their appearance, while they were alive, must have been truly extraordinary. One of them had lost its head, but the scientific value of its body was extraordinary. It measured no less than six and one-half feet in length; it was horn-shaped and partially covered with scales; and it had a large, round fin. Another specimen's head was present, but it had lost its body; the tentacular crown was recognizable—that is, the head, with its eight arms, each of which was almost as large as that of a man, and was equipped with a hundred sucker disks with claws as sharp and powerful as those of the great land predators.

"My naturalists had already explored the stomachs of these specimens and had removed, along with over two hundred pounds of debris, the remnants of several giant octopuses, fairly well preserved, which also belonged to totally unknown species. As one may suspect, the profession of these men requires a great amount of dedication; for, in their work, they were required to stir about in a purple mass, in full fermentation, littered with eyes and

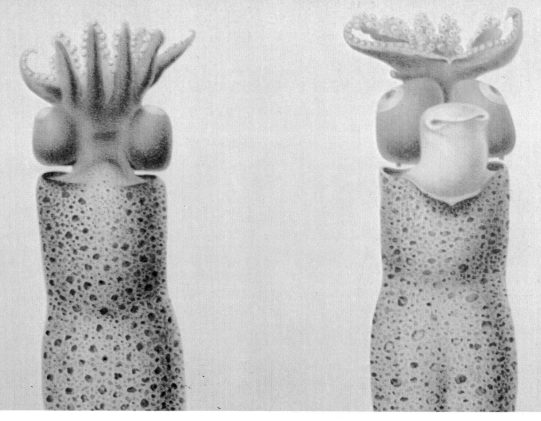

Taonius pavo Lesueur, watercolor by Jeanne Le Roux, reproduced in the work on Prince Albert's expeditions.

Right. Captain Cousteau and Albert Falco returning from a dive in the Persian Gulf, during a 1954 oil-exploration project.

beaks which had resisted the action of the gastric juices. The stench of this mass was most unpleasant. Toward the end, the naturalists' stomachs revolted in a faint echo of the event which, the day before, had given these treasures to science during the final spasms of the dying whale.

"When I returned to the bay where the whale had been killed, it had changed considerably. There were no more birds circling in the air, and no more fish jumping in the water. Both had been chased away by the spreading putrefaction. Only men remained in this infected environment, some for the sake of science, and some for the sake of profit."

A Confrontation in the Depths

"M. Richard pointed out to me certain round marks, accidental in origin and measuring an inch or so in diameter, on the lips of the whale. When we compared these to the sucker disks on the enormous arms of the octopus

found in the whale's stomach, it seemed to us quite clear that the marks had been made by these sucker disks. I could see, in my mind's eye, the colossal struggle in the depths between the great whale and its giant prey. The eight arms of the octopus were wrapped around the cetacean's head and attached to it by its sucker disks, while the rest of its body was already in the whale's mouth. Finally separated one from the other, the head and arms remain attached to the head of the whale, for the disks, even in death, retained their power of adherence.

"The evocation of such a confrontation reminds me of an incident which occurred during my expedition of 1887 aboard the *Hirondelle*. We were in mid-Atlantic, en route for the Azores, when, one day, we sighted great columns of water being thrown up on the horizon of the calm sea. We could see clearly that they were caused by the struggles of a huge creature, the head and body of which rose up occasionally like a tower above the surface, while its tail stirred up sizable waves in the water. Before very long, the water was calm again. But, in the area where we had seen the creature, it was covered with a white slick, visible from a distance of five miles, which may have been either a liquid or simply foam from the recent agitation of the water. Despite our best efforts, the direction of the wind did not allow the *Hirondelle*—a small sailing vessel—to reach the slick before it dispersed, even though it remained visible for several hours. When we finally reached the spot, we found the recently severed head of a giant squid. When the description of this head was later compared by Professor Joubin to several of the cephalopods furnished by the cachalot's stomach, it appeared that it belonged to the same group as the latter, and that it was, like them, an inhabitant of those depths of which we know practically nothing.

"It is not farfetched, now that I have mentioned these two incidents in the same context, to suppose that the disturbance in the sea, which I had witnessed from afar, was caused by the efforts of a cachalot, who had risen to the surface in order to shake from its head the arms of a giant octopus encountered in those depths."

Here is a list of the various species of cephalopods identified as the result of Prince Albert's discovery:

Cucioteuthis unguiculata: a huge crown of arms.

Ancistrocheirus lesueuri: the body of a large specimen, and a separate "plume," probably belonging to the same species.

Lepidoteuthis grimaldii: the bodies of two very large specimens.

Histioteuthis ruppeli: three large specimens, about three feet in length, intact and perfectly preserved.

Dubioteuthis physeteris: the body of a large specimen. In addition to these specimens, some fifty-four beaks were found, all belonging to animals of large size.

An Epic Struggle

The most famous account of a confrontation between a sperm whale and a giant squid is that given by Frank Bullen, in his *Cruise of the "Cachalot.*
The *Cachalot*, a whaler, was cruising in the Indian Ocean in the 1870s. Bullen was on watch one night; and he tells us that he "was so tired and sleepy that I knew not how to keep awake. I did not imagine that anything would happen to make me prize that night's experience for the rest of my life, or I should

*The latest edition of this classic work was published in New York in 1948.

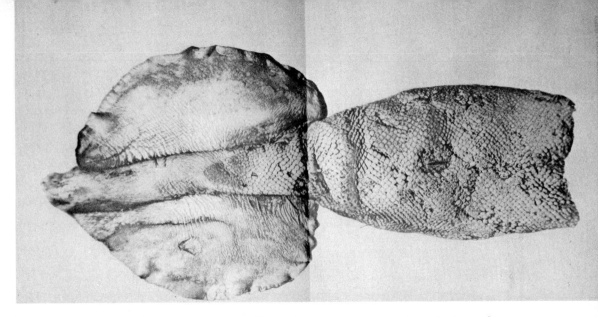

Rear part of the squid *Lepidoteuthis grimaldi* vomited by a sperm whale and salvaged during one of Prince Albert's expeditions. The body, except for the fins, is covered with scales.

have taken matters with a far better grace.

"At about 11 P.M., I was leaning over the lee rail, gazing steadily at the bright surface of the sea, where the intense radiance of the tropical moon made a broad path like a pavement of burnished silver. Eyes that saw not, mind only confusedly conscious of my surrounds, were mine; but suddenly I started to my feet with an exclamation, and stared with all my might at the strangest sight I ever saw. There was a violent commotion in the sea right where the moon's rays were concentrated, so great that, remembering our position, I was at first inclined to alarm all hands; for I had often heard of volcanic islands suddenly lifting their heads from the depths below, or disappearing in a moment, and, with Sumatra's chain of active volcanoes so near, I felt doubtful indeed of what was now happening.

"Getting the night-glasses out of the cabin scuttle, where they were always hung in readiness, I focused them on the troubled spot, perfectly satisfied by a short examination that neither volcano nor earthquake had anything to do with what was going on; yet so vast were the forces engaged that I might well have been excused for my first supposition. A very large sperm whale was locked in deadly conflict with a cuttlefish, or squid, almost as large as himself, whose interminable tentacles seemed to enlace the whole of his great body. The head of the whale especially seemed a perfect net-work of writhing arms—naturally, I suppose, for it appeared as if the whale had the tail part of the mollusc in his jaws, and, in a business-like, methodical way, was sawing through it.

"By the side of the black columnar head of the whale appeared the head of a great squid, as awful an object as one could well imagine even in a fevered dream. Judging as carefully as possible, I estimated it to be at least as large as one of our pipes, which contained three hundred and fifty gallons; but it may have been, and probably was, a good deal larger. The eyes were very remarkable from the size and blackness, which, contrasted with the vivid whiteness of the head, made their appearance all the more striking. They were, at least, a foot in diameter, and, seen under such conditions, looked decidedly eery and hobgoblin-like.

"All around the combatants were numerous sharks, like jackals round a lion, ready to share the feast, and apparently assisting in the destruction of the huge cephalopod. So the titanic struggle went on, in perfect silence as far as we were concerned, because, even had there been any noise, our distance from the scene of conflict would not have permitted us to hear it.

"Thinking that such a sight ought not to be missed by the captain, I overcame my dread of him sufficiently to call him, and tell him of what was taking place. He met my remarks with such a furious burst of anger at my daring to disturb him for such a cause that I fled precipitately on deck again, having the remainder of the vision to myself. . . The conflict ceased, the sea resumed its placid calm, and nothing remained to tell of the fight but a strong odor of fish, as of a bank of seaweed left by the tide in the blazing sun."

In the few accounts of such battles, it seems that the whale is usually the victor. Erling Sivertsen tells of one battle in which the squid's arms and tentacles surrounded the whale's head so tightly that even the mighty muscles of the latter were unable to open his jaw. But then the whale dived—and when it reappeared on the surface it "was chewing happily on the smashed squid."*

Aristotle Was Right

Man has long believed that the depths of the sea are inhabited by giant monsters with long arms, which are capable of drowning swimmers and even of dragging ships to the bottom.

Aristotle reports a squid five ells—fifteen to twenty feet—long. This is not difficult to believe, since our octopuses at Seattle reach that size.

Pliny tells the story of a giant octopus raiding the fishponds of Carthage. This monster's head was the size of a barrel, and its arms measured thirty feet in length—which is not impossible.

The accounts of mariners in the seventeenth, eighteenth, and nineteenth centuries are harder to believe. Many of them take their inspiration from the Norwegian myth of the Kraken, a creature whose arms were larger and

---

*Quoted by Frank W. Lane in *Kingdom of the Octopus*, p. 216.

longer than the largest masts of any sailing ship. According to these accounts, the Kraken was able to lay hold of a ship of a hundred cannon and drag it to the bottom.

Through the portholes of the *Nautilus*, Jules Verne's heroes see a "squid of colossal dimensions, twenty-five feet long," but with only eight arms, twisting "like the tresses of the Furies." Verne estimated the weight of this beast at between 40,000 and 50,000 pounds, which is quite a bit. It is more surprising that Verne's squid had only eight arms, since squids are decapods—that is, ten-armed cephalopods.

The *Nautilus* attacked by seven giant squids, one of which halts the engines by grasping the propellers "with its horned beak." Whereupon, Captain Nemo swears to "slaughter all of this vermin." At that point, an octopus captures, and asphyxiates, a sailor from the *Nautilus*, and Captain Nemo, in the struggle, is red with the octopus' blood. This is perhaps the most extraordinary thing about the story, since the blood of cephalopods, containing as it does a respiratory pigment of hemocyanin, which has a base of copper, is not red but green.

Verne does not try to hide that he was greatly influenced by Hugo's *Toilers of the Sea*. For him, as for Victor Hugo, octopuses and squids are ferocious monsters who must be "slaughtered."

The diving saucer is lowered into the water by *Calypso*'s hoist.

There is much testimony which justifies the belief that there exist cephalopods as large and as formidable as those conceived by the two writers. There is, however, no recent evidence of the aggressive tendencies of such animals; and we cannot, in all fairness, accuse them of having deliberately killed or wounded a human being within the past fifty years. Even the largest of the squids and octopuses seem to be rather lazy and timid creatures.

For centuries, our knowledge about these animals was based upon secondhand information, and the descriptions given of the monsters in question were very vague. Almost always, these stories are about a squid, of which hardly anything was known for certain.

One such story was recorded by Olaus Magnus, a Swede and a Roman Catholic archbishop, in the middle of the sixteenth century, who had heard it from mariners of his country. The "monstrous fish" he describes in his book* "will drown easily many great ships provided with many strong Mariners." And, the good prelate assures us, "their Forms are horrible, their Heads square, all set with prickles, and they have sharp and long horns round about, like a Tree rooted up by the Roots."

In the middle of the eighteenth century, Erik Pontoppidan—also a bishop, but a Norwegian and a Protestant—wrote down various stories which he had heard from seamen of his own country. His *Natural History of Norway*—an English edition of which was published in 1755—records an account of the stranding of a kraken: "In the year 1680, a Krake (perhaps a young a foolish one) came into the water that runs between the rocks and cliffs in the parish of Alstahoug, though the general custom of that creature is to keep always several leagues from land, and therefore of course they must die there. It happened that its extended long arms, or antennae, which this creature seems to use like the snail, in turning about, caught hold of some trees standing near the water, which might easily have been turned up by the roots; but beside this, as it was found afterwards, he entangled himself in some openings or clefts in the rock, and therein stuck so fast, and hung so unfortunately, that he could not work himself out, but perished and putrefied on the spot. The carcass, which was a long while decaying, and filled a great part of that narrow channel, made it almost impassable by its intolerable stench."

There are also more recent accounts of sightings of giant cephalopods. As in older reports, the animal observed is usually described as a "squid," but the descriptions given are vague, and it should be noted that it may be difficult, especially in the open water, to tell the difference between an octopus

---

*A compendious history of the Goths, Swedes and Vandals and other Northern nations. London, n.d. (English edition).

and a squid. The anatomical differences between the two, which readily discernible on dry land or in an aquarium, are not obvious to the untrained eye, especially when the animal is only glimpsed in the sea. These differences reflect very different ways of life. Octopuses, with few exceptions, live on the bottom and feed on crustaceans and bivalves. The squid, on the other hand, is an active swimmer and pursues fish, which it captures by means of its two tentacles armed with sucker disks.

An Unknown Giant

In at least one case, the existence of a giant octopod has been recognized by scientists. The account given by F. G. Wood, in the prestigious *Natural History* magazine, deserves to be repeated here. In researching the archives of the Laboratory of Marine Research in Florida, Wood discovered that, in 1897, the remains of an apparently enormous cephalopod had been found on a beach at St. Augustine. These remains indicated that the cephalopod was larger than any specimen ever observed. The cadaver, which weighed six tons, was examined by an expert, Professor Verrill, of Yale University, who was the discoverer of much of what is presently known about cephalopods. Professor Verrill estimated that the specimen, when alive, had had a stretch of approximately 25 feet, and that its arms had been about 75 feet long. Wood even found in the archives a photograph of the cadaver.

The same author learned that there was, in the Smithsonian Institute, a large barrel containing animal tissue, preserved in formaldehyde, which bore the label, *Octopus giganteus verrill*. This tissue, beyond a doubt, constituted the fragment of the "monster" found at St. Augustine.

Wood asked a friend of his, Joseph F. Gennaro, Jr., to analyze this tissue. Obviously, this was rather difficult to do. After sixty years, the tissue had a very strong odor; and its long bath in formaldehyde and alcohol, after a period on the Florida beach, made a cellular examination precarious. Nonetheless, in comparing histological specimens of the tissue to specimens of cetacean, octopus, and squid tissue, Gennaro was able to establish that the monster of St. Augustine was, in fact, an octopus; and a giant octopus, with arms from 75 to 90 feet long, which measured, at the base, eighteen inches in diameter. "It is difficult," wrote Gennaro, "to believe in the existence of a marine animal the total length of which is more than 180 feet." And yet, it seems that, for the first time, it was proved by Wood and Gennaro that such an animal did exist. Unfortunately, no such specimen has ever been taken alive. Those which have been found on the surface have all been dead, or dying, and were smaller than the St. Augustine specimen.

Between Florida and the Bahamas, in the Gulf Stream, fishermen reported having had their lines broken by an enormous animal which, when sighted, resembled a squid. Incidents of this kind were so numerous and well attested that an expedition was organized. Its purpose was to photograph the animal in question, and, for this, a flash camera was attached to a line in such a way as to be activated by traction. The animal was, in fact, hooked on the line, but broke it. When the camera was recovered, it was found that shots had been taken at 300 and 600 feet, but they showed only an undefinable stretch of brown flesh.

In 1956, *Calypso* was in the Atlantic, studying the Romanche ditch. On that occasion, we established a new record, as well as achieving a "first." At 24,800 feet, we succeeded in the first deep-water anchorage with nylon line. This was something that had hitherto seemed impossible and required special equipment and some very difficult maneuvering. Moreover, thanks to the Edgerton flash camera, we were able to take photographs of the bottom.

On the two nights that we spent anchored in mid-Atlantic, we were surrounded by large red squids which, no doubt, had been attracted by our lights. Once in the vicinity, however, they occupied themselves with hunting flying fish around *Calypso*'s hull. Their attack was so sudden and quick that the fish were unable to rise above the surface of the water in order to escape.

That was seventeen years ago; and, at the time, we had not yet learned that respect for animal life that has since become one of our principles. I allowed our divers to hunt the squids with spears. My son Philippe, who was fifteen, brought back the largest prize: a specimen five feet long.

An Enemy of the Squid

Michel Lerner has specialized in fishing for squids at night, and he succeeded in taking many large ones, especially the *Diosidicus gigas*, which is abundant in the Humboldt Current off the Peruvian coast. One specimen was ten feet long, and weighed over 300 pounds. The tentacles measured 35 feet, and the eyes were sixteen inches in diameter.

Unlike the giant octopuses of Seattle, these equally large squids are capable of very vigorous resistance; but we must remember that these were animals which were fighting for their lives after being wounded by harpoons.

Right. *Melanoteuthis lucens*, according to a watercolor by Mlle. Vesque. This specimen, which was caught in the Saragasso Sea, has two large luminous organs on its back, near its fins. Its body is about nine inches long.

We do not know what would happen if they were approached gently by divers with peaceful intentions. Man seems always to be surprised when an animal which he has attacked fights back; and then he describes it as a "ferocious" beast—as happened with the cachalot and the moray eel.

In any event, the squids in the Humboldt Current react as effectively as they can to the persecutions of which they are the victims. They squirt out their ink, and they shoot a water jet of surprising force out of their funnels. John Manning, of the University of Miami's Marine Laboratory, says that this discharge of water is equivalent to that of a fire hose.*

Michel Lerner's team, like Manning's, was particularly struck by the extraordinary voracity of the giant squids. They devour any individual squid that is wounded—as sharks do with wounded sharks.

We have already had occasion to mention the *Vampyroteuthis infernalis*—the "infernal vampire squid"—which deserves its name, and which is the strangest of the cephalopods. It was christened by Grace E. Pickford, an accomplished biologist. The *Vampyroteuthis* has enormous eyes, luminous organs, and the appearance of a distorted mask leering up from the deep, where it lives at depths between 1,000 and 10,000 feet.

The *Vampyroteuthis* is a living fossil, incorporating characteristics of both the octopods and the decapods. It has ten arms, of which the two thinner ones are actually sensitive filaments. The arms are connected by webbing. The animal has the consistency of a jellyfish and is black and purple. The female, which is larger than the male, reaches a length of fourteen inches.

One of the most curious characteristics of the *Vampyroteuthis* is that at the base of its fins, it has photophores equipped with lids, which can be opened and closed at will.

The deep-water squids discovered by Prince Albert of Monaco all showed unusual characteristics. The *Lepidoteuthis'* body is covered with scales, like a reptile's. The *Grimalditeuthis* is so diaphanous that one can see the various lobes of its brain and the nerves running from them. The *Bathothauma* has its eyes on stalks. The *Histioteuthis* is covered with luminous organs, and its sucker disks are armed with claws or with a jagged circle which serves as a trepan. (This is the species which leaves such terrible scars on cachalots.) The *Cirroteuthis* has a large fin, while the other species just named have fins so small that it is likely they are mostly sedentary.

This is also the case, apparently, with the largest of all the squids, the *Architeuthis princeps*, which lives in equatorial waters and in those of the Humboldt Current. It is supposed, nonetheless, to be ferocious; and it may be

*Cited by Frank W. Lane, *Kingdom of the Octopus*.

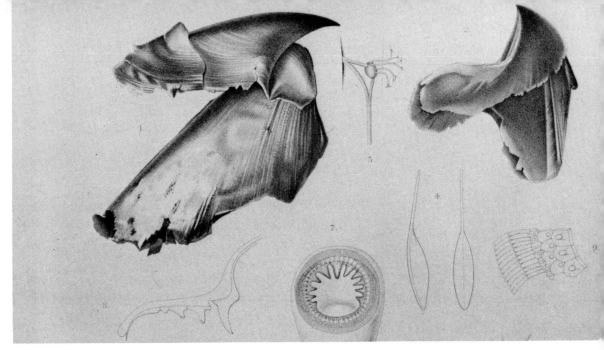

The beak of a squid, from Prince Albert's work on cephalopods.

that these vertical filaments, made of dead matter, floated in the water. Masses of these filaments, lumped together like a loosely woven ball a yard wide, the original Kraken. It is said that its beak is capable of cutting a man in two, or of severing a steel cable.

The only certain data, however, are the following: the mantle of the *Architeuthis* may measure fifteen feet; the arms, from 50 to 60 feet; and it may weigh over four tons.

As all specimens of *Architeuthis* live at depths of between 1,000 and 10,000 feet, it is impossible to know whether or not they are indeed "ferocious." It is likely that the ferocity of this species is simply another example of prejudice born of ignorance and nurtured by fables. We will only know the truth when the great depths of the sea are opened to human exploration, not only for short dives by minisub or bathyscaphe, but for visits and explorations of long duration. As yet, we know practically nothing about life in the deep.

Although I have had only one opportunity to encounter a giant cephalopod in deep water, I have sometimes seen signs of them and observed their traces. On one occasion, during a bathyscaphe descent, I saw before the porthole a group of clouds which seemed to be composed of a white substance. I immediately had the lights extinguished, and I noted that these clouds seemed to be phosphorescent. It was almost certainly luminous "ink" from a cephalopod.

These ink jets leave strange traces in deep water. In the course of minisub dives between 600 and 1,000 feet, and also in the examination of photographs taken with the Edgerton flash camera, it has been established

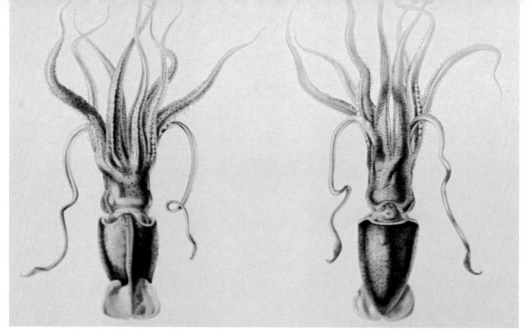

Meleagroteuthis hoylei Pfeffer. This squid has hard, saw-tooth points on its arm and down the middle of its body. It also has numerous photophores on the underside of its body. Watercolor by Mlle. Vesque.

have also been found. They resemble spiderwebs, and, from the minisub, it looked as though we had entered a dusty attic. This ball is made of fibrous elements which eventually dissolve in the water. They are actually the remains of ink clouds emitted by squids.

Calypso in the Indian Ocean, at the entry of the Persian Gulf.

ELEVEN

In Search of a Living Fossil

Personally, I knew the nautilus only by its shell until a day in 1961, when our friend Jean-Marie Bassot, and my old collaborator and diving associate, Henri Goiran (whom we call Riquet), sent us four of the animals. They were packed individually in plastic bags, which had been carefully arranged in a case and shipped by air. The interesting thing about the packing arrangement was that each of the nautiluses' plastic bags was different with respect to its contents. One was filled with sea water. Another contained a little water and a large volume of air. A third held water and pure oxygen. And the fourth had sea water, with a tranquilizer added.

Of the four nautiluses shipped halfway around the world in forty-eight hours (Goiran was stationed at Nouméa, in New Caledonia), two were dead on arrival, and one died almost immediately afterward. The survivor lived for two months in an aquarium at Monaco.

The latter was the nautilus that had traveled in the mixture of water and pure oxygen, without a tranquilizer. To survive for two months in an aquarium is quite exceptional for a nautilus; and this one was quite active in captivity, at least at first. It slept at the bottom of its tank, but it sometimes rose to the surface. It was quite easy to feed, and took eagerly the sardines that we gave it.

An Exercise in Versatility

For two months, I spent an hour a day observing the nautilus in its tank at Monaco. It was an extraordinary sight, and there were many things about this animal that fascinated me. It had a marvelous ability to modify its flotage. These modifications must have been very slight, but they were sufficient to enable the animal to rise and sink, and to stop anywhere that it wished between the surface and the bottom. It therefore had a very delicate and highly controlled static weight.

The nautilus moved horizontally by jet propulsion, which it achieved by the use of its muscular funnel. It could also modify the diameter of that funnel, making it larger or smaller, and turn it in different directions and thus change its course while swimming. The nautilus' funnel is therefore even more effective than that of the octopus.

A Spiral Vaulted with Mother-of-Pearl

The shell of an adult nautilus contains between twenty and thirty separate chambers. The shell itself is a spiral supported by mother-of-pearl vaults. The chambers are joined by a small canal, through which runs a filament or siphuncle. These chambers contain a liquid poor in dissolved salts with respect to sea water and to blood, and rich in nitrogen and argon. By means of an extremely complex mechanism of secretion and absorption, the nautilus uses these chambers as gas ballasts which enable it to rise and descend in the water. The arrangement is one of nature's most ingenious "inventions," though it works relatively slowly. If a nautilus, either through mechanical failure or as the result of human intervention, is brought to the surface by an excess of buoyancy, it takes a very long time for it to correct its weight sufficiently to sink. But, when it is suspended in the water, midway between the surface and the bottom, it requires only a very minor adjustment to be able to rise or to sink; and this takes very little time.

One must admire the nautilus for having perfected a very complex system of vertical displacement. It works well, and it is found only in the nautilus and, to a certain extent, in the cuttlefish.

The secret of this system lies in the siphuncle, about twelve inches long and one-sixteenth of an inch in diameter, which runs from the nautilus' body through all the chambers of its shell. It is, in fact, an elongation of the nautilus' mantle. This threadlike tube contains a large artery and a vein, and is covered by an epithelium the cells of which serve to absorb or secrete the liquid and the gas contained in the chambers. The liquid and the gas are alternately removed from and restored to the animal's blood. These cells therefore play the part of tiny pumps, and are reminiscent of the renal cells of mammals.

The nautilus, in order to rise or sink, modifies the equilibrium between the liquid and the gas within the chambers of its shell. It is not known for certain whether the nautilus also adjusts the interior pressure of these chambers to correspond to that of the exterior environment. It has been established, however, that the nautilus' shell is especially resistant to pressure. Experiments have demonstrated that, when the shell is sealed, it can resist pressures the equivalent of those found at depths of slightly over 1,000 feet.*

Some 600 million years ago, therefore, the nautilus adopted a method of displacement by ballast, which involves an extraordinary "cellular pump" mechanism. It is surprising that it did not adopt, instead, the muscular system which is universal among both invertebrates and vertebrates for displacement of any kind. Only the nautilus makes use of gas, liquid, and hydrostatic principles. The system worked, obviously; and therefore there was no need to change it.

The nautilus, which, until the present time, has been considered a rarity, is, in fact, a living fossil. It is the only living species of cephalopod with an exterior shell. It has survived into the twentieth century absolutely unchanged from what it was during the Primary era, in the Devonian period. In the Secondary era, the seas were invaded by Ammonites which, like the nautiluses, had an external shell; and both are found in the same geological layers.† The Ammonite has since disappeared, but the nautilus has survived unchanged, and without benefit of further evolution. It is one of the rare life forms that have not been modified since the Primary era.

---

*For much of this information, we are in the debt of Dr. Jean-Marie Bassot, and we are grateful to him for his kind collaboration, and for his contribution to science in the form of studies on the histological characteristics and function of the nautilus' siphuncle.

---

†The genus *Nautilus* of the Nautiloidae family appeared in the Triassic period, and its representatives have remained unchanged to this day. It is one of the most remarkable of nature's living fossils; it has been called, and is, "the Coelacanth of the invertebrates."

Above. Michel Deloire films nautiluses on coral plateau, near Amadeus lighthouse.

Left. On the bridge of the *Pilou-Pilou,* Captain Cousteau charts his course through the waters of New Caledonia in order to reach the coral beds where the nautiluses live.

Below. A nautilus hovers above the ocean floor.

The Pendulum

The nautilus uses water jets to move horizontally; but, in watching it, one has the impression that it is hanging from an invisible string which is attached to an invisible nail. It swings back and forth regularly and oscillates. It acts, in fact, like the pendulum of a clock. Yet, the nautilus moves at a fair speed. The rounding of the shell in the form of a bulb is hydrodynamically effective.

The eye of the nautilus is large and flat, and it is marked by a black line which is always vertical. The eye moves in a direction opposite to that of the shell, and thus compensates for the oscillation of the shell. It is as though the entire animal moved on an axis.

Almost as fantastic, and just as mysterious, is the nautilus' method of enlarging its shell by secreting a new and larger chamber, in which it then takes up its residence. It is possible to tell young specimens from older ones by the smaller number of chambers in their shells. The growth of the nautilus seems to take place with the construction of a larger chamber. That is understandable. But it is not known just how the animal moves from the old chamber to the new one, or how it builds the final wall, or how it is able to bring into the new chamber the siphuncle, which runs all the way back into the smallest chamber. Does the siphuncle stretch, or elongate? For the nautilus, therefore, growth is a series of moves. A new chamber, the last one the animal builds before its death, may presuppose the displacement of a body three or four inches long.

It should be noted that the enlargement of the nautilus' shell follows a mathematically rigorous logarithmic progression. The relationship of the volume of the old chamber (N) to the new chamber is $N + \frac{1}{2}$.

At the time that we were studying our nautilus in the aquarium at Monaco, we referred to it as a "living bathyscaphe." And, in fact, it rose and sank like a bathyscaphe; but it moved horizontally like our minisubs, and with the same directional hydrojet (rotary jet) system.

The nautilus' flat vertical form makes one think of the famous "turtle" of Bushnell; that is, a turtle placed on its side, at a 90° angle. This is a form that we discussed at the CEMA for a certain kind of minisub. We wondered whether it might not be worth while to build a minisub with a vertical form, rather than, as we had always thought, with a horizontal form.

Arms with Specialties

We were quite surprised at the number and diversity of the nautilus' arms, which have very different functions. There are several of these arms around the mouth, and these are called labial palps. They are themselves tipped by smaller arms and play an olefactory role.

On the nautilus' head, there are two groups of arms, each containing seventeen individual arms. One group is located on one side of the head; and the second, on the opposite side.

Two larger arms act as a hood, and fold back over the nautilus' back. They serve as a covering for the opening of the shell when the nautilus is in hiding and are rather like the leatherlike hood used by some shell animals for the same purpose.

Finally, there are a pair of small arms near the nautilus' eyes.

The male may be distinguished from the female by the wider opening at the end of its shell, and especially by a smaller number of arms. The male has around sixty, while the female may have as many as ninety. In the male, four arms merge to form a "spadix," which is the equivalent, in the nautilus, of the hectocotylus among other cephalopods.

The arms of the nautilus are able to grasp and adhere, like those of many other cephalopods; and yet, they have no sucker disks. They do have small ridges, however, which serve to adhere like tiny sucker disks, and allow the nautilus to exercise a firm grip.

The arms, moreover, are more or less retractable. They may be elongated, or shortened, by being pulled back into fleshy sheaths located at their base.

For five or six hundred million years, the nautilus, from inside its shell, has been in a position to observe the parade of animals which gradually populated the sea. All in all, there have been some 3,000 such species of nautilus. Today, there are only six remaining says Frank W. Lane. The seas of the world, millions of years ago, contained myriads of nautiloids, scattered everywhere. Their fossils have been found in the most unexpected places—such as present-day London. It has seen life come and go, species rise and fall. And, though fragile in appearance, the nautilus, through all of this, has continued to lead its strange life, to swing with its geological pendulum. It has, however, become relatively scarce. The nautilus is found today only in the waters of New Caledonia, the Fiji Islands, the Philippines, and parts of Indonesia. Along the coast of Malabar, the nautilus is sufficiently abundant to be prized as food. Some are also found at New Guinea, where Davydof led an expedition, as dramatic as it was unsuccessful, in order to observe the embryology of the nautilus—which was the dream of his life.

Few animals are as little known as the nautilus, and few are so complex in their being. Perhaps the mystery which envelops it, along with its intricate beauty, is the reason why the nautilus is one of the few cephalopods mentioned in modern poetry. Oliver Wendell Holmes could not resist the charm

230 OCTOPUS AND SQUID: THE SOFT INTELLIGENCE

of the "Chambered Nautilus," as he called it,

". . . the ship of pearl, which, poets feign, Sails the unshadowed main."

Holmes was more than sufficiently astute to realize that the "sailing" of the nautilus was nothing more than poetic fantasy. But one wonders whether he was aware that the mechanism which enables the nautilus to swim, and to rise and descend in the water, is no less marvelous than anything which the most ingenious poet could devise.

The beauty of the nautilus has had commercial as well as esthetic appeal for man. The shell of the pearly nautilus is highly prized by collectors, and highly priced by vendors. According to some observers, it was greatly valued by natives of the South Pacific islands as an item of exchange; and it is still used by some of them for the fashioning of ornaments of rare beauty.

The Living Fossil at Home

For years, I treasured the remembrance of the nautilus which I had observed and studied at Monaco. I was particularly interested in its means of locomotion by jet propulsion, because they were similar to those of the engines which I had designed and which had been built by the French Bureau of Marine Research—and are being built today by CEMA.

Therefore, in the second series of films that we made for television, I wished to devote, not an entire film, but at least some important sequences, to the nautilus.

I had decided to shoot a film in New Caledonia, where reef fauna is particularly abundant. The working title of this film, which reflected its original concept, was *The Living Desert of the Sea*. But, as we were shooting, we realized that the true subject of the film was diurnal and nocturnal life in tropical waters. It was the nautilus, in fact, which made us decide on this new subject. It is one of the many marine animals which remains deep in the water during the day, and rises to the surface at night.

The Pilou-Pilou

I therefore sent to Nouméa a team composed of my son Philippe, our cameraman, Michel Deloire, a marine photographer, François Dorado, and our divers, Prezelin and Sumian. They rented a handsome boat, the *Pilou-Pilou*, as captain of which I appointed Alain Bougaran. I joined this team as soon as I was able.

The weather was then very bad. The sea was often rough, and our work

Dominique Sumian and Jacques Delcoutère shine a light on a nautilus which they have just found.

The *Pilou-Pilou*—the boat used in searching for nautiluses.

was made correspondingly more difficult. The trade winds blew unceasingly. New Caledonia is bordered by two barrier reefs which form a lagoon in which the water is quite rough. We found nothing but dead and dying nautiluses, which had been carried into the lagoon by waves and ended up by washing ashore onto the beaches.

Given the continuously inclement weather, it was very risky to anchor the *Pilou-Pilou* off the reef. It was only there, however, that we could hope to find any nautiluses. They are never seen during the day, in any case, but it is likely that they are present all around the island, deep in the water.

As always, the expectations that one may have with respect to certain marine animals change, according to whether one listens to the experts or one goes to see for oneself *in situ*—in the ocean. We discovered that the nautilus, while not abundant, was less rare than was generally believed. They are not animals in imminent danger of disappearing. The fact is that they live perhaps between 300 and 1,000 feet below the surface, and they rise only at night to between 125 and 175 feet of the surface. Any nautilus that is encountered closer to the surface, or on the surface, is either wounded or diseased.

We have been able to establish that the species is not in danger. Unless the requirements of shell collectors lead to the wholesale massacre of nautiluses, this fossil of six hundred million years can look forward to a bright future. It belongs to an order which stretches back to the very beginning of animal life on earth, and it has survived to witness the rise to supremacy, and the final extinction, one after another, of mighty animal dynasties. There is no reason to believe that the nautilus will not be here, unchanged, when *homo sapiens* himself is but a faded page in the book of evolution.

The Amadeus Lighthouse

We found that the most favorable location for our dives was directly opposite Nouméa. The *Pilou-Pilou* went through Boulari pass and anchored off the reef where the Amadeus lighthouse is located.

There, the coral barrier drops, by means of an almost vertical cliff, to a plateau. This plateau slopes gently downward from a depth of 125 feet to about 175 feet. Then there is another cliff, also vertical, which goes down into deep water: 1,000 feet and over.

We chose this particular spot because the plateau was, for us, an ideal place for observation. The lighthouse was an excellent reference point and would, in case of really bad weather, make it less difficult for the *Pilou-Pilou* to get through the pass again, especially at night.

The undersea terrain here was beautiful; almost as beautiful as that of

Above left. Captain Cousteau and Philippe Cousteau examine the "owl eye," the device which we used during nighttime dives in order to be able to observe the nautiluses without disturbing them.

Above right. Jacques-Yves Cousteau laying hold of a nautilus.

the Red Sea. The first cliff was decorated with large patches of sea fans. The multicolored fishes of the reef swam among heads of coral. But we soon realized that, splendid as our surroundings might be, our job would be difficult. In order to find nautiluses during the day, we would have to go down into very deep water, and we were not even sure of being able to go down deep enough to find them. If we were going to study them, we would therefore have to dive at night, and somehow to solve all the new problems that this would involve.

One of the stages of our preparation for diving, given the exceptional nature of the nautilus and the little that is known about it, was to study whatever scientific data were available. There is, at Nouméa, a truly extraordinary tropical aquarium founded by Dr. Catala. He and Mrs. Catala are devoted to their work. They often exhibit nautiluses, which they catch by means of special traps placed outside of the reef in about 175 feet of water. Dr. and Mrs. Catala were very helpful throughout our quest for the nautilus.

Since we wanted to have with us an eminent specialist on nautiluses, we had asked our friend in Miami, Dr. Voss, a distinguished authority on cephalopods, to recommend someone to us. As it turned out, there were experts on the liver of the nautilus, and on its kidney, but there seemed to be absolutely no one who knew much about the nautilus in general. We had Jean-Marie Bassot, of course, who was part of *Calypso*'s team. But, for television, what we needed was not merely an expert, but an English-speaking expert. We were fortunate enough, eventually, to secure the services of a well-known British authority, Miss Anna Bidder, of Cambridge University.

The Traps

Like Dr. and Mrs. Catala, and like Goirand and Bassot before us, we began by setting traps for nautiluses. These traps were on loan to us—or rather, to Michel Deloire—from ORSTOM, the Office of Overseas Scientific and Technical Research, at Nouméa. They were boxes, with one end—the entry—covered by a grill. We lay these traps at night, in water 125 to 175 feet deep, and baited them with fish or crustaceans. The next morning, in each of the five traps, there were at least two nautiluses. In the days following, however, our catch diminished. Three days later, we took only four; and, six days later, we caught nothing. It is likely that the number of nautiluses in any one spot is rather small, and I suspect that we had "fished out" that particular site. This probably affects only a limited area, for it is clear that nautiluses are found on all the coasts of New Caledonia.

In order to preserve the natural environment of the nautilus for our captives, we had established a preserve in 140 feet of water. This was simply a large cage, in which the animals had adequate space to move about. And, of course, we provided them with ample food.

We then spent two days experimenting. First, we turned loose one or two specimens to see what they would do. I witnessed once more that strange pendular movement, and I saw the round eyes, the delicate arms, and the perfect shell that I remembered so well from Monaco. Unfortunately, few people have seen the nautilus in the open sea, and few can appreciate its true beauty.

The nautiluses, once free, sank to the coral floor. As soon as they had "touched" bottom, they rose slightly and, following the slope of the plateau, headed for the vertical cliff which marked the beginning of deep water. Until they reached the cliff, they remained a constant four inches above the bottom, navigating so as to avoid obstacles. Then, at the cliff, they sank into the deep, eager to escape the light. It was not possible to ascertain the depth to which they ultimately sank, or at what depth they normally lived during the daylight hours. According to some theories, the makeup of the nautilus does not allow it to go deeper than 1,000 or 1,200 feet. At that depth, in fact, unless the internal pressure of the gas within the shell is regulated in accordance with the external pressure of the water, the shell reaches the limit of its resistance to pressure and implodes. If that theory is correct, it is likely that the nautilus stops when it has reached a depth of between 300 and 900 feet.

We do not know what the life of the nautilus is at these great depths. Do they, despite their protective shells, hide in holes, like octopuses? There is no real evidence for this. It seems likely that they live along the cliff, in holes or crevices.

Two nautiluses probably mating. This is the first photograph of its kind ever taken.

The funnel of the nautilus. One can make out the artery, the veins, and the epithelium. (With the kind permission of Jean-Marie Bassot.)

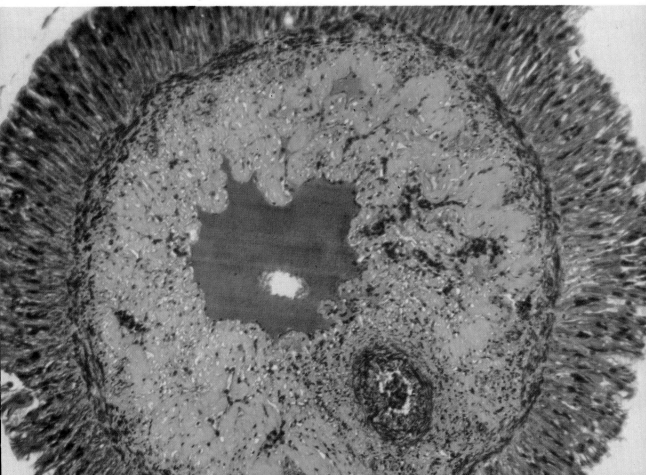

During the daylight hours, I took another of our captive nautiluses and placed it near an underwater cavern. As soon as I released it, the nautilus immediately went into the darkness of the cave. Whatever else it may be, it seems obvious that the nautilus loves the dark.

Although there is no evidence of the kind that gives certainty in such matters, we have been able to make certain assumptions concerning the mode of life of the nautilus. This is a step forward, for, until now, nothing was known in this area. We have been able at least slightly to advance knowledge of these mysterious animals.

The Dives

The moment had now come for us to begin our nocturnal dives. For this, we needed fair weather outside the reef, which happens very seldom. In the three months that we spent off Nouméa shooting our film, we had few such days.

Every dive at night was an enormous strain for a boat the size of the *Pilou-Pilou*, and a strain on everyone; for, since we were so few, everyone aboard had to be pressed into service. For every sequence, we needed a cameraman, two divers, two "grips" to handle the lights, a photographer, a diver, and myself. To add to our difficulties, we were shooting in deep water, which meant that our return to the surface would have to be interrupted by long decompression stages.

Obviously, we could make only one such dive in a twenty-four-hour period. And there was never any assurance—or even much chance—that the weather would be good during the following period. In fact, we often dived when our mooring was not at all secure; which was disagreeable for everyone concerned, and especially for the divers and Captain Bougaran.

Here is an extract from Captain Bougaran's ship's log, concerning one of our nocturnal dives:

December 22, 1971. The trade wind from the southeast which, this morning, was only a breeze, gained in strength as the sun rose in the sky.

"At 4 P.M., we hoist anchor and leave our excellent anchorage at Point Nokoué, off the island of Ven. We proceed at 16 knots toward the white tower of the Amadeus lighthouse. We will have to find anchorage at least one hour before sunset, since securing the boat is a complicated and lengthy operation. At this latitude, we cannot count on the light lingering for any time at all, for dusk is extremely brief.

"We soon pass the lighthouse to our starboard and head for Boulari pass. A long swell, breaking on the reef, outlines the pass very clearly. It is a

From left to right: Ann Bidder, Captain Cousteau, and Philippe Cousteau observing a nautilus in an aquarium aboard the *Pilou-Pilou*.

southwest swell—long, very long. It breaks on the reef with a great crash, throwing white foam onto the green surface of the lagoon, and then disappears.

"We have gotten through Boulari pass and we are cutting our speed to 9 knots as we approach the reef to the wall of which our nautilus traps are attached. However, we cannot see the buoy which marks the location of the traps. I am nonetheless certain that this is the correct position. We quickly put down a diver's buoy to serve as a reference point for the *Pilou-Pilou*'s anchorage. To our anchor line, which is forward, there is attached a 250-pound fluked anchor and four lengths of chain. There is also a lighter anchor, with 600 feet of nylon line.

"The *Pilou-Pilou* is turned into the wind about 750 feet to the west of the reef. The long swell from the southwest makes us roll slightly, and the sea, stirred up by the trade wind, is pushed out of the lagoon between the reefs. The water is rough, but this does not bother the *Pilou-Pilou*, whose stem is now quite securely anchored.

"Two divers quickly suit up and go down to find the traps. Fifteen minutes later, they are back. The traps are in place, squarely under our stern. The divers report that there are seven nautiluses in them. But there has been a tragedy in the preserve. Two of the nautilus shells were found to be empty. Their occupants were apparently eaten by the other nautiluses when they became hungry.

"Our divers made another discovery. The buoy that we were looking for is at the bottom, among the traps, covered with the toothmarks of sharks. It was a large red buoy, of the kind that can be submerged in deep water

This nautilus in the open water is holding between its tentacles a piece of fish given to it by a diver.

without damage. The sharks no doubt saw it moving in the swell and thought that it was edible.

"We are ready now for the dive. The camera teams are ready on the rear deck. But then we discover that the diver's buoy we set out is no longer near the *Pilou-Pilou*. The significance of this is that the boat's anchorage is now threatened by a change in the direction of the current—as we can see by observing the water moving alongside our hull. We are now much too far from the traps, and it is impossible to dive.

"We try to pick out the buoy with a projector, but we cannot locate it. We estimate that we are about 250 feet from the buoy, and south of it. It should therefore be to our port.

"The launch goes out to look for it. It tows a diver carrying a powerful underwater light. The buoy is located in ten minutes; and we tie a large buoy to the buoy rope of the anchor to make certain that it will be visible at all times. But we are pursued by bad luck. The diver has not left enough slack in the buoy rope, and the buoy, under the impact of the crests of the swell, gets stripped of its ballast. We lose our reference point to the current. Then, there is another shift in the current—which takes us back to our initial position.

"We know very well that, anchored at two points, we are at the mercy of such changes in the speed and the direction of the wind and the current. And so, here we are, back over our traps, thanks to the unpredictable current. Over the starboard aft we drop 100 feet of nylon line, to which we have tied 125 pounds of chain. This will be the ladder for the camera teams to get down into the water. It will also be their means of getting back aboard. Also, the divers will be able to hold onto it during their decompression stages on the way to the surface. At night, one cannot be too careful.

"The dive went very well. The current remained constant in both strength and direction all night. We made about fifteen dives in this same spot without incident, during the day as well as at night. But weather, however, forces us to abandon it for an entire week. Then, we have two days of almost dead calm; but, other than that, we spend much of the time rolling. Nonetheless, the teams beneath the surface were never in danger."

Miracle Equipment

We would never have been able to undertake, or to finish, our observations at night if it had not been for a piece of American equipment that we used for the first time at New Caledonia. It is called an "owl eye," and its purpose is to increase night vision. It works so well that, even when the water is black, we can see a nautilus. The owl eye works in any faint light, even one so faint as to be virtually nonexistent. When the moon is full, the device enables us to see beneath the surface as though it were broad daylight. It "intensifies images," as the sales literature says, and is composed of a photographic lens with a wide opening which transmits an image onto an electronic screen, a little plate, which is an extremely sensitive iconoscope.

The owl eye has a series of stages with varying degrees of power. Each photon of the initial image thus creates a flow of electrons which gradually increases in power, until, finally, they appear on a television screen in a reinforced form. This device is battery operated. It is therefore autonomous, and ideal for our purposes. There are no wires, which is very convenient for diving. It is expensive, of course, but it gives a very well-defined image—much better than that given by television. It is equal in quality to a black and white photograph.

We thought that it would be sufficient to multiply the actual light 20,000 or 25,000 times, but the owl eye can multiply it up to 80,000 or 100,000 times. Which is to say that one ends up with an image 100,000 times brighter than that which one sees with the unaided eye. At times, a multiplication of 20,000 times was not quite adequate for our purposes.

When we lighted a small diver's lamp—which is rather weak—under the surface and shone it onto a subject, it gave sufficient light for the owl eye. If we put a floodlight on the subject, however, the owl eye would shut itself off—as it did whenever the light was too strong. This was a built-in safety device, intended to protect the owl eye's electronic system.

The owl eye is used in the United States by customs officials to patrol the Mexican border at night. It must be an effective weapon against smugglers—as it is intended to be. It was adapted for underwater use by the Center of Higher Marine Studies of Marseilles, which designed and manufactured a watertight case for it.

A Mating

We arranged our dives in such a way that they would be staggered throughout the night. We dived at 10:00 P.M., midnight, and 2:00 A.M. We hoped in this way to learn whether the nautiluses were more plentiful at one time than at another; but there seemed to be no significant difference from one hour to the next. We found nautiluses at every depth, from the surface down to 325 feet. They were attracted by the bait in our traps, and this nocturnal migration upward is apparently motivated by a search for food.

Michel Deloire, during one of our dives, held a nautilus by the base of its shell with one hand, and with the other held out a small fish. The nautilus, which had not even pulled in its arms, immediately took the fish. Deloire picked up the nautilus again a few minutes later and noted that the fish had already been torn to pieces. This seems to indicate that, unlike the octopuses, nautiluses ordinarily use their beaks to lacerate their prey. A nautilus six inches long has a beak as large as that of an octopus weighing seven pounds.

The owl eye turned out to be extremely useful for observing animals at night without disturbing or frightening them. With it, we were able to watch two nautiluses face to face, bound together by their intertwined arms. Around them in the water was a whitish secretion: a cloud in the sea. We did not disturb them. It is very probable that they were mating; and Ann Bidder confirmed this opinion when we described the scene to her. The mating of the nautilus had never before been observed, not even in aquariums.

I would like to explain the impression made by the sight of a nautilus moving gently in the dark sea. Its behavior seems strange, exotic, not because of its unusual means of locomotion, but because of the relative slowness of its movements. We are accustomed to seeing rapid motions and quick reactions. But the nautilus is not built for such things. In the course of its horizontal movements, for example, its muscular funnel contracts, and shoots out a jet of water, only once per second.

The means of locomotion at the disposal of the nautilus are certainly not ineffective. It happened once that we accidentally allowed one to escape, and

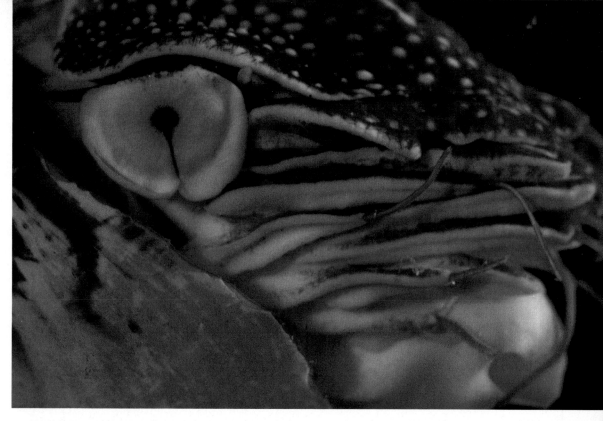

The head of the nautilus.

it disappeared immediately, as though it had simply vanished. We found it in a hole in the coral, in which it had cleverly hidden itself. It seems, nonetheless, that the life of the nautilus takes place in slow motion, as in a dream. It is as though one had returned to a time when life was still precarious, less sure of itself. One could be in a Paleozoic or Mesozoic sea, in which ten thousand

Frontal view of the nautilus. Under the tentacles, the round hole in the funnel orifice, which is used to eject the water jet by means of which the nautilus moves.

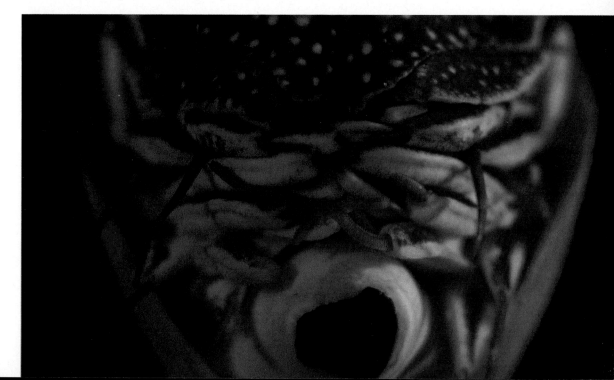

transient species of ammonites, along with the nautilus, were rising and sinking.

The slowness of the nautilus does not mean that its nervous system is primitive. Quite the contrary. While it is not so well developed as that of the octopus or the squid, it is compact, very complex—and quite extensive for a mollusk.

The nautilus' knowledge of the world around it is very different from our own. The arms that it stretches out to explore the sea are not, like those of the octopus, tactile organs. The nautilus' sense of touch seems barely to play even a secondary role in its life. Its "palps" are, above all, chemical and olfactory detectors. The nautilus lives by odors. And this is what guides it to our traps, for it smells the bait.

The eye of the nautilus is not as good as that of the squid or octopus. It is constructed in such a way that the anterior chamber is in direct contact with the sea water. Since it has no lens, the image it gives is not well defined. Compared to the eye of the other cephalopods, which is strangely similar to that of vertebrates, that of the nautilus is not highly developed. It is, nonetheless, quite sensitive to the intensity of light; and it is probably the eye of the nautilus which furnishes the animal with information on the depth of water. This opinion seems corroborated by the fact that a nautilus will react to the shadow of a diver passing over it.

Even though the nautilus does not share the ability of other cephalopods to change color according to its emotions, it is no stranger to aggression and self-defense, or even to panic, which causes it to cling, with all the strength in its grooved arms, to the enemy which has seized it—a diver, for example.

Night in the Sea

Night in the sea is sometimes eerie, and a bit frightening. We were often brushed by small sharks, but they never bothered us and there were no incidents. We had heard talk at Nouméa of very large sharks which were supposed to live beyond the reef, but we never saw them. Our lamps apparently did not attract them.

It is a marvelous feeling to discover nautiluses, one by one, with the owl eye, and to see them appear in the green light of the owl eye's screen. Sometimes a diver would shine a weak beam of light on the shell of a nautilus, and then return it to darkness. In this brief illumination, the pink and red hues of the shell stood out with extraordinary brilliance. Its pendular equilibrium was more exotic than ever. The fixed eye sparkled, and the brightly colored hood moved like the visor of a glistening helmet. The nautilus can withdraw completely into its shell, and then the hood comes forward and seals the shell. The animal is then completely sheltered.

It is difficult to imagine what enemies the nautilus could have. Even sharks cannot have much appetite for a hard shell. I think that the chief dangers to the nautilus must come, not from other animals, but from nature—storms and currents. If they rise too near the surface, they are carried away by waves, washed into the lagoon, or thrown against the coral. They are poorly equipped to struggle against the sea; and, after three months spent in observing them at New Caledonia, we are aware of the dangers to which the nautilus is exposed in the rough waters around the reefs.

We can only admire these marine animals who, 600 million years ago, found unusual, and still mysterious, solutions to the problems of life.

TWELVE

The Reconciliation

Our purpose in recounting our experiences with octopuses has been to help put an end to misunderstandings between them and man. There is no doubt that the poets, and especially Victor Hugo, have been largely responsible for these misconceptions. But Jules Verne has also contributed his share.

Long before these writers, however, there were already many tales about the octopus; myths spread by mariners whose words were accepted as fact. Throughout the nineteenth century, it was believed that there were monsters in the sea, capable of dragging ships to the bottom. Obviously, one cannot say that that legend is entirely without foundation in fact. It is true that there are giant squids, weighing several tons, in the deep. But that they rise to the surface to attack ships remains to be proved.

Man claims to be the judge of the universe, and he brings his moral sense to bear on everything in creation. This is at once his greatness and his weakness. He describes animals as "good" or "bad," as "gentle" or "ferocious,"

Left. A diver lying in wait for octopuses among the sea fans of the Mediterranean.

not according to the animals' own acts, but according to the fear that the animals inspire in man.

The animals of the sea have not been spared this simplistic division of the world into good and bad. And yet, for most of his existence, man has barely known anything about these creatures. He has approached them only to kill them, to tear them from their environment with his fishhooks, his nets, his spears, and harpoons. He has known only dead or dying animals; fish and mammals taken from the water which supported their weight, moistened their gills, and conditioned their lives. Then he rendered his verdict, and there was no appeal from it. He ruled that the cachalot, for example, was ferocious because it did not always die after the first stroke of the harpoon, and because it defended itself as best it could until its last breath.

As for the octopus, it has been pulled from the water, killed with a bite between the eyes, reduced to a gelatinous mass, thrown onto the sand of a beach or the concrete of a pier; and then it has been judged to be slimy and repugnant, without beauty or intelligence.

A Tradition of Discrimination

There was once a people who were the exception to the rule. The Aegean artists,* three thousand years before Christ, painted the arms of the octopus and the cuttlefish around their ceramics and around the anchors of their ships. But that lesson was soon forgotten. The Greeks, it is true, still honored the cephalopods enough to strike a few coins with their image. But the Romans, a "practical" people, lost the secret of the octopus, as they did so many others, and the octopus was consigned to the black night of the sea.

The Middle Ages populated the oceans with monsters. An entire bestiary of fantastic beings was said to inhabit the waters, hideous and bloodthirsty creatures—who belonged less to nature than to the interior life of man himself. There were giant octopuses, dragons, sea serpents, cachalots and whales, all creatures out of a painting of Hieronymus Bosch. And these, too, rose, not out of the sea, but out of the troubled depths of the human soul.

And this is why the large animals of the sea have remained the object of man's fear and disgust.

It has taken centuries to begin to dissipate the hideous images, representing man's own vices and sins, that were associated with the octopus and the whale, among others. The Kraken, terror of the Norwegians, lived until the end of the nineteenth century; and the sea serpent is not yet wholly dead.

*See Appendix II.

Debbie, with Captain Cousteau's encouragement, works up the courage to pet an octopus.

Life has so many forms, and the oceans are so deep! If even now we do not know the number and the appearance of the giant squids, we know at least a little about how a squid—even a giant squid—behaves in the presence of man. It was necessary to wait until the twentieth century, until the invention of scuba equipment and the development of diving techniques, to learn the truth about this unknown, misunderstood, and grossly slandered animal. It was necessary to wait until we could go down to its habitat, and swim in the same water, to discover that it was, in fact, beautiful. It was not without reason that the squid once evoked the admiration of the artists of Crete, who used its supple grace to lend beauty to their greatest works.

Discrimination against animals, like all discrimination, is rooted in contempt—that is, hatred—for what is unknown and for what is different.

A Victory of Evolution

It is true, of course, that cephalopods belong to a sector of creation other than our own. The solutions that they have found to the vital problems experienced by all beings on this planet—movement, hunting, food, reproduction—are different from ours as well as from those of other animals. Their

Above. A Cretan wine cup decorated with an octopus. (Louvre Museum. Photo: Chuzeville.)

Right. Fixed animals on a rocky wall of the Morgiou cove. A spirograph is in the center.

Left. A stylized octopus-design cup from Rhodes. (Louvre Museum. Photo: Chuzeville.)

arms and sucker disks are radically different from claws and paws, and different also from hands. But their efficiency is at least as great as that of the latter. They have beaks like birds; venom like snakes; chromatophores like certain fishes; and eyes like mammals. And yet, they are invertebrates.

They represent one of the most astounding victories of evolution in a given line, and they are gifted with an intelligence all their own. Cast in the anatomical mold of mollusks, they have far surpassed the gastropods and lamellibranches with their limited mobility and even more limited brains. They have attained a freedom in the sea, and achieved a double means of movement: swimming, and, above all, jet propulsion. And, so far as their intelligence goes, we have only begun to suspect its breadth.

At the risk of seeming to venture into science fiction, we might say that, if there exists a group of invertebrates which may one day rise to unexpected heights, the cephalopods are that group. For their story is far from over.

The gifts and talents of the cephalopods deserve better than our contempt; and our reaction would have been different in the past if we had been able to observe the octopus in its own environment, where it had been evolving, in the full sense of the term, for hundreds of millions of years. Even observation in an aquarium does not offset the calumnies of which the octopus has been the victim. What is required is contact in the open sea and the same benevolent attention that we give to animals on land. But then, man has never known more than three elements: air, land, and fire. Water, the sea, has remained a mystery to us until the middle of the twentieth century. Just as the octopus is ignorant of fire, so we are ignorant of water. The ocean was closed to us, and it has only just been opened.

Man's penetration of the sea offers us not only the possibility of discovering mineral wealth, but also innumerable new animals to study, understand, and appreciate. The most striking example of this has been that of the cephalopods.

If there is to be a reconciliation between man and the octopus, the responsibility for it lies with the diver. This book represents an attempt to fulfill that responsibility. Whether we are talking about the lazy giants of Seattle, or the lively little octopuses of Riou and Alicaster bay, we hope it is clear that communication is possible between us and them. If we have not understood one another until now, the fault lies with man, who habitually underestimates other species as a prelude to slaughtering them.

The Curse of the Speechless

We have been able to determine that the curiosity of the octopus is virtually without limits. Their sole misfortune is that, with all their extraordinary physiological equipment, they lack the means to hear and to speak. Sound, beyond a doubt, is the best intermediary between man and animal. The only senses common to us and the octopus, however, are touch and sight. And these must suffice to establish a mutual understanding.

The time is not far off when the trained octopus will become the companion of the diver. Octopissimus, the large octopus at Alicaster, did not hesitate to emerge from its shelter to greet Falco. Joanne Duffy has her favorite octopus at Seattle, which she pets and which strokes her in return. Our friend Jerry Brown is in the midst of an exciting experiment with a giant octopus which lives in a sunken ship in the Straits of Juan de Fuca.

Before long, friendship between cephalopods and divers will become one of the pleasures of life in the sea. Even then, of course, we will have to remember Joanne's warning, and not disturb the cephalopods or interfere with their lives. Man goes very quickly from ignorance to exigence. He feels that all animals must be his subjects, regardless of the effects of subjection upon the animals themselves.

The New Generation

It is not our generation, but the generation of the future, which will finally discard all the legends and live on terms of familiarity with the octopus. I have already had an experience which has been very enlightening in that respect, at the Lindero Canyon School in Aguora, California, where I sat in on a natural history class. The teacher had brought to class a group of small octopuses in a tank. We asked the pupils—boys and girls about nine or ten years old—if they would put their hands into the tank and touch the octopuses. They were slightly uneasy, but, with only a minimum of hesitation, put their hands into the tank and touched them.

I then had an interesting conversation with one of the pupils, a girl named Debbie. "You see that little octopus," I said. "I bet that it is able to show affection. Why don't you shake hands with it?"

Debbie hesitated a bit, and giggled a little, but bent over the tank and put her arm into the water. The octopus, naturally, put out an exploratory arm of its own.

"It's funny," Debbie said. "It has so many hands to shake. It's kind of sticky."

"Are you afraid?"

Following page. An octopus and diver swimming around in a thicket of sea fans.

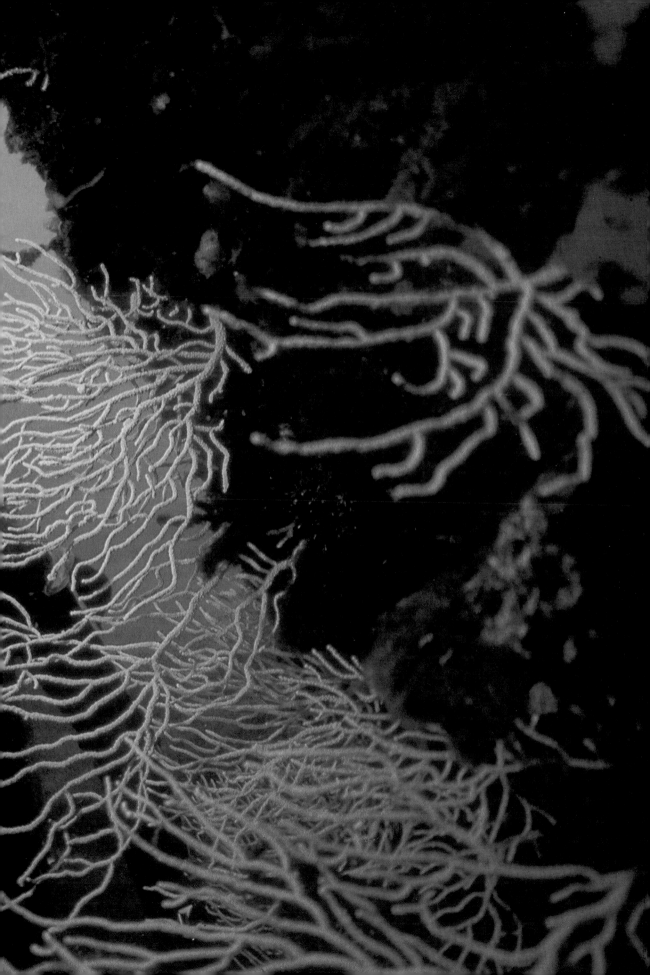

"Oh, no. Of course not."

Debbie and her friends did not believe the legends about the monsters which sink ships and drown divers. I showed them the old engravings that had been used to illustrate *Toilers of the Sea* and *Twenty Thousand Leagues Under the Sea*, and I asked them what they thought about them. Everyone answered that they were fairy tales and that people shouldn't be fooled by them.

And yet, one must admit that not all cephalopods are like the friendly little Pacific octopuses that the children saw and touched. In the depths of the sea, there are giants which, if we can judge from the fragments found on the surface, are sixty feet long and weigh four tons. As imaginary as the old stories may be, they do have a basis in reality. Until the present time, the giant cephalopods seen on the surface have all been either dead or dying. Until the contrary is proved, we may assume that these "monsters" do not leave deep water, even though they may vary the depth at which they live according to whether it is day or night.

I myself, from the minisub, saw an unidentified cephalopod which, while not a giant, was of considerable size. How is it, then, that we see these animals so rarely? For the past fifteen years, dives in bathyscaphes and other similar enclosures have been undertaken in increasing numbers by the Russians, the French, and the Americans. These dives have been made by experienced observers. One would think that they would have seen specimens of giant squids if there were such animals.

The explanation may be that these exploratory devices are slow, and

Creto-Mycenaean vase with stylized octopus design. (Louvre Museum. Photo: Chuzeville.)

Left. The Gournia octopus vase, a realist representation. (Photo: Giraudon.)

A porphyr anchor decorated with octopuses, from the Palace of Knossos in Crete. (Photo: Giraudon)

An octopus, in the open water, moves by jet propulsion.

they move within a very restricted area. This is especially true of the bathyscaphe. Also, as our own experiences would indicate, the squids are rather timid animals. The appearance of a submersible apparatus in their environment may well frighten them and awaken a desire to escape—which they have all the time in the world to do before the bathyscaphe reaches its proper depth. This was precisely the reaction of the only large cephalopod that I have ever met underwater.

Despite all the progress that we have made in discovering the secrets of the sea, those of the deep still elude us. We cannot be content with brief visits at 10,000 feet and even beyond. We must learn to remain at those depths and to explore large areas, just as we have learned to do on the Continental Shelf. It is, after all, only a question of technology.

The future may well reveal to us those great and mysterious beings, inoffensive and luminous, at the bottom of the sea. That alone is an expectation that makes life worth living.

Photo Credits

Acknowledgments

We owe a particular debt of gratitude to Mme. Katharina Mangold-Wirz, of the Arago Laboratory at Banyuls-sur-Mer, who kindly consented to read the manuscript of this work and to make many helpful suggestions.

Our special thanks also go to M. Jean-Marie Bassot, Director of Research of CNRS, for sharing with us the results of his study of the Nautilus.

Dr. N. Chalanozitis, also of CNRS, made available to us his findings on the value of the giant nerve fiber for cellular neurophysiological research, for which we are most grateful.

Finally, we express our thanks to Miss Anig Toulmont, ecological assistant at the Oceanographic Institute, for her valuable help in solving some of the difficulties presented by this manuscript.

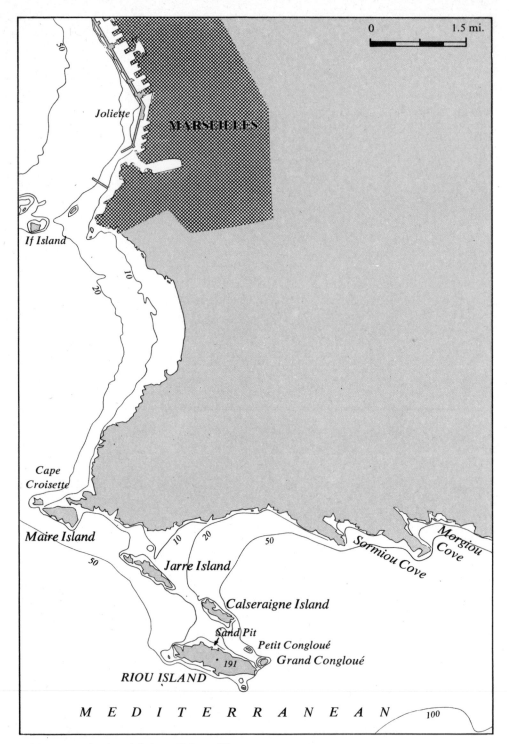

1. The coast in the vicinity of Marseilles.

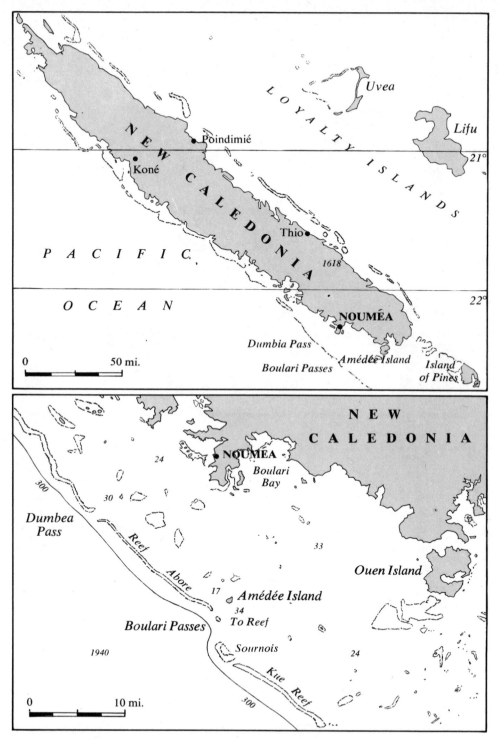

2. New Caledonia.
   Offshore at Nouméa: the inlets and the Amadeus lighthouse.

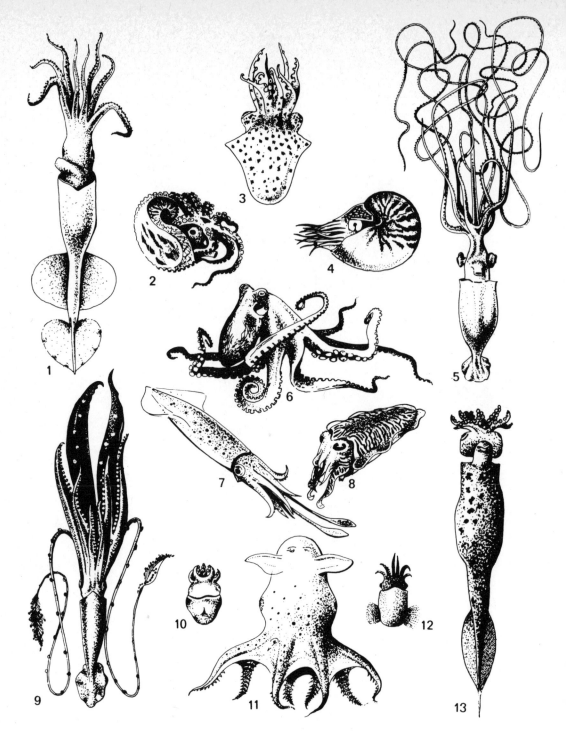

Some Cephalopods

1. *Grimalditeuthis richardi*
2. *Argonauta argo*
3. *Tremoctopus hyalinus*
4. *Nautilus pompilius*
5. *Chiroteuthis portieri*

6. *Octopus vulgaris*
7. *Loligo pealeii*
8. *Sepia officinalis*
9. *Chiroteuthis lacertosa*
10. *Tremoctopus hirondellei*

11. *Vampyroteuthis infernalis*
12. *Sepiola*
13. *Taonius pavo*

Appendix I

THE CEPHALOPODS

Cephalopods are invertebrates and constitute a class of the phylum Mollusca. The term *cephalopod* dates only from 1823, and is derived from two Greek words: *kephalè*, head; and *pous* (the root is *pod-*), meaning foot. They are marine animals only and are found in all the oceans. Their bodies have two basic parts: first, the cephalopodium (the head and arms), and, second, the palliovisceral complex, which is the mantle serving as a cover for the viscera.

A Simplified Classification*

The class *Cephalopoda* may be subdivided into three subclasses:

> Nautiloidea
> Ammonoidea
> Coleoidea

---

*The Cephalopoda were formerly divided into two subclasses—Tetrabranchiata and Dibranchiata—depending upon the number of gills present in the animals. This classification was abandoned because it was impossible to tell the number of gills from fossils. Even today, systematists do not agree on all details of the family tree of the Cephalopoda, and the reader will find differences between the above classification and that found in other works.

A. *Nautiloidea*

The Nautiloidea were very abundant in the Secondary era. Today, however, only one family remains, the Nautilidae, and, within that family, there is a single genus: *Nautilus*.

B. *Ammonoidea*

The Ammonoidea are known only as fossils by their shells divided into a series of chambers. The funnel is not axial but is found near the outer edge of the shell. The *Ammonites* flourished from the early Devonian to the end of the Cretaceous periods.

C. *Coleoidea*

There are four orders of Coleoidea:

Sepioidea
Teuthoidea
Octopoda
Vampyromorpha

I. The Sepioidea include five families:
Spirulidae
Sepiidae
Sepiardariidae
Sepiolidae
Idiosepiidae

II. The Teuthoidea are divided into two suborders:

Myopsidae (having the cornea almost closed) represented by two families:
Pickfordiateuthidae
Loliginidae

Oegopsidae (whose cornea is not closed) composed of twenty- three families:

Gonatidae	Lycoteuthidae	Chiroteuthidae
Enoploteuthidae	Histioteuthidae	Mastigoteuthidae
Octopoteuthidae	Bathyteuthidae	Joubiniteuthidae
Onychoteuthidae	Psychroteuthidae	Cycloteutidae
Lepidoteuthidae	Neoteuthidae	Promachoteuthidae
Ctenophterygidae	Architeuthidae	Grimalditeuthidae
Batoteuthidae	Ommastrephidae	Cranchiidae
Brachioteuthidae	Thysanoteuthidae	

III. Octopoda have small, compact bodies and arms that are longer than their body. There is no shell, and the sucker disks are sessile—that is, attached directly to the base. The integument, or skin, has no iridocytes. Octopoda are generally sedentary animals.

There are two suborders:

Cirromorpha, which includes three families:

  Cirroteuthidae

  Stauroteuthidae

  Opisthoteuthidae

Incirrata, which has nine families:

  Bolitaenidae Amphitretidae

  Idioctopodidae

  Vitreledonellidae

  Octopodidae, with three subfamilies:

    Octopodinae

    Eledoninae

  Bathypolipodinae

  Tremoctopodidae

  Ocythoidae

  Argonautidae

  Alloposidae

IV. Vampyromorpha, represented by a single family:

Vampyroteuthidae, which has one species: *Vampyroteuthis infernalis.*

THE NAUTILUS

The *Nautilus* is the only surviving genus of the subclass Nautiloidae. It is found nowhere but in the tropical waters of the Indo-Pacific, at depths of between 175 feet and 900 feet, and especially near the coasts.

The *Nautilus* has a spiral shell divided into successive concave chambers. Through these chambers runs a siphuncle—a threadlike tube about twelve inches long, which is an extension of the animal's mantle. The last and largest chamber contains the body of the animal, while the other, smaller chambers contain the liquid and gas by means of which the animal controls its buoyancy. These constitute its means of vertical movement.

The arms of the *Nautilus* number between forty and fifty. They have no sucker disks, but, at their tips, there are ridges or folds in the skin, which enable them to adhere to any object.

When the *Nautilus* is entirely within its shell, the opening is closed by means of a leathery membrane, or hood, which blocks it completely.

It has no ink sac, no chromatophores, but it has four gills. Its eyes, which have no lens, are more simple in structure than those of other cephalopods, and they do not perceive colors.

The Nautiloidea appeared on earth during the early Cambrian period, some 600 million years ago. For 400 million years they flourished, then began to decline 200 million years ago, during the Triassic period.

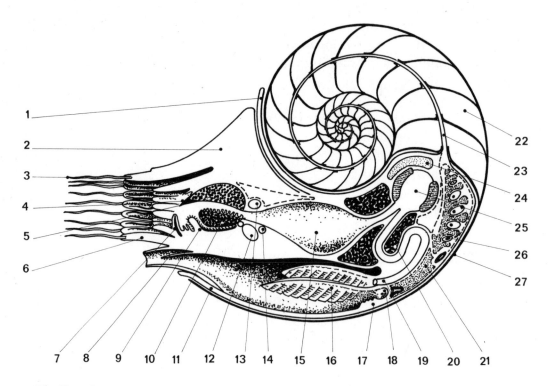

The Nautilus

1. Dorsal part of the mantle
2. Hood
3. Arms
4. Upper jaw
5. Mandibular (lower jaw) muscle
6. Arms
7. Lower jaw
8. Obturating (sealing) muscle of the funnel
9. Radula
10. Tongue
11. Ventral region of the mantle
12. Cartilage
13. Cerebral ganglia
14. Pleurovisceral ganglion
15. Crop
16. Gills
17. Gland (secretion of shell)
18. Renal pore
19. Anus
20. Digestive gland
21. Pericardial region
22. Chambers
23. Funnel
24. Genital area
25. Stomach
26. Ovaries
27. Shell

THE SPIRULA

The *Spirula* belongs to the family Spirulidae, order Sepioidea, subclass Coleoidea.

It is, with the *Nautilus,* the only cephalopod in existence today which has a shell divided into between 25 and 37 walled chambers connected by a siphuncle. These chambers, like those of the *Nautilus,* are filled with gas and liquid. The work of Anton Bruun in 1945, and that of E. J. Denton in 1962, on the hydrostatic mechanism of the *Spirula,* shed a great deal of light on this animal which, until then, was very little known. It is widely distributed in the oceans, but rarely caught alive.

The *Spirula* is one of the smallest of the *cephalopods.* When it is disturbed, it retracts its arms, tentacles, and head under its mantle. The latter is very tough, and its edges can be sealed.

The "normal' position of the *Spirula* is vertical, with the arms, eyes, and head pointed toward the bottom.

The *Spirula* has two small fins located at the top of its shell,   which   are used in moving. Between these fins is a luminous organ, pointing   toward the surface which can be "shuttered" by means of a mobile diaphragm.

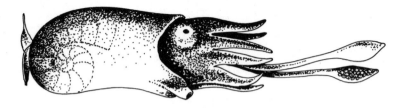

The Spirula

THE CUTTLEFISH

The cuttlefish belongs to the family Sepiidae, order Sepioidea, subclass Coleoidea. It lives in coastal waters among vegetation and on sandy bottoms, where it finds the shrimp which are its usual diet. There are approximately eighty species of cuttlefish, most of which are found in the tropical and subtropical waters of the Indo-Pacific. There are only a few Atlantic species. They are abundant in the western Pacific and in the Indian Ocean. There are none, however, in American waters.

The body of the cuttlefish is oval in shape. At the edge of the mantle there is a ribbonlike fin running the length of the body. Around the head there are eight arms and two tentacles which are used to capture prey. Ordinarily, the two tentacles are retracted into two cavities under the eyes.

The body of the cuttlefish is strengthened by an internal shell, the

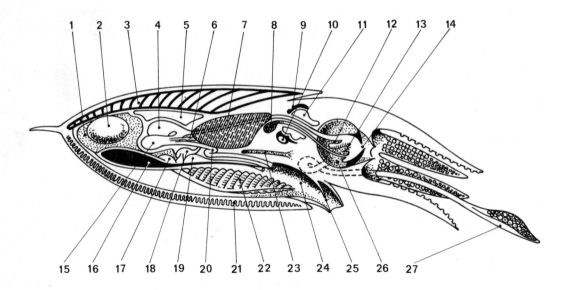

The Cuttlefish

1. Body cavity
2. Gonad
3. Shell
4. Stomach
5. Dorsal part of kidney
6. Pancreas
7. Liver
8. Salivary gland posterior
9. Skull
10. Statocyst
11. Brain
12. Salivary gland anterior
13. Radula
14. Beak
15. Caecum
16. Ink sac
17. Branchial heart
18. Systemic heart
19. Kidney
20. Gut
21. Muscular mantle
22. Gill
23. Cephalic vein
24. Funnel
25. Funnel valve
26. Buccal mass
27. Tentacle

"cuttlefish bone," which contains chambers filled with gas and which serves as the cuttlefish's hydrostatic equipment in swimming and floating.

The best-known species is the common cuttlefish, *Sepia officinalis.*

Sepia officinalis was observed and commented upon by Aristotle some twenty-three hundred years ago. It is found in the coastal waters of the Mediterranean, and all authorities agree that it is a strictly coastal species which rarely is found in water deeper than 450 feet.

Only a part of the cuttlefish population reaches the age of three or even four years. Its ordinary life span appears to be between two and two and one-half years. However, according to J. Kristensen, writing in 1959, cuttlefish live for at least three years, since the females of three distinct generations take part in the migrations to Dutch coastal waters.

The length of the cuttlefish's mantle is rarely more than sixteen to twenty inches. The smallest of the cuttlefish is the *Hemisepius typicus,* which measures about 2-3/4 inches; and the largest is the *Sepia latimanus,* which reaches a length of five and one-half feet.

The mating season is usually in spring and summer.

THE SEPIOLA

Sepiola belongs to the family Sepiolidae, order Sepioidea, subclass Coleiodea. They reach a length of slightly less than two inches and have a rudimentary shell or chitinous "pen."

THE LOLIGO

Loligo, or common squid, is of the family Loliginidae, suborder Myopsidae, order Teuthoidea, subclass Coleoidea. Its body is cigar-shaped and ends in a point.

The *Loligo paeleii* or common squid, has a pair of triangular lateran fins and an internal chitinized shell. It is found in the Atlantic, the North Sea, the Mediterranean, and the Red Sea. Most specimens of this species, in the Atlantic as well as in the Mediterranean, probably reach the age of two or two and one-half years.

The film we shot off the California coast had *Loligo opalescens* as its subject. Both the male and the female of this species reach a length of about eight inches, but the male's arms are longer than those of the female.

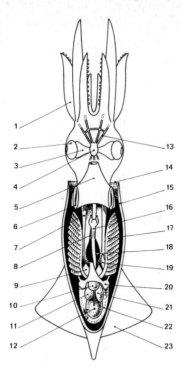

1. Tentacles	13. Arm nerves
2. Eyes	14. Neck
3. Optic ganglion	15. Mantle
4. Brain	16. Gut
5. Funnel	17. Gill
6. Funnel cartilage	18. Ink sac
7. Funnel retractor	19. Genital opening
8. Cephalic vein	20. Branchial heart
9. Kidney	21. Caecum
10. Systemic heart	22. Body cavity
11. Stomach	23. Fin
12. Gonad	

The Squid (Loligo)

HISTIOTEUTHIS

Family Histioteuthidae, suborder Oegopsidae, order Teuthoidae, sub-class Coleoidea. *Histioteuthis* lives in deep water and has luminous organs. Its arms are joined by means of a highly developed interbrachial membrane. *Histioteuthis bonellii* is found in the Atlantic, the Indian Ocean, and the Mediterranean.

ARCHITEUTHIS

Family Architeuthidae, suborder Oegopsidae, order Teuthoidea, sub-class Coleoidea. *Architeuthis* is a giant squid living in open sea at depths of between 1,000 and 4,000 feet. It is the largest of the cephalopods, and the largest of known invertebrates. It is the favorite food of the sperm whale.

A specimen of *Architeuthis* was found in 1878, near Newfoundland. Its body was almost twenty feet long, and its two tentacles measured thirty-five feet in length. Some pieces of flesh found floating on the surface or washed up on beaches, however, are evidence that specimens reach even greater sizes. It is not known whether or not the *Architeuthis* exists in large numbers.

DOSIDICUS

The *Dosidicus* belongs to the family Ommastrephidae, suborder Oegopsidae, order Teuthoidea, subclass Coleoidea. It is found off the western coast of South America, in the Humboldt Current, in the Pacific, and near the Australian coasts.

In 1930, in Talcahuano Bay, the bodies of thousands of these squids were washed up on the beaches and into the ports. Those found in California are about four and one-half feet long and weigh about 28 pounds. In the waters off Chile, they are larger—sometimes as much as ten feet long.

Very little is known about the eggs and embryology of these squids. It is thought that their eggs are deposited at a depth of approximately 3,000 feet. Very few have been found on the surface.

The maximum life span seems to be about three years.

CHIROTEUTHIS

Chiroteuthis belongs to the family Chiroteuthidae, suborder Oegopsidae, order Teuthoidea, subclass Coleoidea. It is a deep-water animal. Two of its arms are disproportionately long and non-retractable, while two others are broad and flat.

The *Chiroteuthis lacertosa* reaches a length of about two and one-half feet.

GRIMALDITEUTHIS

Suborder Teuthoidea, subclass Coleoidea. The mantle is not attached to the underside of the *Grimalditeuthis,* but is fused to the funnel. The funnel is very large and reaches the level of the eyes. The mantle has large, round fins. The body ends in a point, which has additional heart-shaped fins.

TAONIUS PAVO

The *Taonius pavo* belongs to the family Cranchiidae, suborder Teuthoidea, subclass Coleoidea. The members of this family are characterized by the
peculiarities of their larvae, which are so different from the form of adult
specimens that they have often been mistaken for entirely distinct species.

Taonius pavo has a gelatinous, colored body. The mantle ends in filaments. An adult specimen has no tentacles. The ocular bulges have two
photophores.

This species is found widely in all the oceans.

CIRROTEUTHIS

The *Cirroteuthis* belongs to the family Cirroteuthidae, subclass Coleoidea, suborder Cirromorpha. It is a deep-water animal, and an octopod with
very thin, flat fins. Its arms contain between fifty and sixty sucker disks. It has
a small funnel.

A specimen caught by the Prince of Monaco off the Azores, in 13,000
feet of water, was two and one-half inches long (60 millimeters).

OPISTHOTEUTHIS

Family Opisthoteuthidae, suborder Cirromorpha, subclass Coleoidea.
The palliovisceral complex, or body, is quite flat, and the funnel is turned
toward the rear. The arms are connected by a large interbrachial membrane.
The eyes are large; the body cavity, small; and there is no radula.

The *Opisthoteuthis,* of which there are about seven species is found in the
Atlantic and in the Indo-Pacific area.

OCTOPUS

The octopus belongs to the subfamily Octopodinae, family Octopodidae,
suborder Incirrata, order Octopoda, subclass Coleoidea.

The common octopus is the *Octopus vulgaris.* It has eight arms, each with
two rows of sucker disks. The third arm of the male has a groove which runs
the length of the arm, and this is used to convey the octopus' spermatophores
into the body cavity of the female. This arm is known as the hectocotylus.

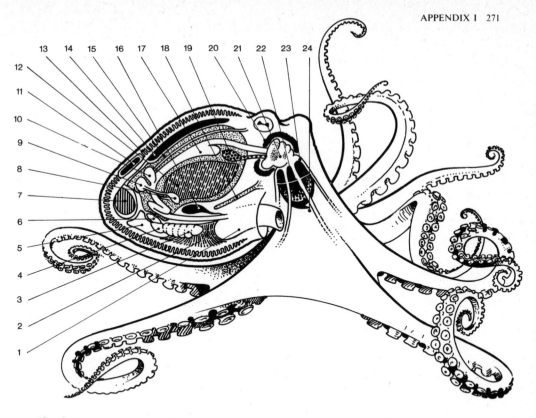

The Octopus

1. Funnel
2. Muscular septum of ventral mantle cavity
3. Gill
4. Branchial heart
5. Kidney
6. Systemic heart
7. Gonad
8. Pancreas
9. Caecum
10. Stomach
11. Shell rudiment
12. Liver
13. Mantle musculature
14. Dorsal mantle cavity
15. Intestinal blood space
16. Ink sac
17. Crop
18. Cephalic vein
19. Poison gland
20. Skull
21. Brain
22. Buccal mass
23. Arm nerves
24. Beak

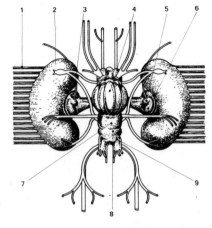

1. Optic nerves
2. Optic lobe
3. Optic gland
4. Vertical lobe
5. Olfactory lobe
6. Pedunculate lobe
7. Superior frontal lobe
8. Inferior frontal lobe
9. Buccal lobe

The Brain of the Octopus (dorsal view)

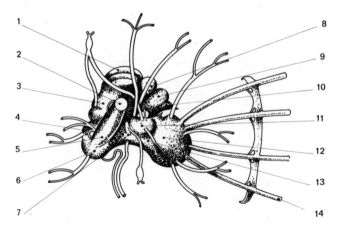

The Brain of the Octopus (side view)

1. Vertical lobe
2. Optic stalk
3. Posterior basal lobe
4. Posterior chromatophore lobe
5. Magnocollular lobe
6. Pallioviseral lobe
7. Nerves to the statocyst
8. Superior frontal lobe
9. Inferior frontal lobe
10. Buccal lobe
11. Anterior chromatophore lobe
12. Brachial lobe
13. Pedal lobe
14. Nerves to arms

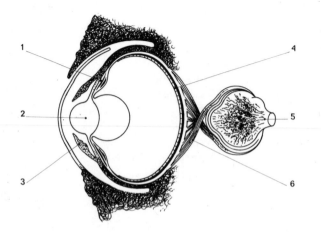

1. Ciliary muscle
2. Lens
3. Iris
4. Retina
5. Optic lobe
6. Optic nerves

The Eye of the Octopus

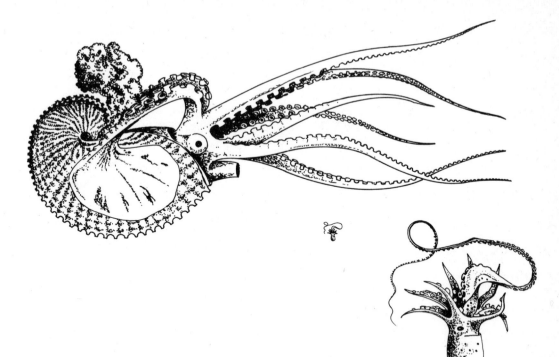

A Female Argonaut with a Cluster of Eggs

Bottom left: A male Argonaut, greatly enlarged

Above: The size of the male Argonaut compared to that of the female

The globular body of the octopus is slightly indented where it is joined to the head. The arms are located around the beak, which resembles that of a parrot. The ink sac contains the ink, which the animal emits from its funnel to throw an adversary off the track.

The eyes of the octopus, like those of the Coleoidea generally, are comparable in development to those of vertebrates. The nervous system is also highly developed.

Some octopuses have only a vestigial shell, as a thin plate. Some have no shell remnant at all.

It lives in coastal waters, in caves, or beneath rocks.

The *Octopus vulgaris* is found along the coast, close to shore. It is rarely found in water deeper than 450 feet, even though some specimens have been found off the Irish coast at 1,200 feet.

ELEDONE

Family Octopodidae, suborder Incirrata, order Octopoda, subclass Coleoidea.

The arms of the *Eledone* have a single row of sucker disks (unlike those of the *Octopus vulgaris,* which have two rows).

The *Eledone* lives in coastal waters in the Mediterranean and North Atlantic. It is smaller than the *Octopus vulgaris,* but lives in deeper water.

One species of this genus is called *Eledone moschata* because of its odor of musk. In the Catalan gulf, it is found exclusively in water between 45 and 300 feet deep. Off the Algerian coast, however, it is found as deep as 600 to 900 feet.

Eledone cirrosa, which ordinarily is found in coastal waters from 60 to 90 feet in depth, at the Faeroe Islands, lives in water up to 200 feet deep. In the Mediterranean, the *Eledone cirrosa* lives in deeper water than the *Eledone moschata.*

TREMOCTOPUS HYALINUS

Tremoctopus hyalinus belongs to the family *Tremoctopodidae,* suborder Incirrata, order Octopoda, subclass Coleoidea. Its body is translucent and only the head and the arms are opaque.

The anus is located on a tube which may be extended or retracted into a papilla which bears black stripes.

The female has luminous organs on the interbrachial membrane. The hectocotylus of the male is detachable, like that of the Argonaut and the *Ocythoë.*

OCYTHOË

Ocythoidea, suborder Incirrata, order Octopoda, subclass Coleoidea. The female *Ocythoe* weighs from two to five pounds, and the male, who is smaller, lives in the branchial cavity of a deep-water ascidian called *salpe.* He emerges only during the mating season. The hectocotylus, like that of the Argonaut, is detachable, and moves through the water until it reaches the mantle of the female, to which it attaches itself by its suction disks.

ARGONAUT

Family Argonautidae, suborder Incirrata, order Octopoda, subclass Coleoidea.

The Argonaut is found in warm waters, near the surface. It is also found in the Mediterranean. The female reaches a much larger size than the male; she is sometimes twenty times the size of the latter.

The hectocotylus of the male is curled in a sack, where it grows. It detaches itself from the male's body and carries the spermatophores to the female.

The female swims using six of her arms. With the other two, she secretes a "nacelle," which she uses as a receptacle for her eggs.

The species are:

Argonauta nodosa Solander, about eight inches long, found in Australian waters;

Argonauta argo Linné lives in the Mediterranean and in the waters of South Africa;

Argonauta Hinus Solander, found in the Pacific;

Argonauta tuberculosa Lamarck, found in the southwest Pacific.

VAMPYROTEUTHIS INFERNALIS

The "infernal vampire squid" belongs to the family Vampyroteuthidae, order Vampyromorpha, subclass Coleoidea. Grace E. Pickford, the biologist, established that the dozen species described as Vampyroteuthidae, and considered as a family of the suborder Cirromorpha, were, in fact, a single species. This species is so different from the Octopoda and the Teuthoidae, however, that it constitutes a new order, the Vampyromorpha, of which the *Vampyroteuthis infernalis* is the single species.

Pickford gave this species its name because of its enormous eyes and luminous organs, which resemble those of a hideous mask. In her opinion, *Vampyroteuthis infernalis* is the sole species surviving of an order which has been otherwise extinct for millions of years. It is called a "living fossil."

The *Vampyroteuthis infernalis* has ten arms, of which two—which seem to play a sensory role—are more slender than the others and are able to be folded into two pockets located at the base of the mantle.

The *Vampyroteuthis infernalis* is neither a squid nor an octopus. It has the consistency of a jellyfish and is dark violet in color. The female is larger than the male and may reach a length of about fourteen inches. The male has no hectocotylus, but ejaculates its spermatophores, probably through its funnel.

The species is found in subtropical and tropical waters, and it seems to live at a depth of between 1,800 and 10,000 feet.

The *Vampyroteuthis infernalis* was formerly known as *Melanoteuthis lucens,* among other names.

APPENDIX II

The Octopus and Man

The octopus, the squid, and the cuttlefish have not always been considered "monsters." The ancient civilizations of the Mediterranean were on better terms with the cephalopods than our own contemporaries have been, and, early in recorded history, the people whose existence was linked to the sea were able to appreciate the beauty of the octopus. Far from thinking of it as repulsive, or as an enemy to man, they depicted it with obvious sympathy.

Between the second and third millenium before Christ, the artists of the Creto-Mycenaean civilization often used *Octopus vulgaris* as a subject. The lifelike quality of these images, their grace, and the decorative role which these artists assigned to the octopus, indicate that they had observed it in the water, that they were aware of its special beauty, and, above all, that they were very familiar with it. The octopus was not, for them, the gelatinous mass of cold flesh that one sees washed up on a beach, or for sale in a marketplace.

It is not impossible that, in Minoan civilization, a special place was reserved for the octopus, just as one was reserved for the dolphin. The octopus was not regarded as man's enemy, but probably as a useful friend. The fact that it was sculpted on the two sides of a stone anchor, found in the Palace of Knossus,* is an indication that the octopus was believed to exercise a protective influence. (The figures appearing on anchors in antiquity were always those of objects or beings considered favorable to man, or which, by their nature, might be expected to bring good luck—the sea fan, dies, etc.)

There are many such representations also on Creto-Mycenaean and Greek ceramics The octopus vase of Gournia and the Palaikastro pitcher (1600-1550 B.C.) are examples of naturalism in Cretan art. The animal, depicted with extraordinary fidelity, seems captured in mid-movement; and its arms, depicted in the midst of algae, convey not only intense realism, but also a highly developed decorative sense on the part of the artist.† It is interesting to note how carefully, and how capably, these artists stylized the octopus, enlarging the eyes, detaching the oval body, disposing the arms in such a way as to achieve a unique and maximum decorative effect.

It is known that there was a close relationship between the Creto-Mycenaean civilization and that of Egypt. The Egyptians, however, do not appear to have been inspired by the octopus to the same degree as the Minoans. All that is known is that, two thousand years before Christ, the Egyptians were fishing octopuses by the same method employed today by the fishermen of Provence; that is, by submerging jars and waiting for the animals to move into them.

The Greeks and the Romans

Classical Greece discovered the octopus as part of its Aegean heritage. We find it appearing not only on vessels, from the sixth and fifth centuries before Christ, but on coins of Dikaia in Macedonia (520-510 B.C.), Syracuse (470-460 B.C.), Messina, Populonia, Alontinon, etc.

The role of the octopus as protector seems demonstrated by the fact that its image appears on a shield held by a warrior and on a vase dating from the fifth century before Christ. (The vase is presently in the Louvre Museum.)

---

*This stone is presently at the Museum of Heraklion. It is triangular in shape and was long believed to be a weight. Other discoveries, however, especially in the Palace of Mallia, have led to the conclusion that it is in fact an anchor. (See Honor Frost, *Under the Mediterranean*.)

†"The genius of the Cretans for perceiving life by means of its essential traits, their sense of movement and color, the combination of grace and preciosity which their work illustrates, all demonstrate that they were in permanent contact with nature itself. It was through nature that they succeeded in expressing all the qualities of their race which distingusished them so vividly from contemporary civilizations." Guy Rachet, *Civilisation de la Grèce préhistorique,* p. 178.

The octopus was also an item of food, and an inexpensive one, for Greeks of the classical period. They had their own method of obtaining octopuses, which was different from that of the Egyptians. Aristotle noted that the octopus adhered so firmly to rocks that it was impossible to detach it, even with a knife. But, he said, if leaves of *Inula viscosa* (a plant) were held near the animal, it would release its hold. This same method is used in present-day Greece—where it has been discovered that tobacco has the same effect as Aristotle's *Inula viscosa*.

The Romans, who were very partial to fish, were also aware of cephalopods to the extent that we find them often depicted, in exact detail, in mosaics. A beautiful specimen, preserved in the Naples Museum, shows an octopus in the center, and a squid to one side. Another mosaic, devoted to fishing and fishermen, shows an octopus and a cuttlefish.

The Kraken

To a large extent, the Middle Ages are responsible for the tales of the gigantic monsters of the deep. The legend of the Kraken, for example, originated with reports by Norwegian fishermen that they had found an animated mass, floating in the sea, a mile and a half long. From its body, they said, there were shining "horns" scattered about upright like masts. These were the arms of the Kraken, which were so powerful that, if they seized a ship's lines, the vessel must inevitably end up at the bottom of the sea.

For centuries, mariners handed down, from generation to generation, stories of terrifying sea serpents and of giant octopuses which specialized in sinking ships. This school of thought was reinforced in the nineteenth century by Victor Hugo, (*Toilers of the Sea*), and by Jules Verne, (*Twenty Thousand Leagues Under the Sea*), whose stories increased man's dread of octopuses and squids. From this perspective, cephalopods, with their many arms, their soft flesh, their unusual eyes, could only be "ferocious monsters."

Strangely enough, in the midst of all this artificial drama, Mediterranean fishermen continued to fish for octopuses. In these relatively clear waters, a man could make out the true dimensions of the "monster" and could easily catch it. Thus, octopus fishing continued without interruption from the days of ancient Greece until our own time. One of the steps in the pursuit of the octopus used today goes back at least two thousand years: the fishermen

The Colossal Octopus — Engraving by Denys de Montfort (Bibliothèque Nationale)

spread oil on the surface of the sea to make the water calm in that spot. This makes it easier to see beneath the surface to the bottom, where the octopus is hiding.

Today

At present, octopuses, cuttlefish, and squids are still fished. The Greeks and the Turks are so fond of these delicacies that they import them dried. The Italians and the Spaniards are very fond of squids, while the North Africans prefer cuttlefish.

Although the traditional method of catching octopus is by submerged jars, other means have now been added. One such method is to lower a lead bar, covered with barbs, into an octopus' house. Octopuses are also hunted with spears, and caught in nets baited with crab. According to Duhamel du Monceau, "the cuttlefish was caught in previous ages by using a line weighted by lead. The weight was smeared with grease and had two rows of hooks. The line was towed through the water. A wooden prism, painted red and with mirrors glued to its side, serves the same purpose."*

Even today, around Port Vendres, octopuses rising to the surface at night are caught by means of a spindle-shaped lure (called a *turlutte*) made of lead and covered with hooks. A variation of the *turlutte* is a cuttlefish bone also covered with hooks.

A more original method is that called "cherchez la femme." Fishermen know that cuttlefish move in groups, with a female leading and the males following. They therefore capture a female alive and tow her behind their boat. The males in the vicinity are thus attracted and, sooner or later, one of them embraces the female. The fishermen then haul both of them aboard, remove the male, and begin towing the female again.

Along the North African coast, especially at Gabes and at the Kerkenna islands, where octopuses are abundant during the winter, fishermen submerge palm branches covered with algae. The octopuses attach themselves to these branches and are brought aboard.

The octopus is a naturally curious animal and, as we have seen for ourselves, is attracted to anything that moves. Many methods of octopus fishing are based upon that characteristic. One such is the use of the *arpetta,* a long piece of bamboo ending in a hook with several points. A piece of red cloth is attached to the hook, and the fisherman lowers the pole to the entrance of an octopus hole and then moves it about slowly. Other devices which employ a

*Quoted by A. Thomazi, *Histoire de la pêche*, Paris, 1947.

similar principle are not submerged vertically but are thrown out into the water and then hauled slowly back to the boat. One of these is the *supion* mirror—*supion* being the Provençale word for "little cuttlefish"; another is the *tautenière*, which is a small board to which hooks, a weight, and a crab are attached.

Octopus Fishing

The fisherman is using an *arpetta*—a bamboo pole, at the end of which is a hook with several points. There is a red cloth attached to the hook, which the fisherman waves in front of the octopus' hole. In order to see the bottom clearly, the fisherman is using a glass-bottomed box, which neutralizes reflections from the surface.

Various devices used in octopus fishing:

1. The *Tautenière*—a piece of lead with hooks attached, and a red cloth.
2. A piece of wood, with hooks attached to the top and a lead weight to the bottom. For bait, a crab or a fish is used, or even a piece of red cloth. The fisherman throws the wood out as far as he can and then hauls it slowly back toward the boat.
3. A *supion* (little cuttlefish) mirror.
4. An octopus jar.

The natives of Maurice Island and of Polynesia are very fond of octopuses. They catch them in great numbers and then dry them on racks on the beach.

The greatest fans of the octopus are the Japanese, who especially prize the eyes. They have developed a method of breeding octopuses in submerged cages, each measuring about six feet by six feet. The octopuses are well fed and grow rapidly. Dr. Catala has recorded, on the basis of his observations in the aquarium at Nouméa, in New Caledonia, that a small octopus, captured when it was four inches long, reached, in fourteen months, a length of four feet.

On the coasts of Annam, the natives fish at night, using the luminous organ of a squid—a photophore which, even when removed from the animal, continues to give off an intense green light. Thomazi reports that "the fisherman, with amazing dexterity, removes the luminous organ by means of a sort of scalpel made of bamboo. He then rubs it with his fingers, which seems to increase the amount of light the organ emits. The organ is placed into a small sack made of fish skin, and the opening of the sack is closed tightly so as to make it waterproof.

"The fisherman attaches the bag to the end of his line, an inch or so away from the hook. The hook is concealed within a piece of white fish flesh, and the flesh is illuminated by the light within the bag, which lasts for about six hours. Many fish are caught in this way, but none of them ever touches the luminous organ, which is used over and over again."

Salvage

Thomazi also cites a case of an ingenious utilization of a cephalopod's talents. During the First World War, some coal was lost offshore by a ship. The natives brought it up by attaching a large octopus to the end of a line. They would wait until the octopus had a firm grip on a piece of coal, and then haul it to the surface. It was a slow process, but, nonetheless, an effective one.

It is recorded that, on several occasions, Chinese, Vietnamese, and Japanese salvage workers have used octopuses to bring up objects from sunken ships. The octopus, in other words, took over the role of a human diver.

Appendix III

The Giant Nerve Fiber

In 1936, J. Z. Young, the English biologist, for the first time, noted and described the giant nerve fibers in the nervous system of the squid (*Loligo*). The diameter of such fibers, Young recorded, measured up to 500 microns (0.5 millimeter); that is, from 50 to 100 times larger than human nerve fibers. The fiber of the squid attains such giant size because it is formed from the fusion of a number of small fibers, each one of which emanates from its own nerve cell. Its function is to register the electric signals, or the "nervous influx," coming from the neurons and transmit their message to the muscles by synapses. When the signal, which is passed along at a rate of 60 feet per second, reaches the muscle, it results in contraction.

The ability to experiment with the giant nerve fiber of cephalopods has opened up the way to a new area of physiological and electrophysiological research. Since this research began, in 1936, the results of the exploration of the giant fiber have led to the establishment of a new branch of cellular biology: cellular neurophysiology.

The history of the exploration of this giant nerve fiber (or cylindrax, or giant axon) is as follows. Four laboratories have a claim to being the first to have undertaken the experiments the results of which are still valid:

1. The Cambridge Laboratory—Professors Hodgkin, Huxley, and Keynes, in 1949, for the discovery of the ionic currents which play a part in the formation of the electric signal which runs along the fiber and which causes the muscles to contract. For this discovery, as well as for others concerning the giant fiber, Hodgkin and Huxley were awarded the Nobel Prize in Medicine.
2. Two American laboratories of international renown. One of these, under the direction of Professor K. S. Cole, measured, with utmost precision, the electrical properties of the membrane of the giant fiber (1938). These properties are the fiber's electrical capacity and resistance, and its electrical potential. The second, under the direction of Professor Tasaki, undertook studies of the electrochemical properties of the giant fiber.
3. The French laboratory of the CNRS, at the Oceanographic Museum of Monaco. Dr. N. Chalazonitis and Dr. Arvanitaki studied the giant fiber of the *Sepia*, or cuttlefish, which measures 0.3 millimeters. It is therefore smaller than the fiber of the squid and more difficult to study. The results of this research are important in both the physiology and the pathology of nerve cells.

In 1939, Mme. Arvanitaki recorded, for the first time, the existence of local electrical responses on the isolated giant nerve fiber. Thus, in addition to the electrical signal communicated from one end of the fiber to the other, even a weak local irritation is capable of causing a localized, and non-communicated, electrical signal. This local response demonstrates clearly that the fiber's membrane gives off graduated electrical responses—a discovery which later was found to be very important in the analysis of the mechanism which effects the passage of the electrical signal from one nerve cell to another in the human brain. Moveover, Mme. Arvanitaki was able to construct a model of the passage of the electrical signal from one fiber to another by dissecting two giant fibers and connecting them together. She was therefore able to demonstrate that, normally, the electrical signal does not go from the first (the transmitter) to the second (the receiver). But, if the receiving fiber is chemically sensitized (by removing calcium, for example), it may be seen that the electrical signal crosses the junction of the two fibers and stimulates the receiving fiber.

This biological model, illustrative of an electrical transfer from one fiber to another, has found innumerable applications in neurology and neurophysiology, in the study of the transmission of electrical signals among the nerve cells of the brain.

Finally, one of the most important of Mme. Arvanitaki's discoveries has to do with the creation of oscillations in the electrical potential of the giant fiber. This discovery opened the road to numerous experiments concerning the stimulation of electrical oscillation in the nerve cells (which are normally stable) by chemical substances which produce epileptic seizures.

In tracing the history of experimentation with the giant nerve fiber of the *Sepia,* it should be noted that a substantial contribution was made by Dr. N. Chalazonitis. The photosensitization of the fiber's membrane—that is, the infusion of certain non-toxic coloring agents—gives it photoelectric properties. When a light is turned onto a photosensitized nerve fiber, its electrical potential is diminished and a number of local electrical responses occur. The giant fiber thus functions as a model photoreceiver; that is, as a converter of luminous energy into electrical energy. This discovery has proved to be very useful in the analysis of the mechanism of retinal function.

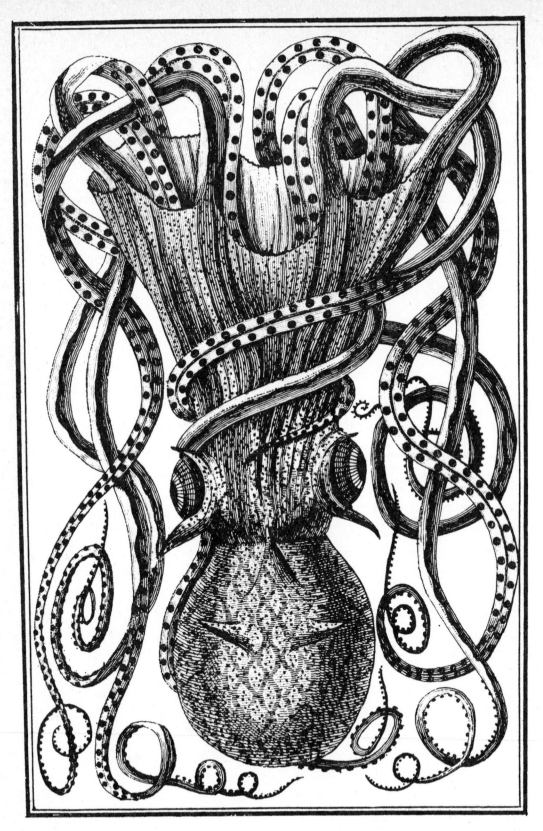

Aplysia

Illustrated Glossary

AIR LIFT

A device used to draw sand, sludge, or gravel into a metal pipe by means of a powerful suction created by air pressure.

The air lift is used to clear sunken ships. The octopuses living in the amphorae at Grand Congloué were sometimes "inhaled" by the air lift and deposited on *Calypso's* rear deck in place of the coins and pottery fragments for which our resident archaeologist was waiting.

APLYSIA

A mollusk, subclass Opisthobranchidae, order Anaspidae, with tentacles located on top of its head like long ears—which has earned it the nickname of "rabbit of the sea." The Aplysia, whose body may measure a foot in length, feeds on algae and is harmless. It has a gland which secretes a liquid of violet color. The eggs are joined together in a long cord which is more or less rolled up.

AUTOTOMY

A frequent phenomenon among crustaceans, by which they can simply shed a limb if held by it. The break is caused by a violent contraction and takes place along a predetermined line.

We know very little about the mechanism—no doubt analogous to that of the autotomy—by means of which the male Argonaut, for an entirely different reason, detaches its hectocotylus.

BARRACUDA

The barracuda is a well-known flesh-eater of the tropical seas. In appearance, it somewhat resembles the pike, with its prominent teeth, well-defined jaw, and its elongated body the color of steel.

The largest species of the barracudas sometimes reaches a length of over six feet. When fully grown, it is solitary or forms small shoals. Young barracuda are often found in schools comprising individuals all of the same size and of the same age or generation.

Barracuda

BATHYPELAGIC

Bethypelagic animals are those which live in mid-water at depths of between 2,000 and 6,000 feet. Epipelagic animals are those which lie between the surface and 600 feet; mesopelagic, between 600 and 2,000 feet. Those which lie between 6,000 feet and the bottom are called abyssopelagic.

The same terms are applied to benthic life forms; that is, to those which live on the bottom*:

Littoral benthic—down to 600 feet. Mesobenthic—from 600 to 2,000 feet
Bathybenthic—from 2,000 to 6,000 feet
Abyssobenthic—from 6,000 feet to the bottom of the deepest part.

BATHYSCAPHE

The first bathyscaphe was designed and created by Auguste Piccard in 1948. The FNRS-2, as it was called, went down to 1,380 meters (slightly over 4,000 feet) off the coast of Dakar.

In October 1950, an agreement reached between the French Navy and the Belgian National Fund for Scientific Research made it possible to undertake the construction of a new cable buoy and a new hull for the steel inner sphere of the bathyscaphe. This improved model, the FNRS-3, went down with Commandant Houot, and an engineer of the Naval Engineers named Wilm, to 4,050 meters (12,500 feet) off Dakar, in February 1954. Later in 1954, and in the ensuing period until 1958, there were deep-water dives in the Mediterranean, the Atlantic, and in Japanese waters. After its ninety-fourth dive, the FNRS-3 was retired from service.

Auguste and Jacques Piccard had constructed another bathyscaphe, the *Trieste*, which, in September 1953, had gone down to 3,150 meters (9,500 feet). Subsequently, the *Trieste* was acquired by the U. S. Navy, and, in January 1960, off the island of Guam, went down to 10,916 meters (33,000 feet)—the deepest spot known in the ocean.

The French Navy decided to build a new, improved bathyscaphe, with the cooperation of the National Center for Scientific Research and of the Belgian National Fund for Scientific Research. This Model, the *Archimède*, was launched at Toulon in July 1961. In July 1962, in a series of six dives, it reached a depth of 9,000 meters (27,500 feet) in the Kuriles ditch. Later, it was used by scientists and researchers in the deep off Puerto Rico in Madeiran waters.

BUSHNELL'S *TURTLE*

An American named David Bushnell (1742-1826) was the inventor of the first workable submarine, which he called *The Turtle*. It was a wooden structure resembling two turtle shells joined by their undersides.

Bushnell conceived and worked out all the equipment used by most of his successors: propellers, water ballast, pumps, depth indicator, etc.

Bushnell's submarine was actually built and used in the Revolutionary War, in 1776. It was able to approach an English warship undetected, but its pilot was not successful in attaching a charge of gunpowder to the hull of the warship. Bushnell, discouraged by his failure, abandoned the idea of subsurface navigation.

---

*"A species may be called benthic when it exists on or near the bottom. It may be fixed on the bottom, or burrow into it, or move on it, or even swim a short distance about it—so long as it never moves any distance away from the bottom." J. M. Pěres, *Océanographie biologique.*

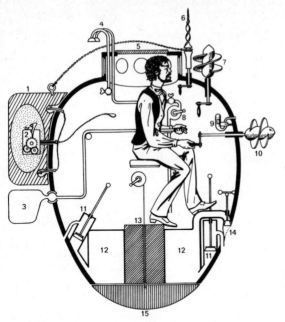

1. Torpedo
2. Clock movement regulating launching of torpedoes
3. Rudder
4. Air tube
5. Entry hatch
6. Drill for attaching torpedoes to keel of ships
7. Propeller on vertical shaft for diving
8. Ventilator
9. Water-level depth indicator
10. Traction propeller for forward movement
11. Pump for emptying ballast tanks
12. Ballast tanks
13. Ballast
14. Valve for taking on water
15. Security ballast

Bushnell's "Turtle" Submarine (1776)

CACHALOT, or SPERM WHALE

The sperm whale is a toothed cetacean of the family Physeteridae. It lives in equatorial waters in groups of 20 to 50 individuals. It is the largest of the toothed cetaceans, and males sometimes reach a length of sixty feet and weigh from 35 to 50 tons.

It differs from other toothed whales by its spout, which is oblique; this is the result of the fact that only one blowhole (that on the left) is functional.

The enormous square head of the cachalot may account for as much as one-third of its body length. Only the lower jaw is endowed with teeth, and these are formidable weapons, weighing as much as two and one-half pounds each.

The period of gestation is sixteen months, and the female bears a calf once every three years.

CALYPSO

Calypso is a former minesweeper, a vessel of 350 tons built in the United States in 1942 for the British Navy. It has a double wooden hull and two engines and attains a maximum speed of 10 knots.

J.-Y. Cousteau found *Calypso* after World War II at Malta, where it was being sold as surplus. He was able to acquire it through the generosity of an English patron, Loël Guinness.

Calypso's maneuverability and its shallow draught enable her to navigate in shallow water and among coral reefs.

Several modifications were necessary to convert the old minesweeper into an oceanographic research vessel. An underwater observation chamber (which we call the "false nose") was installed in front of the stem and under the water line. An observation tower was constructed on *Calypso*'s foredeck to help in navigating her through coral waters, and also to provide a point of elevation from which to observe marine life.

CEMA

Acronym for *Centre d'Études Marines Avancées* (Center of Advanced Marine Studies). It is an agency established for the manufacture of prototypes, and was founded in 1953 by Captain Cousteau, at Marseilles. It includes a laboratory for the study of high-pressure physiology, which is equipped with deep-water diving simulators and equipment for analysis and control.

CEPHALOTHORAX

The anterior body region of crustaceans, in which one or several thoracic segments are fitted to the head.

CEPHALOTOXIN

Toxin contained in the venom of cephalopods which has a paralyzing effect. It is secreted by the salivary glands.

CHORION

Chorion is a membrane in which is contained the squid embryo, or the cuttlefish embryo. In order to burst the sac, the embryo makes use of a special organ—a protrusion, in the form of a Y—located between the two fins. This organ secretes an enzyme which, in effect, digests the chorion's membrane.

CHROMATOPHORES

Chromatophores are the pigmented cells which work color changes among cephalopods. These cells, which are round and have elastic walls, are located in the epidermis. Each chromatophore is attached, by several branches, to relaxed muscle fibers which, when they are stimulated to contraction, stretch the cell. The chromatophore then spreads out into a flat disk and the surface of the skin takes on its color. The basic colors shown by the chromatophores are brown, black, red, yellow, and red-orange. The largest chromatophores are dark colored, while the smallest are yellow.

CONNECTORS

Among such decapods as the cuttlefish, there are knob and socket cartilages which lock funnel and mantle together when the mantle contracts. They are referred to as "connectors," like snap fasteners or poppers, which clip the sides of the mantle to the head.

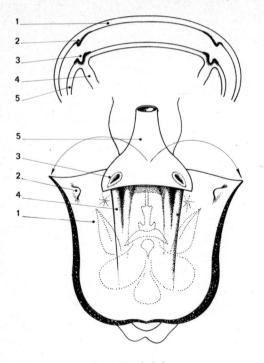

1. Mantle
2. Knob
3. Socket
4. Funnel-retractor muscle
5. Funnel

(Internal organs are indicated by
   broken lines)

Connectors of the Cuttlefish

CUTTLEFISH BONE

The cuttlefish "bone" is the internal shell of the cuttlefish, secreted by the mantle which envelops it. Its underside shows growth stripes. It is composed of a calcium mass containing, in its center, tiny alveoli or compartments filled with gas (97 nitrogen, 3 oxygen and carbon dioxide). It has a horned, calcareous border which, in most cuttlefish, ends in a small ledge. This "bone" has a hydrostatic function.

DEEP SCATTERING LAYERS (DSL)

The name given, during World War II, to mysterious layers detected by sonar at various depths and different places in the ocean. Study has since revealed that these layers rise toward the surface during the night and sink toward the bottom during the daylight hours. It seems that they are composed of marine animals—life forms which Professor H. E. Edgerton, of the Massachusetts Institute of Technology, photographed from *Calypso* with electronic flash equipment. Chief among these animals are jellyfish, siphonophores, copepods, and also eggs and larvae.

DIVING SAUCER

There are several types of diving saucer (or minisub) designed by Captain Cousteau and built by the Center for Advanced Marine Studies of Marseilles:
    - The *SP-350*, which carries two passengers. It has a movie camera, a still cam-

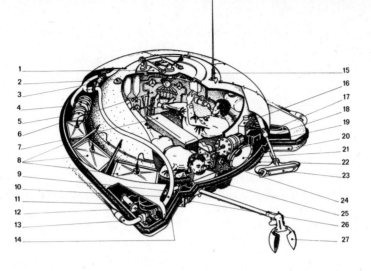

The SP-350 Diving Saucer (or Minisub)

1. Entry hatch
2. Wide-range portholes
3. Water distributor (right or left, for water jets)
4. Pump
5. Electric engine (2 hp.)
6. Interior
7. Water ballast
8. Submersible batteries
9. Control lever for pincer arm
10. Jet tube
11. Lever for front and rear jets
12. Transducer
13. Jets
14. Headlights

15. Radio antenna
16. Contact box
17. Upper transducer
18. Forward transducer
19. Forward mercury-equilibrium apparatus
20. Flash apparatus
21. Portholes
22. Sample basket
23. Telescopic projector
24. Film and photo porthole
25. Detachable kentledge
26. Photostereo apparatus
27. Pincer arm

era, a hydraulic pincer arm, and a storage basket. It has been used in more than 600 dives.

-The *SP-1000,* or "sea flea," is a one-passenger vehicle, and it was designed to dive in tandem with a second SP-1000. It has two outside cameras (16mm or 35mm) which are remote controlled, and tape recorders to record marine sounds. It has made over 100 dives.

- The *SP-4000,* or *Deepstar,* is able to go down to more than 3,500 feet. It was built for Westinghouse and was launched in 1966. It carries two passengers and has a speed of three knots. It has been used in over 500 dives.

- The *SP-3000,* built for CNEXO. It has a speed of three knots and will carry three passengers.

ECHINODERMS

The echinoderms constitute one of the primary divisions of the animal kingdom and include sea stars (or starfish), sea urchins, sea cucumbers, and the crinoids. They are distinguished by the fact that they are radial animals with five sectors. All echinoderms are marine animals. They have a vascular system that circulates sea water which enables them to move their suckerlike tube feet. This is the only phylum in which tube feet are found

EDGERTON FLASH CAMERA

The Edgerton flash camera was designed by Professor Harold E. Edgerton of the Massachusetts Institute of Technology specially for the "Troika"—a marine-research device perfected under the auspices of the French Bureau of Marine Research. It is basically a trailer towed on the bottom by *Calypso* and is used for close-up photographs. It is composed of a camera and a flash device operated by battery, and it becomes operational automatically, as soon as it touches bottom.

GUY GILPATRIC

Guy Gilpatric, an American writer living at Cap d'Antibes, France, became in 1920 one of the first practitioners of underwater hunting. He developed the first equipment used in such hunting, consisting of a harpoon and aviator goggles. His first book on diving, *The Compleat Goggler,* was published in 1938.

GRAND CONGLOUÉ

Between 1952 and 1957, during five years of very hard work, *Calypso*'s divers excavated a sunken Roman ship loaded with amphorae and pottery from the Campania. The ship had belonged to a man named Marcus Sestius, a native of Delos, and dated from the second half of the third century B.C. It was found at a depth of 125 feet, at the foot of an island off the coast of Marseilles: Grand Congloué.

HEMOCYANIN

A copper-based respiratory pigment found in the blood of mollusks and crustaceans, to which it gives a blue-green or bluish color.

HEMOGLOBIN

An iron-based respiratory pigment which constitutes the coloring matter of red blood cells as found in man, all mammals and most fish.

HOMOCHROMISM

The quality, possessed by cephalopods, of being able to change color in accordance with the color of the object or place on which they are resting.

HYALIN

From the Greek word *hualos,* meaning "glass," and signifying "diaphanous" or "transparent."

HYDRA

One of the twelve labors assigned to Hercules was the death of the Hydra of Lerna. This monster lived in a swamp and was said by some to have seven heads. Others claimed that it had nine heads; and still others, fifty or a hundred. These heads were at the end of a neck so long that it resembled a serpent—or the arms of an octopus. As soon as one of the heads was cut off, it grew back, and it could be destroyed only if the wound was seared with fire.

Hercules forced the Hydra to come out of its swamp, and then crushed its heads with a hammer and applied fire to the wounds. There was one invulnerable head, which he buried under a rock.

The struggle of Hercules against the Hydra is symbolic of that of man against his vices, sins, and interior demons, all of which are reborn incessantly.

KELP

Kelp is the name commonly given to various large algae, most of which are Pheophytes and are found especially off the coasts of California but also around New Zealand, Argentina, Chile, and Peru.

Macrocystis pyrifera attains a length of 175 feet. It is strongly anchored on the bottom by means of crampons, and floats by means of its air-filled vesicals. It grows very rapidly, and some experts believe that this species may reach a length of from 1,000 to 1,500 feet.

Other algae often called "kelp' are *Pelagotphycus porra* and *Eisenia arborea*.

KÖLLIKER CANAL

A tube, with one closed end, located in the cephalic cartilage. Among cephalopods, it begins at the statocysts—the organs which control the orientation and balance of the animal. This canal, at least among octopuses, is the vestige of a tube with an exterior opening.

MANTLE

A complex membrane which, in most mollusks, secretes a limestone shell which encloses the animal's viscera. A fold in the mantle constitutes the body cavity, in which are the animal's gills.

When a cephalopod contracts the muscles of its mantle, the water in the body cavity is expelled through the funnel tube—which constitutes the cephalopod's means of jet propulsion. Water then enters into the body cavity between the mantle and the edge of the funnel. This alternating motion also circulates water over the animal's gills.

MESOZOIC ERA

The geological span following the Paleozoic era. It lasted 167 million years and ended 130 million years ago. It is divided into three periods: Triassic, Jurassic and Cretaceous.

MOUTHPIECE

A rubber element which the diver holds between his teeth. It is attached to the diaphragm of the Cousteau-Gagnan Aqua-lung by means of two flexible hoses, one of which is used for inhalation and the other for exhalation.

NEEDHAM'S SAC

A reservoir for the temporary storage of spermatophores in male cephalopods.

The male cuttlefish uses its hectocotylus to remove spermatophores from the opening of this sac. In *Octopus vulgaris,* the spermatophores are expelled spontaneously and then carried along the groove of the hectocotylus. A male squid can store 400 spermatophores in its Needham's sac.

OCEAN SUNFISH

The ocean sunfish, or headfish, belongs to the Plectognathic order. It has the shape of a disk and may be as much as nine feet in diameter and weigh close to a ton.

Its disklike body has a strange fringing tail fin, above and below which are high paddlelike fins. These can scull the fish along quite efficiently in the water, and its very size protects it from predators. The fact that it has often been seen lying on one side at the surface of the sea has lead to a widespread misconception that this is its normal attitude.

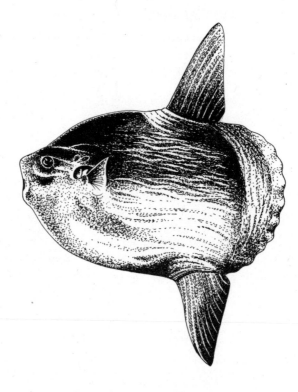

Ocean Sunfish (or Headfish)

OSMOTIC PRESSURE

The difference in pressure on opposite sides of a differentially permeable membrane, due to solutions of different concentrations on the opposite sides of it, is called osmotic pressure.

OTHOLITH

A calcium formation contained in the ear of the fish which helps the animal to keep its balance. It serves to indicate the age of fish since, every year, a fresh layer forms around the existing stone. A count of these layers therefore reveals the age of the fish.

PALEOZOIC ERA

The period from which date the oldest animal fossils. The Paleozoic era lasted 370 million years and ended 230 million years ago. It is divided into seven periods: Cambrian, Ordovician, Silurian, Devonian, Mississippian, Pennsylvanian, and Permian. The three last are often grouped together as the Carboniferous.

PENIS

The copulatory organ found in vertebrates and some invertebrates. It is generally well developed among the octopods, but less so among the decapods.

PILOT WHALE

The pilot whale is a toothed cetacean and a member of the family Delphinidae. Its length is usually between 12 and 25 feet. It is black, has a dorsal fin, and between seven and eleven teeth in each jaw. Its head is very rounded.

Pilot whales move in groups of as many as several hundred individuals, and they are led by a leader whom they follow blindly. They are found during the summer off the coasts of Newfoundland, and during the winter in warm water where the females bear their young. Mating takes place in the fall, and gestation lasts twelve months.

Pilot-whale hunting is the chief occupation of the natives of Newfoundland.

Pilot Whale

PLANKTON CAMERA

The plankton camera was designed and conceived by a CEMA team under Armand Davso. It enables one to study the micro-organisms contained in plankton. The camera is composed of a plankton trap made of a square plastic syringe which takes in a certain volume of water. The liquid is then carried by the syringe to a screen, which is about the size of a matchbox. The organisms in the water are then filmed.

PORPOISE

The porpoise is a toothed cetacean of the family Delphinidae, genus *Phocoena*. It is found widely in the North Atlantic, especially in coastal areas.

Its length varies from four feet to six feet, and it weighs about 160 pounds. It is white on the underside and almost black on the back. There are fifty-four blade-shaped teeth.

Porpoises travel in couples and also in groups of about one hundred individuals. They swim a short distance below the surface and rise to the surface to breathe approximately four times per minute.

They feed on schools of small fish found very near the surface.

Porpoise

POSIDONIA

An aquatic plant of the family Naiadacea. It is common along the coasts of the Mediterranean, where it grows in great profusion. It blooms from June to September.

PROTEUS

A god of the sea, son of Neptune and Tethys, who had the ability to change his shape in order to escape from his enemies. He could take on the appearance of a lion, or a tiger, or even transform himself into water, a tree, or fire.

RADULA

A part of the buccal apparatus of mollusks. Among the cephalopods, it is found on the upper front surface of the tongue and is composed of a row of teeth. Among octopuses, it is a ribbon of tiny hornlike teeth surrounding a larger tooth. These teeth can be replaced as they became worn.

The cuttlefish does not appear to use its radula as frequently as the octopus. The former uses it less to grind its food than to make the food pass into the esophagus.

The radula of the squid is relatively small.

SEA CUCUMBER

The sea cucumber is an echinoderm, class Holothuroidea. At the anterior end of its soft, tubular body is the mouth, through which the ten tentacles draw mud, which passes through the body and is expelled through the cloaca at the other end. Around the cloaca, or rectum, are two branchlike growths, the "lungs," which act as gills. Males are more numerous than females.

The sea cucumber is called *Trepang* by the Chinese, who regard it as a potent aphrodisiac.

SEA FANS

Sea fans belong to the class Anthozoa, subclass Octocorallia, order Gorgonacea. It takes its popular name from its fan-shaped branches, and is found in yellow, mauve, and rose pink. Like all Anthozoa, the animals are exclusively polypoid, having no medusa stage. Sea fans are fixed to the ocean floor or to rocks by means of branches, or tufts, and are sometimes found in tight groups. They have an encrusting base, which allows them to remain attached to their support.

They are found in warm or temperate seas. In many tropical regions, they attain a height of over three feet and are one of the most beautiful objects of the underwater décor. Their abundance and diversity were first revealed with the advent of scuba diving.

SEA SQUIRTS

The sea squirt, or tunicate, is a protochordate. It looks like a small bag, and may be colored bright red or yellow, though the color is not fixed until the sea squirt is an adult. Its larva is free-swimming.

The small sac or tuna (hence the name Tunicata for this group), which is the sea squirt's body, has two openings: the anterior buccal siphon, which takes in the sea water on which the animal feeds, and the dorsal siphon, which ejects water containing the animal's waste.

Despite its rather primitive appearance, the sea squirt has gills, a stomach, an intestine, and a V-shaped heart the contractions of which push the blood first in one direction and then in the other—80 directions one way, and 40 the other way.

Sea squirts are hermaphroditic; self-fertilization may occur, but in many species fertilization is the general rule.

SESSILE ORGAN

An organ which is attached directly to its base, without a peduncle or stem.

STAGES OF ASCENT

Decompression accidents during a diver's ascent to the surface are due to the fact that the diver breathes compressed air, and that the gases dissolved in his system by water pressure are liberated during the ascent. The faster a diver rises, the larger are the air bubbles that may be generated—depending also upon the depth of the dive and its duration. These bubbles block the circulatory system and may result in "gaseous embolism."

The diver's ascent is therefore slowed in order to allow the gases sufficient time to dissolve. Tables have been worked out which give the number and duration of the stops a diver must make during his ascent in relation to the depth of his dive and the time spent at that depth. These stops are the "stages of ascent."

STARFISH (SEA STARS)

Starfish are echinoderms. Their bodies are in the shape of a star with five branches or "arms." Some species have more than five. At the tip of each arm there is a short tentacle and, at the base of the tentacle, there is a bright red, light-sensitive organ. This is the optic cushion at the base of the terminal tentacle. It consists of many sensory cells (called retinal cells) surrounding a cup-shaped area overlaid, in many species, by a lens, thereby forming a pigment-cup ocellus. There are many ocelli (80 to 200) in each optic cushion. In addition, each arm carries, on its underside, hundreds of tiny podia, or tube feet, equipped with suction disks. A starfish, therefore, is more mobile than its appearance would suggest.

Starfish are carnivorous and feed on mollusks and crustaceans both living and dead. Rather than swallow its victim, however, the starfish everts its stomach and applies it to its prey, whereupon the latter is dissolved by the starfish's digestive juices.

STATOCYSTS

The equilibrium of the octopus is assured by two statocysts located in the cephalic cartilage. These organs are filled with endolymph and contain an irregularly shaped statolith. The system is analogous to that of the semicircular canals among vertebrates.

The epithelium of the vesicles have two points on which there are large cells covered with stiff cilia. These are the "acoustical spot" and the "demicircular crest," at which the acoustical nerves end.

Despite this somewhat elaborate acoustical apparatus, it seems that the octopus is deaf.

TEUTHOLOGY

The science of cephalopods. A teuthologist is a zoologist specializing in the study of cephalopods.

BIBLIOGRAPHY

Appelöf, A., "Die Schalen von *Sepia, Spirula* und *Nautilus*," K. Svenska Vetensk, Akad. Handl. 25, no. 7, 1893.

Aubert, Maurice, "Cultiver l'océan," P.U.F.

Barber, V. C., "The Fine Structure of the Statocyst of *Octopus Vulgaris*," Z. Zellfrosch, 70, 1966.

Bassot, Jean-Marie, and Gabe, Manfred, "Caractères histologiques généraux des centres nerveux du nautile," C. R. Acad. de Paris, 263, 1966.

——— and Martoja, Micheline, "Histologie et fonction du siphon chez le nautile," C. R. Acad. Sc. Paris, 263, 1966.

Bidder, A. M., "Use of the Tentacles, Swimming and Buoyancy Control in the Pearly Nautilus." *Nature* 196, London, 1962.

Boycott, B. B., "Learning in the Octopus," *Scientific American,* Vol. 212, no. 3, 1965.

——— and Young, J. Z., "A Memory System in *Octopus Vulgaris,* Lamarck," Proc. Zool. Soc. 126, London, 1956.

Catala, Dr. René, *Carnaval sous la mer,* ed. R. Sicard, 1964.

Chun, C., "Die Cephalopoden," Wiss. Ergebn *Valdavia,* 18, 1910.

Delaitre, J. J., *Le poulpe, biologie et valeur alimentaire,* Thèse de doctorat no. 27, 1965.

Denton, E. J., "Some Recently Discovered Buoyancy Mechanisms in Marine Animals." Proc. Roy. Soc. 265, 1962.

Gilpin-Brown, J. B. "The Effect of Light on the Buoyancy of the Cuttlefish," J. Mar. Biol. Assn. U.K. 343, 1961.

——— "The Distribution of Gas and Liquid Within the Cuttlefish," J. Mar. Biol. Assn. U. K. 41, 1961

——— "On the Buoyancy of the Pearly Nautilus," J. Physiol. 168, 1963.

Dilly, Noel, Nixon, Marion, and Packard, Andrew, "Forces Exerted by *Octopus Vulgaris*," Pubbl. Staz. Zool. Napoli 34.

Dragesco, J., "Le monde extraordinaire des pieuvres," *Science et Avenir* no. 68, 1952.

Gilpatric, Guy, *The Compleat Goggler,*, Dodd, Mead and Company, New York, 1938.

Goldsmith, M., "Quelques réactions du poulpe, contribution à la psychologie des invertébrés." *Bull. Inst. Gen. Psychol.* 17, 1917.

Gouret, P., *Les pecheures et les poissons de la Méditerranée,* Provence, Paris, 1894.

Heldt, J. H., *"Observations sur une ponte d'Octopus vulgaris,"* Bull. Soc. Scie. Nat. I. Tunis, 1958.

Heuvelmans, B., *Dans le sillage des monstres marins. Le kraken et le poulpe colossal,* Plon, Paris, 1958.

Holmes, W., "Les changements de couleur des céphalopodes," *Endeavor*, Vol. 14, no. 54, 1955.

Lane, Frank W., *Kingdom of the Octopus,* Sheridan House, New York, 1960.

Mangold-Wirz Katharina, "Quelques problèmes actuels de la teuthologie méditeranéenne," Rapp. Comm. Int. Mer Medit. 14, 1959.

——— *Biologie des céphalopodes benthiques et nectoniques de la mer Catalane,* Thèse doctorat E. Sciences, 1961.

Albert, Prince, of Monaco, *Campagnes Océanogràphiques,* Imprimerie de Monaco.

Harvey, E. Newton, *Bioluminescence,* Academic Press, Inc., New York, 1952.

Ozeune, D., *Essai sur les mollusques considérés comme aliments, médicaments et poisons.* Thèse de doctorat de Médecine, Paris, 1958.

Packard, Andrew, "The Behavior of *Octopus vulgaris*," *Bull. Inst. Océanographique,* no. Special ID, 1963

———and Sanders, Geoffrey, "Ce que la pieuvre montre au monde," *Endeavour*, Vol. 28, no. 104, 1969.

Pérès, J. M., "Océanographie biologique et biologie marine," P.U.F., 1963.

Pieron, H., "Contribution à la psychologie du poulpe," *Bull. Ins. Gen. Psych.* II, 1911.

Portmann, A., "Observations sur la vie embryonnaire de la pieuvre, *Octopus vulgaris*," Lamarck, *Archives zool. Exp. Gen.* LXXVI-I, 1933.

Racovitza, E. G., "Notes de biologie I: accouplement et fécondation chez *Octopus vulgaris.*" *Arch. Zool. Exp. Gen.,* ser. 3-11, 1894.

Rullier, F., "Répartition et reproduction d'*Octopus vulgaris,* Lamarck dans les eaux françaises" *Bull. du Laboratoire Maritime de Dinard.* no. 39, 1953.

Ten Cate, J., and Ten Cate, B., "Les *Octopus* peuvent discerner les formes," *Arch. Neerl. Sc.* 23, 1938.

Thomazi, A., *Histoire de la pêche,* Payot, Paris, 1947.

Verany, J. B., *Cèphalopodes de la Méditerranée observés à Nice et Genes.* Turin, Imprimerie Royale, 1840.

Mollusques Méditerranée observés décrits, figurés et chromolithographiés d'apres le vivant. I. céphalopodes de la Méditerranée. Genes, Imprimerie des Sourds-muets, 1851.

Verrill, A. H., *Moeurs étranges des mollusques,* Payot, Paris, 1952.

Wells, M. J., *Brain and Behavior in Cephalopods,* Heinemann, London, 1962.

Young, J. Z., *A Model of the Brain,* Clarendon Press, Oxford, 1964.

——— "The Central Nervous System of *Nautilus*," *Proc. Roy. Soc.,* 249, 1965.

——— *Mollusques Méditerranée,* etc.

Index